Warning - Disclaimer

Blue Water Hunting

and

Freediving

Dedication

To my parents, who always supported my freediving endeavors; to my mother, who taught me to read.

To my lovely wife Beth, my freediving companion and first editor. Beth read every word on every page, and helped me place all the illustrations. I am grateful for her love, encouragement and understanding.

To my friend Al Schneppershoff, who ignited in me, as well as many others, a deep love for bluewater hunting and the sea.

BlueWater Hunting and Freediving

Terry Maas

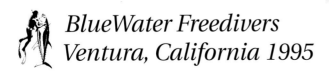

BlueWater Freedivers
Ventura, California 1995

First printed August 1995
8 7 6 5 4 3 2 1

Library of Congress Catalog Number 98-070237

ISBN 0-9644966-3-1

CREDITS

Cover design: Vance Carriere.
Art:
Darrell Hattingh 20, 25, 38, 41, 47, 113, 121, 127, 139, 145,
150, 151, 157, 161, 166, 171, 179.
Eva Askay 5, 49 ,61, 85, 93, 101, 184.
Chris Martinez 58, 73, 88, 91, 191.
Color photgraphy:
James D. Watt 4, 16, 26, 30, 34, 40, 42, 128, 130, 163.
Rick Rosenthal 12, 14, 22, 24, 132, 152, 186.
William Boyce 100, 104, 140.
Black and white photography:
Wes Morrissey 62, 63, 64, 65, 66, 68, 71, 72, 80, 81, 187.
Digital retouching: Vance Carriere, Elena Trevino.
Editing: Beth Maas, Suzanne Schlosberg, Susan Smith,
Angel Zobel Rodriguez, Paul and Janet Greenberg.

Manufactured in South Korea with acid-free paper

BlueWater Freedivers
552 N. Victoria Ave
Ventura, California 93003
www.freedive.net

Acknowledgments

Thank you to all the divers who contributed to individual chapters. Told with candor, not all stories glorified you; some reveal your mistakes and misjudgments. I am confident that your honesty will help aspiring bluewater hunters develop their skills more rapidly, and hopefully save them from injury or death.

One of the most stimulating and gratifying things about writing this book was the unselfish and enthusiastic help I received from respected freediving experts. Hearing about the project, professionals and amateurs generously contributed their stories, pictures and editing skills. Thank you to those of you whose assistance spanned two or more chapters: Howard Benedict, Fred Biller, Tom Blandford, Tommy Botha, Bill Boyce, Carl Butler, Cuan Cronje, Darrell Hattingh, Skip Hellen, Terry Lentz, Gerald Lim, Milton Love, Jim Mabry, Ron Merker, Ian McGonagle, Peter McGonagle, Tom Millington, Greg Pickering, Jack Prodonavich, Wally Potts, Dave Reid, René Rojas, Rick Rosenthal, Andy Ruddock, Linda Schneppershoff-McWhorter, Al Schneppershoff Jr., Terry Schuller, Dave Sipperly, Adam Smith, Mark Steele, Robert Torelli and James D. Watt.

My special thanks:

To women bluewater hunters, your accomplishments speak for themselves as the following pages reveal. In addition, as organizers and record-keepers, women like Jessica Jones of South Africa and Carol Rose of the United States have given decades of unselfish service to their respective country's spearfishing communities. Readers, please note: for simplicity, I use the masculine gender throughout this book. Where you see "he," please read he/she, and where you find "spearfishermen" read spearfishermen and spearfisherwomen.

To Milton Love, Ph.D., author of *Probably More Than You Want to Know About the Fishes of the Pacific Coast,* for his assistance in developing the natural history of many of the bluewater species profiled.

To bluewater hunter, marine journalist, and artist Darrell Hattingh. His beautiful line drawings illustrate most of the bluewater species, sharks and the flasher. Darrell was instrumental in developing and coordinating information from his South African countrymen. His work is available through BlueWater Freedivers.

To Australian Rob Torelli, who assisted me with personal introductions to the finest bluewater hunters in his country. Many in the freediving world appreciate his ground-breaking work with the *Australian Spearfishing and Freediving News.*

To bluewater hunter and Long Beach Neptune Wes Morrissey, for his assistance in providing most of the black and white photographs used to illustrate the sections on gear and photography.

To the medical professionals who reviewed my sections on shallow-water blackout: tuna hunter and physician, Andreas Agathos; Frank Farm, director of the Hyperbaric Treatment Center, University of Hawaii School of Medicine; William Hurford, M.D.; and Tom Millington, M.D.

To the major color photograph contributors; Howard Benedict, William Boyce, Bob Caruso, Greg Pickering, Rick Rosenthal, Robert Torelli and James D. Watt.

To the three major Southern California spearfishing clubs whose members have given support and valuable contributions: my own club, the Long Beach Neptunes; our sister club, the Los Angeles Fathomiers; and the grand members of the San Diego Bottom Scratchers.

To the record-keepers of the major English-speaking bluewater hunting countries: Mel Brown of the Australian Underwater Federation; Jessica Jones of the South African Spearfishing Federation; Carol Rose and Dan Mosier of the Underwater Society of America.

To Harry Davis for his friendship, his bluewater hunting experience and his scientific approach.

Contents

Left to right: Al Schneppershoff, Terry Maas and Carl Krupansky on a mid-1960s trip to the Sea of Cortez, Mexico.

PHOTO BY CARL KRUPANSKY

Introduction

"MAN ATTACKED AND KILLED BY GREAT WHITE SHARK," the *Los Angeles Times* headline screamed. It was September 1973 and my friend Al Schneppershoff was dead.

During the 1960s, Al Schneppershoff was California's consummate bluewater diver. He was a big man, over six feet tall. His roly-poly appearance imparted a jovial look that belied an underlying muscular strength and incredible stamina. Al was always the first diver in the water and the last one to leave it.

The Long Beach Neptunes offer a special award for a single year's effort. Earning a "King Neptune award" requires spearing fish—one each from selected species weighing 25, 40 and 100 pounds. Few divers have achieved this goal. The ones who succeed take years in the effort. Al got his King Neptune award in one day. Twice!

Al owned a boat and delighted in taking fledgling divers to his favorite fishing holes. Much of our time on the boat trips to Catalina Island was spent with stories about the times we let a fish get away. Al would make us all laugh, even when the story was about our own dubious exploits. We adored Al and we learned from these exchanges. Al taught us to love the ocean.

Two of Al's protégés are Skip Hellen, who now holds the world's record for white seabass (80 pounds), and James D. Watt, whose beautiful bluewater images adorn many of the pages of this book. Skip remembers Al driving over to his house at 4 a.m., boat in tow, enthusiastically honking the horn. Skip, too young for a driver's license, was thankful for Al's efforts because otherwise he could not dive.

James remembers hunting for kelp paddies with Al, Skip and another diver in the open ocean. Approaching a paddy, the excited divers saw a lone yellowtail swimming around the submerged kelp stringers. While James and the others were frantically putting their gear on, each trying to be the first in the water, Al ignored them all and slipped into the cold water. Stark naked and glowing like the moon, he shot the yellowtail.

Another day, young James swam up to Al off the kelp beds of Santa Cruz Island, off the central coast of California. "Here, hold my gun," Al said. Sure he was doing his mentor a favor, 14-year-old James took the gun. He had no idea that minutes before, Al had shot a giant black seabass. Moments later, James went on the ride of his life. An hour after being alternately dragged under the surface and hydroplaned across it, he was rejoined by a laughing Al, and together they landed the 350-pound fish.

Al and I met in the early 1960s as participants in the U.S. national spearfishing championships in Port Townsend, Washington. Like many bluewater divers, I began my spearfishing days competing in freediving spearfishing contests. We remained friends because of our passion for bluewater hunting. The thrill of stalking and landing exotic fish and the possibility of setting a world record motivated us. In 1972 I moved from Northern California to Southern California to complete my residency in oral surgery and to stay close to the bluewater action in the warmer, more hospitable waters. In 1982, I reluctantly resigned from the U.S. national spearfishing team. My busy professional life left little time for competitive diving. I wanted to spend that time bluewater hunting.

Four divers accompanied Al on his fateful trip to Guadalupe Island off Baja California, Mexico. (I was unable to make the trip.) Their vivid report of the events surrounding Al's death had a profound effect on his protégés, including me. One of Al's last shouts, "Tuna! Three hundred pounds!" and two hours later his final word, "Shark!" represent the yin and yang of bluewater hunting. The image of monstrous tuna captured our imaginations and drew us to Guadalupe Island. "Shark!" told us, "Stay away from Guadalupe Island. Guadalupe means death."

In the months following Al's death, the cry "Shark!" interrupted my every dive. I spent an inordinate amount of time looking behind myself. Whenever I had a premonition that a shark was near—and I had these premonitions frequently—I nervously scrutinized the water around me. Sometimes I simply got out.

Nine years passed before the words "Tuna! Three hundred pounds," acted again as a siren's call. The siren said, "Come to Guadalupe Island. Find the big tuna." I had settled in Ventura, where I met another ad-

venturous bluewater hunter, Jim Mabry. Jim and I organized the first trip to Guadalupe Island after Al's death. We returned in quest of the now legendary giant bluefin tuna.

Thirteen adventurous freedivers from California and one from Connecticut made the trip. Seven days later, we returned to San Diego with two consecutive world records. With a 175-pound fish, I eclipsed the previous record of 52 pounds taken by Ron Merker some 20 years earlier. Just two days later, I shattered this new record with a 398-pound bluefin tuna.

That trip galvanized the freediving community's interest in bluewater fishing and led to the production of the PBS television documentary, "Blue Water Hunters," stimulating countless questions from freedivers across the country. This book—with chapters on gear, hunting techniques, sharks, shallow-water blackout and more—answers these questions. Sprinkled throughout the chapters are stories and anecdotes from divers around the world. Bluewater hunters have accumulated nearly 40 years of unpublished stories. These stories illustrate important points on safety, technique, and the behavior of fish and humans.

Twin themes of resource conservation and diver safety are woven throughout these chapters. Conservation will guarantee game for future generations of bluewater hunters. How we accomplish this is important. The general public, as well as our fellow fishermen, need to understand our sport so they can appreciate our efforts and respect our place as legitimate sportsmen. Safety is important because bluewater freediving is a very dangerous sport. I will identify many hazards and present methods of surviving them.

* * * *

The breath-holding freediver is the Native American Indian of the ocean. His speargun replaces the bow and arrow—otherwise the analogy is complete. Both hunt wild animals under conditions where only primitive skill and guile prevail. Conditions can change quickly, with the hunter becoming the hunted.

Follow the freediver into his world. After a deep breath, feet raised, he tips over and slips effortlessly head-first beneath the waves into the liquid world of the open ocean. The enveloping water is supportive and filled with beauty. The diver is free. Free of bulky and noisy scuba gear. Free to roam with the wild animals. Free to fly gracefully in any direction.

Armed with only his speargun, the streamlined diver levels off easily at 25 feet. He experiences an exhilaration known only to trained freedivers. His mental ease and special physiological adaptations make him feel as if he has no need to breathe—now or ever. It is narcotic. Peaceful. Part of him feels as if he could remain suspended beneath the waves forever.

The open ocean seems limitless. Molecule after molecule of bluewater connect in endless chains encircling the globe, allowing fish to journey between continents. The diver cannot always predict what type of fish will appear out of this fenceless world. The oceans are the wildest places left on earth. The animals roaming there completed their evolutionary development long before man's presence, yet he can still watch them acting out their ancient rituals of hunting and survival.

Alert and filled with anticipation, the diver is focused entirely on the present. There is no room for terrestrial thoughts here. He conserves vital oxygen by remaining relaxed, even limp, but his head and eyes are in constant motion. His movements are smooth, as fluid as the water enveloping him. As his vision sweeps side to side, up and down, he is alert for game and trouble.

The diver senses a shift in the current as he adjusts his position with subtle fin movements. He can hear a variety of sea creatures without the noisy interference of escaping scuba bubbles. Ghost shrimp click and pop, whales sing and dolphins whistle. Now his ears provide the first evidence of approaching game. Frenetic bait fish send out sonic waves as they flee. Next he watches the bait fish dart past and knows from which direction his prey will be coming. His eyes strain as he focuses into the distant blue void. His heart starts pounding. First, shadows appear. They materialize into bodies of giant tuna, regal and aloof. Subtle tail movements propel them as they glide past—apparitions just out of range.

Finally, the diver feels the need for air as his chest begins to burn and his breathing muscles pull against his closed throat. He has been down for more than a minute and a half. Just three strong kicks initiate the ascent. The glide upward is effortless. He hardly notices the waves slapping against him as he takes a giant breath. The cool air, scrubbed by ocean waves, quenches his lungs as it supercharges them. Ten breaths are all he needs before diving back down. He is certain that this will be the dive when the big ones come within range.

It takes courage to make the transition from the shore waters into the open ocean. Most scuba and freediving activities are oriented toward getting to the bottom. The bluewater freediver severs his psychological tether to the security and familiarity of the inshore reefs and bays. He swims far from shore, feeling naked, into waters many hundreds, even thousands, of feet deep, where any animal can appear, and from any direction. He becomes part of the food chain. While the risks seem great, the rewards are tremendous, and the lure of the open water increases as divers return with incredible catches and stories.

I cannot help but wonder what tales Al would have contributed to this book. My bet is that he would have offered a colorful story or two about his own personal world-record tuna, white seabass or yellowtail.

Bluewater hunting

HUNTING WITH SPINNER DOLPHINS

Forty miles from the Pacific shores of Costa Rica, I am about to experience what the local fishermen call "a happening." I ease off the end of the drifting boat into blue water 2,000 feet deep, just ahead of an advancing school of dolphin. The water is quiet. It appears as clear and insubstantial as air; the uninitiated would surely fear an immediate plunge into the abyss.

Suddenly, the silence is broken by sea birds, screeching and wheeling into high-speed dives. As they crash through the water around me, I see a blue football-shaped tuna squirt by, followed by others of increasing size. Now the ocean is full of yellowfin tuna streaking beneath me, intent on driving up the bait fish layered a hundred feet below.

A giant tuna, weighing over 200 pounds, changes direction and swims toward me. He turns just a few feet away and presents an image of incredible beauty. Dancing shafts of penetrating surface light play over his cobalt blue body. His center and finlets are highlighted in intense canary yellow. In a second he is gone, called to join his mates in the hunt below. There are fewer tuna streaking by now; their departure is heralded by an increasing cacophony of clicks and whistles as the dolphin catch up and feast on the morsels left behind by the marauding tuna ahead.

There are at least a thousand spinner dolphins in the approaching school. Many of them prove that they are appropriately named by making spectacular vertical and horizontal leaps incorporating multiple, twisting mid-air

A spinner dolphin jumps in a Hawaiian sea.

PHOTO BY JAMES D. WATT

spins. A vanguard of seven adult males protects the school by challenging me with their penetrating clicking and close circling behavior. They quickly lose interest and rejoin the main school, its members swimming and leaping by. There are many pups sheltered against their mothers' sides. A surprising number of dolphin are engaged in sexual intercourse, with the female on the surface and the male undulating below, as they, too, speed by.

Within three minutes "the happening" is over. The animals are traveling at a speed of six knots. It is quiet again. Only fish scales remain, a mute testament to the passing of this ancient ritual. The flurry of iridescent blue and purple sequins shimmer and dance in the reflected sunlight as they slowly make their way to the ocean floor a third of a mile below.

GENERAL BLUEWATER SPEARFISHING TECHNIQUES

Some say successful bluewater hunters, with their trophy fish, are lucky. I define "luck" as the meeting of *opportunity* and *preparedness*. Create your opportunity by carefully studying fish and their habits. Prepare yourself and your gear for that one chance at a big fish.

Freediving clubs are an excellent source of knowledge and companionship. Find a buddy and grow together. Discuss your observations—this will accelerate your learning. As you become more educated about the sport, you'll worry less about the risks of drowning and shark attack. Your fears of the unknown will be replaced with a wary confidence that you have the skills to manage these problems.

Mentally prepare. Expect 99 percent of your diving time to be spent waiting, but tell yourself on every dive that this time "the big one" will

appear. Do not allow your mind to wander. Do not think about your work or how cold you are. Instead, focus on the important questions:

- Am I quiet?
- Am I at the right depth?
- Is my gun in position and ready to go?
- From which direction do I expect the fish to approach?

This is a time for profound physical relaxation. Every part of your body should be relaxed, including your gun grip. A little anticipation, however, goes a long way in sharpening your scan. If you have just sighted a large school of fish, you will be alert. Hours later, as your enthusiasm wanes, imagine a record fish lurking just outside the limits of your visibility. The belief that "I am going to see a big fish *this* dive," produces fish. Every dive must contain this affirmation.

Let us review a typical dive. It starts as you surface from your last dive. Your snorkel is already clear of water. The first surface breath is as deep as you can manage. Hold it for a few seconds before letting it out slowly. Start slow, deep breathing that gradually increases in tempo. Generally, you are ready for another dive after 10 breaths. Make your last three breaths quick and deep.

Excessive hyperventilation is dangerous. Hyperventilation is rapid and/or deep breathing practiced long enough to cause lightheadedness and dizziness. Avoid hyperventilation. Hyperventilation will be explored in the chapter on shallow-water blackout.

Surface dives must be quiet because noisy dives scare fish. Tuck dive, up and over, raising one leg in the air for momentum and using the other to bite the water for the first kick. Break the snorkel seal around your mouth and let water enter. This maneuver prevents noisy bubbles from escaping your snorkel and alerting the fish. Level off your dive at the depth you see fish, anywhere from 15 to 40 feet. Weight yourself so that you neither sink nor float at that depth, usually 25 feet.

Pace yourself. Settle into a pace you can maintain for hours. Seventy-five seconds under the water and 45 seconds on the surface is a good rhythm. A well-trained diver can keep this pace up for hours, spending 40 minutes of every hour under water!

Level off so that you are oriented into the current, at or near the bait boundary. Your head must be in constant but smooth motion, swiveling 180 degrees horizontally, and moving up and down to cover the three-dimensional space surrounding you. Look for fish and sharks approaching you from behind. You must keep your eyes focused at the far edge of your visibility; try focusing on a distant bait fish. Do not worry about missing something close—you won't; a study of airline pilots revealed that as their eyes tire they tend to focus only a few feet ahead. Do not allow your eyes to fixate. It takes constant effort to focus toward the distance, but the reward is spotting fish before they enter your target zone, allowing you to prepare for the shot.

Develop your scan. I learned scanning from Al Schneppershoff, who constantly spotted fish before the divers around him did. Your scan should be fairly rapid. Pause only slightly to identify objects in the distance. You will not see a complete fish. Initially, all you will see of the white seabass are its fins. Tuna frequently swim straight at you, presenting a circular, bullet-like profile.

Many times, a subtle change in the hue of the water color provides the first visual clue of approaching fish. Most fish appear dark, but some are light. In low-visibility water, the yellow finlets of a larger tuna's tail may be the first thing you see.

Modify your scan when you dive against a current. Confine your scan to the 220-degree window in front of you, keeping the bait fish just behind you. Approximately every 10 to 20 seconds, scan the 140 degrees behind you where the bait is concentrated.

Manage your speargun. Hold the gun in your hand with your trigger finger resting against and outside the trigger guard, or behind the trigger. The best technique is to hold the gun close and slightly elevated in front of you. Estimate the fish's path. Slowly turn the gun toward that direction. Now slowly extend the gun and wait.

Sometimes a fish will come from behind or from your side. In this case, slowly retract the gun to your chest using the "soldier-at-arms" position with the handle at your hips and the muzzle near your face. Turn yourself ahead of the fish's path and re-extend the gun. This is how South Africans handle their guns in dirty water; otherwise they would lose sight of their spear tips. This technique works equally well in clear water because turning a fully extended gun will frighten your fish. The initially high angle of the gun can be adjusted as the gun sinks slowly. (The muzzle end of most guns is heavy.) Most fish will dive beneath you when they pass. Just allow the sinking gun to follow them.

The ideal shooting range is 10 to 15 feet for horizontal shots. Gravity has a remarkable effect on your spear. Shooting downward will add five feet to your range. Gravity will also increase the punch of your shot. Consequently, your best shot will be made at a downward angle with no more than 15 to 20 feet separating you and your target. Conversely, shooting upward will shorten your range and decrease the spear's penetration.

Ascend quietly, using smooth fluid motions. This will help avoid distressing approaching fish that are out of your range of vision. Plan to ascend 15 seconds before you run out of air. This will allow you enough air to approach, aim and shoot a trophy you may encounter on the way to the surface. Be sure to hold the gun at the ready on the way up and avoid the temptation of letting it drag behind you. Look for the direction of your next dive and orient yourself facing that way.

Release air into your snorkel within one foot of the surface. This serves two very useful functions. First, the air rising in the snorkel pushes water ahead of it. You will not have to expend valuable energy blowing water out at the surface.

Second, you can immediately take a breath when breaking the surface.

HUNTING AND SHOOTING

The following comments apply specifically to bluewater fishing. While many of these techniques work well for shallow-water reef fish, others do not. Refer to the sections on individual species for specific recommendations, some of which are contrary to the following generalizations.

Be underwater before the fish approach. Your chances of getting close to fish are greatly increased if you are underwater, and level, *before* they appear. Bluewater divers would never get within range of pelagic fish if the fish were not curious. They can outswim and outmaneuver us. They can see us and sense us well before we see them. It is their sense of curiosity that brings them close. (See the chapters on individual gamefish to see how divers use this curiosity to their advantage.)

Freeze your position and analyze the course and number of approaching fish. Gradually ease your gun to their level and position it ahead of their expected course so they swim in front of your spear. Don't swing your gun directly toward the fish. Set up an intersecting course. Avoid swimming after a fish; this usually spooks the fish as well as all of the surrounding game, even fish not yet in sight. A solitary fish generally continues in the same direction; it will not change course as it swims away. Be on the lookout for fish following this leader; he may be part of a group. With luck, there will be a second or third group following the first.

Schooling fish are very sensitive to gun movement. It is much better to accept the first fish within range than to swing the gun on a larger specimen. I generally recommend taking your closest shot, keeping gun movement to a minumum. Avoid desperation shots. Do not shoot at a fish that is out of range or poorly positioned. A spooked or injured fish may scatter the school, ruining a better shot later. Alternatively, you might find yourself faced with a beautiful shot and an unloaded gun. If you run out of air, ascend quietly, angling away from the school. Chances are, the unmolested school will return, probably closer.

Remain motionless when a school of fish circles you. Many times they will come closer as their circle tightens. Keep a close watch for a straggler that cuts the corner around you, trying to catch up with others in its school. This fish will frequently come within range. Extend your gun ahead of you and do not move it laterally. Wait for the school to complete another circuit. Adjust the vertical position of your gun as they come around for another pass. You might have to wait for several circuits for a good shot. More than once I have found myself in 60 feet of water, drifting down, waiting for a closer shot as the fish circled. It takes skill to get the largest fish in the school. (Al Schneppershoff was a master at this.)

Think about your profile and reduce it during your final approach to the fish. Imagine the picture you present to a fish viewing you from the side. Your gun, fully extended six feet ahead, and your fins trailing another two feet behind, make you a 15-foot monster. Retracting your gun will help, but there is not too much you can do with the appearance of your fins. The sooner you can present a straight-on profile, the better.

Bluewater diver Gerald Lim demonstrates "the soldier-at-arms" position.

Photo by Terry Maas

This circular profile, perhaps two feet in diameter, is much less imposing and allows you to get closer to your game.

Surface approaches are very difficult, if not impossible, with some species. Solitary gamefish are even more difficult to approach from the surface than schooled fish. One technique usually doomed to failure is diving directly to your prey. (Spanish mackerel and large tuna are exceptions.) Fish are very sensitive to anything approaching them directly. Instead of diving toward the fish, take a deep breath and dive vertically at the first sight of fish. Make little attempt to keep them in sight, as you will tend to angle toward them, spooking them. (Many divers say direct eye contact will spook them as well.) Calculate where they will be when you level off, and look in that direction. Generally, the lead fish of a school will not present the best shot because he will have already passed out of range. Try for another member following the leader. Once you are under, it may be more advantageous to swim away from the lead fish. Often, the group following the leader will circle behind you and then pass around in front of you.

Position your shot carefully. Thin fish like sailfish or wahoo require the most accurate shot. A shot on the lateral line, just behind the gill plates, generally "stones" the fish, rendering it immobile. Any shot striking the spinal cord is a winner; it will disable the fish. Tuna, on the other hand, can be shot anywhere as long as the shot is placed in a bulky area forward of the tail section. Even the gill plates are good. Their speed is what makes tuna difficult to shoot. It takes great discipline on the part of the diver to aim at a position six inches ahead of a tuna's head. Yet this is exactly where you must aim. Fish shot in the tail region are especially difficult to land. Line tension pulls the tail toward you, which constantly positions the fish's head away from you, providing the fish with a maximal swimming advantage.

Clear water causes perception problems. Clear water, with visibility in excess of 100 feet, presents a special problem for the bluewater diver. This problem is compounded with big fish. I remember our first record-breaking trip to Guadalupe Island, Mexico. I watched a competent diver aim at a school of eight 150-pound bluefin tuna. The fish were 60 feet away. The diver shot. His spear streaked straight out for 20 feet and then, its force spent, arced toward the bottom. The fish were so far away that, to my amazement, they did not even flinch at the shot. This diver had problems accurately judging the fish's size and distance. These very large fish, 60 feet away, appeared to the diver as 50-pound fish just 20 feet away.

The solution is to study the approaching fish carefully. Look for details in their scales, eyes and finlets. Looking for these details should remind you of the adage, "Don't shoot until you see the whites of their eyes." Force yourself to see *detail* before taking a shot. Judge distances another way by looking at your spear tip and multiplying this distance two or three times. This is your maximum effective range.

Silence is golden. Gamefish are sensitive to any sound. The only sound a diver should make purposefully is to attract fish. (These sounds are discussed in the section on how to attract fish.) Check your fins for squeaking. Nothing on your weight belt should slide or rub. Learn to hold

Bluewater divers Gerald Lim and Mark Barville demonstrate the marked decrease in profile divers make when they approach fish straight-on.

Photo by Terry Maas

your gun just far enough from your body to prevent the sound of accidental contact with your belt. Float lines should be free of connections that might clank against your gun or belt. Even a poorly attached snorkel can make an undesirable squeak as it rubs your face mask.

Air trapped inside wetsuits will alert fish as it bubbles around inside. Remove this air during your first few dives. Stop in a vertical position on ascent, just below the surface, and let water into your suit. Do this by first pulling open your suit around your feet, allowing water to follow the rising air. Next, open your hood to expel it. I hate this! Just writing about it makes me shiver. Some divers place a permanent hole in the top of their hood to help air escape.

Squeaky ear clearing will scare gamefish. Try to clear your ears continuously, starting with the surface dive. Use several small, quiet clearings instead of a few noisy clearings. Be sure your ears are adequately cleared when you level your dive. Being under-cleared when you level off gives you little leeway if you have to descend while tracking a fish. I have watched big fish bolt after an untimely, noisy ear clearing.

Boat engines alert gamefish. Shut off every possible engine and motor. Have pickup boats circle out, away from divers. Keep them away from the expected path of incoming fish. Your chase boat is best left tethered to its mother boat with all engines off.

FINDING FISH

We need to know our quarry, its habits and its haunts. The bluewater is so vast that finding fish can be an exercise in futility. So how do we increase our chances of locating gamefish?

By looking for areas of fish concentrations. Fish congregate around shallow, rocky structures next to the deep blue. They also gather at feeding locations, on migration paths and around flotsam.

Fish congregate around a high spot in an area known to have lots of fish activity. This underwater structure of coral or rock provides a safe haven for the bait fish. Bait fish aggregations attract larger pelagic fish. Most of the bait fish school up-current from submerged structures. Since their food is borne by the current, each small bait fish tries to get ahead of the other to be first to the food source. Fear of predators keeps them from venturing too far from the safety of their sanctuaries of caves and crevices.

How far bait fish venture from these homes in any one circumstance depends on food abundance, visibility and current velocity. These variables determine the bait fish's sense of safety. This is a fixed distance and it forms a wall. I call this the "bait barrier," and it forms one side of a "fish street." The other side of the fish street is the open ocean. Pelagic predators patrol this street. The best location for fishing near a high spot is just ahead of the bait barrier facing the bluewater.

I am convinced many gamefish approach a location out of curiosity, not hunger. It is as if they are taking a stroll through town. Maybe the noisy ghost shrimp, clicking madly away in their protected caves, attract them. Maybe it is the noise bait fish make when they become alarmed that attracts gamefish. In any case, an area known to be productive will continue to be productive year after year.

Previous experience with a given rock or coral structure gives you a starting point from which to patrol the bait barrier. Open water

Terry Maas hunts the edge of the bait boundary on a "fish street."

predators frequently make circular approaches, with extensions far out to sea. They often follow the same path day after day. This path may be altered by subtle changes in current direction, velocity, visibility and time of day.

"You must remember every day you spend in the water and catalog all variables in the computer of your mind," says Terry Lentz, North America's only individual world spearfishing champion. After years of input, one develops a feeling for an area. It is absolutely uncanny when this feeling translates into palpable anticipation, an anticipation for the moment the big ones arrive. You actually "feel it in your bones."

The following are examples of various locations known to provide productive gamefishing:

Pinnacles. The submerged pinnacle at San Benedicto Island, Mexico, is one-half mile from the island. Its top is 20 feet from the surface. The surrounding bottom is 300 feet deep. You will find the tuna and wahoo up-current just ahead of the bait barrier.

Reefs. There is a fabulous gently sloped reef at San Benedicto Island. It tapers gradually from shore for a quarter mile to 60 feet deep where it drops precipitously into 400 feet of water. Drift parallel to the half-mile-long reef. Stay just outside the bait fish congregations.

Walls. One side of Socorro Island, Mexico, forms a cliff that continues into 300 feet of water. It begins at the mouth of a shallow bay. Tuna and wahoo leave the bay headed down-current. They come to within 50 feet of the shore along this wall. Hunt this structure by swimming into the current. Expect to encounter fish swimming straight toward you, down the current.

Banks. Cortez Bank is 100 miles off the California coast, 60 miles away from the nearest island. It is several square miles in area. Both sides of the bank can be productive, depending upon the direction of the current. Hunt the side that faces into the current. This reef structure steps down from 60 to 90 feet and steps again from 90 to 100 feet. Hunt either of these step-offs where bait fish congregate. Continue out into the bluewater until the bait fish just begin to disappear.

Kelp beds. Pacific Coast kelp beds from California to Baja California, Mexico, attract white seabass, yellowtail and bluefin tuna. Generally the deepest part of the bed, facing into the current, offers the best opportunity for game. Stay with bait fish schools.

Feeding fish. Feeding gamefish offer us an excellent opportunity. Birds are the best indicators of feeding tuna. They can be spotted miles away crashing into the feeding frenzy below. Dolphin are often associated with feeding tuna. Dive underneath passing dolphin because they often swim with yellowfin tuna.

Flamingo Bay, Costa Rica, is an excellent location for yellowfin tuna. Tuna sometimes feed only five miles from shore. Locate dolphin and tuna by following the direction that departing sea birds fly in the morning. White speckles in the air, just above the horizon, indicate feeding sea birds. Move close and the tranquil sea appears rippled. Closer still, the rippling sea transforms into a full-blown feeding frenzy. What an incredible sight! Sea birds dive to attack the bait. Tuna and dolphin are jumping everywhere. The sounds of screeching birds, jumping fish and breathing dolphin amplify the excitement.

There are two special techniques required to fish these schools effectively. First, anticipate the direction the school is moving. It will generally be moving in one direction for a period, however it is not uncommon for it to make radical changes, even reversals are possible. Position

Look for tuna and other bluewater gamefish under dolphin like these.

yourself ahead of the school. The fish travel as fast as six knots, making a fast boat imperative.

Second, get into the water quickly. Sprint on the surface, following the boatman who directs you with hand signals. He will indicate the direction the school is swimming. As the first tuna appears, dive to 40 feet and position yourself against the increasing numbers of tuna as they shoot past. The tuna are pursuing bait fish they drive up from deep water.

It is difficult to prepare for a dive under these conditions. Imagine pursuing the school, then jumping into the water and diving, all within several minutes. It is possible. I used this technique to spear five tuna with five shots. The smallest was 100 pounds and the largest was 256 pounds. I took these fish 40 miles out to sea in 2,000 feet of water.

Carl Butler, a world record holder from the U.S. Virgin Islands, says this technique won't work there. "When the tuna migrate through, they come layered with other fish," he says, "bait fish on the top, tuna below, and a whole bunch of sharks below them both!"

Buoys are excellent fish attracters. Hawaiian and Virgin Island divers find many of their bluewater fish around offshore buoys. The buoys attract bait, which, in turn, attract pelagic gamefish. Divers use a "live boat" technique when the current is impossible to swim against. They drop off up-current and drift through the fishing grounds. They are then picked up when they signal the boatman. This technique has some obvious safety considerations discussed later in the chapter on survival.

Flotsam holds fish. Almost anything adrift on the sea will attract fish—cargo nets, burlap bags, logs and kelp paddies. Flotsam collects marine life. Barnacles form. Immature fish and bait fish congregate. Schools of intermediate predators such as bonito, skip jack and dorado breeze by picking off stray bait fish. Apex predators like the tuna, wahoo, sailfish and marlin hunt the periphery of this micro-ecosystem.

Do not pass up flotsam without making a quick investigative dive. The Global Positioning System (GPS), using satellite navigation, allows a return to the exact area of productive flotsam. Simple drift calculations allow you to relocate flotsam the next day. Fishermen off Baja California, Mexico, anchor radar reflectors to large floating kelp beds to relocate them. Enterprising fishermen make their own flotsam, called "fish aggregation devices" (FADs). Some FADs, made of plastic sheets and ropes, are designed to mimic floating seaweed patches. Fishermen launch these FADs at the beginning of a vacation week and monitor them daily. The use of FADs deserves further investigation by skindivers. Perhaps a dive club could manufacture and loan out such devices to its members.

Known migration paths provide fish concentrations. Some species travel the same route yearly. Australian divers eagerly anticipate the migration of the spanish mackerel as they travel south during the summer. New England divers look for striped bass as they migrate out of their shallow spawning grounds into the deeper offshore waters to the north. The Atlantic bluefin tunas migrate in shallow water from the Gulf of Mexico to the North Atlantic. They appear in shallow water off the Bahamas and off Nova Scotia.

Fish follow currents. Be alert for subtle differences in the current as changing current conditions invariably mean a change in the fishing

Note how bait fish gather around the ropes of this fish aggregation device. Bluewater gamefish will be near.

PHOTO BY JAMES D. WATT

conditions, sometimes quite dramatic. I have seen reversals within minutes, for the better and for the worse. For example, shifts in the direction of the current can bring in clear water loaded with bait and game.

Changes in water clarity and temperature suggest a change in the current. Clouds of dirty water can shut off bluewater fishing. Conversely, cloudy water containing pelagic bait fish can herald the arrival of gamefish. I will discuss current prediction later in this book.

You can recognize a current shift by observing the bait fish. Bait fish intent on swimming in one direction indicate a moderate current. Meandering bait fish, swimming here and there, indicate little or no current.

The time of day has an effect on gamefishing. Yellowfin tuna are most commonly seen during the early morning and late evening. I see most bluefin tuna during the middle of the day. Evening is the best time of day for striped bass and white seabass. Yellowtail (kingfish) prefer the sunny side of a pinnacle in the early morning or late evening. Sea water changes character during the day. The sun warms it one or two degrees. Growing plankton causes water visibility to decrease steadily throughout the day. As evening approaches, the bluewater becomes black and the imagination soars.

ATTRACTING FISH

You can attract fish by a variety of methods, including the use of sounds, baits and lures.

Sounds attract some fish. Use a "croaking" sound generated deep in your throat. Drop your jaw, letting air pass through your vocal cords into your mouth. Make room for the air in your mouth to prevent expelling this valuable commodity. Try varying the note, volume and cadence of these "croaks" until you find a combination that works. Croaking helped me win the national individual championships in Hawaii. Time and again, I attracted the open-water opelu kala from their position over the deep-water drop-off. They swam directly to me from as far as 100 feet away.

Croaking will attract white seabass. Use this technique as a desperation ploy, too. When it seems certain that a gamefish will swim away, try croaking. I have turned wahoo and tuna around with this technique. Try slapping the water over bait fish schools; some divers have successfully attracted surface gamefish using this trick.

Chum, chunk bait and burley, all synonyms for fish attracters, are made primarily from dead fish. One popular method for using these fish attracters is to anchor your boat along a drop-off or pinnacle. Cut fish into one-inch square chunks and cast them behind the boat. This method of chumming works best in clear water with a slight current.

World champion spearfisherman Terry Lentz, Hawaiian champion Dennis Okada and I used a variation of this method in the Hawaiian Islands for yellowfin tuna. We chose a fish aggregation buoy anchored in 4,000 feet of water, 20 miles from shore, as our target. The night before our dive, we packed one-inch pieces of squid mixed with mashed squid and oatmeal into 15 plastic bags.

According to our plan, one diver "rode shotgun" on the surface armed with a powerhead. Another diver dove to 40 feet and released the chum up-current from the buoy. The third diver then descended into the burley ball and waited

An example of the Australian method for making burley.

PHOTO BY GREG PICKERING

19

for the tuna. We were totally unprepared for the tunas' speed. They inhaled our bait ball in seconds. They swam so fast and erratically that only Dennis' quick aim connected with a 20-pounder which quickly escaped. Seconds after the tuna ate the last chunk of bait, they disappeared.

Both divers on the surface filled their masks with water, laughing at the spectacle of the third diver below, who was frantically shifting his aim at the 50-knot missiles devouring our precious bait.

Australian divers sometimes use "live burley." They will shoot a suitable bait fish and drop it. Alternatively, they might carry a bait fish with them and drop it when gamefish appear.

The obvious problem with chunking is that it attracts sharks. It is time to try another location when the first shark appears.

Artificial lures attract fish. Lures will attract specific fish such as wahoo, king mackerel and yellowtail. Try trailing a bright-colored lure or striping your gun with reflective tape. I made a flexible plastic fish that trails 20 feet behind me on my float line. It works well for yellowtail, which are often attracted to a speared member of their school.

The Australians are starting to use a lure they learned about from the South Africans. Their "flasher" is as simple as several pieces of mirror tied together or as complex as plastic lures, with bright colors and mirrors embedded in them, trailing long colorful ribbons. When the flasher is lowered on a line, it flashes, attracting fish. One California hunter reports that reflective tape stripes on his float line attract bluefin tuna, which follow the line straight up to him, joining him in formation swimming. He also recommends placing reflective tape, shaped like bait fish, on his fins in non-sharky waters (are there any?).

Blending in with the surrounding water is my preference for hunting large tuna. My wetsuit is blue and my fins and face mask are black. My float line is dyed black to prevent it

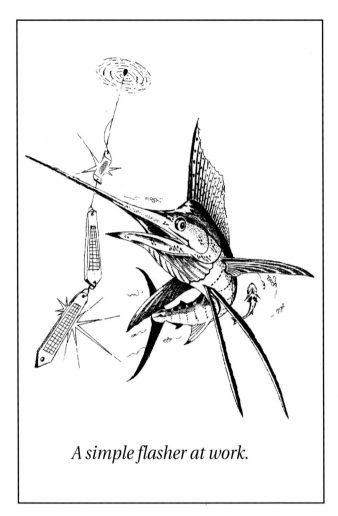

A simple flasher at work.

from reflecting light. Tuna will swim within range, especially if I am submerged. I prefer not to be too conspicuous in the water for fear of attracting sharks. I definitely avoid anything on my body that reflects or contrasts greatly with the water.

Consider fish repellents. Wetsuits are difficult to don. Many divers use fragrant soap, hair conditioner or body lotion to help them slip into their wetsuits. Any artificial scent will alarm fish. Their sensitive olfactory apparatus warns them of danger. Sea water is the best suit lubricant. If the water is too cold, use an unscented, all-natural diluted hair conditioner. Fortunately for the serious diver who spends many hours in the water, urine is regarded as a "neutral" scent. It does not repel fish.

LESSONS FROM THE EASTERN TROPICAL PACIFIC

One of the world's best bluewater hunters does not carry a speargun. Trim and fit, freediver Rick Rosenthal carries a camera. He was an accomplished open-ocean diver even before he devoted over 170 days in the offshore waters of the eastern tropical Pacific (Nicaragua to Columbia) filming his BBC/PBS special, "Hunters of the Sea Wind." Few can equal his bluewater expertise. He enthusiastically embraces the athletic challenge of freediving for large pelagic fish species.

You might ask how a solitary diver, armed only with a camera, defends himself. Have there been any close calls?

Rick answers, "I have had two pretty scary incidents, both involving Pacific sailfish. The first occurred while filming 'Sea Wind.' I was shooting an incredible sequence of courting sailfish off Cocos Island, Costa Rica, with fellow freediver and photographer Flip Nicklin of National Geographic Magazine. Four mature fish were circling in a train-like fashion, furling and unfurling their capes, their colors changing from dark blue to silver. They rubbed each others' sides as they passed, leapfrogging their position in the circle. Suddenly, one broke from the school and flared his bill directly in front of my face plate in an unmistakable act of aggression. I could clearly see the deadly point of its bill as it passed just a couple of feet in front of the camera. That sailfish made it clear to me that I was intruding and in danger.

"The second event occurred far off the Pacific coast of Costa Rica. I was filming a sequence for a TV fishing program. We caught a sailfish on a very light line. I was snorkeling on the surface next to the boat with my large 16-millimeter underwater camera as the sailfish circled some 30 feet below me, languidly pulling at the line. Quickly, its blue color changed to jet black and it charged my silhouette.

Luckily, just in time, I positioned my big movie camera upward in front of my face and shoulder. When the fish struck, it ripped off the light meter, leaving bits of flesh and scales in its place. The sailfish continued upward, leaping completely free of the water. The line parted and it disappeared.

"When Captain Richard Chellemi realized I was not injured, he asked, 'Do you want to get out of the water?' I answered, 'No, not now. Everything happened so fast, I didn't even have time for an adrenalin rush.' Eventually, I swam back to the boat where I promptly threw away the bright red tank top that Captain Richard had me wear. He thought the bright red color would make it easier for him to see me in the turbulent sea. We don't know if billfish see color, but this fish acted as if I were waving a matador's cape!"

Rick received his bachelor's and master's degrees and finished his doctorate research work in marine biology. While a student, he also became a professional scuba diving instructor. He liked to illustrate his course work with underwater photographs. His professional underwater film career began fulltime when he accepted a proposal to shoot a one-hour documentary on Pacific salmon. Keeping up with these elusive fish required Rick to rely on his freediving skills. He enjoyed the freedom and challenge of freediving. His fascination with freediving into the bluewater continued with his filming of whales and dolphin in the tropical Pacific. Freediving allowed him to get close to these relatively shy creatures. Later, after spending a week on a boat with six bluewater spearfishermen, he hatched an idea for a new film. That idea developed into another PBS special, "Bluewater Hunters."

Rick filmed one of the sequences for "Bluewater Hunters" off the west coast of Mexico, hitching a ride on a sportfishing boat. The fishermen hooked striped marlin they found feeding on a ball of anchovetas that the marlin had forced to the surface. After finally catching several fish, the tired fishermen let Rick in the water. The anglers estimated there were four to

five marlin in the school. Once in the water, Rick found upward of 30 striped marlin herding the bait fish.

"They came from below, their mouths gaped wide," Rick remembers. "Making no attempt to use their bills, they just took turns filling their mouths. These marlin were really 'lit up.' Their iridescent, vibrant, horizontal body stripes appeared to glow, illuminated from within. Filming that sequence really hooked me on bluewater hunting."

Rick's countless hours of filming whales, marlin, sailfish, tuna and dolphin certainly qualifies him as an expert bluewater hunter. While the following observations were drawn primarily from his experience in the eastern tropical Pacific, they have relevance for bluewater conditions worldwide.

Feeding birds indicate fish. One of the best and most reliable signs of gamefish are the terns. Typically smaller and whiter than gulls, they fly erratically over the sea surface. Be especially alert when they begin to vocalize, as this means that tuna and bonito are beginning to get active and feed. Boobies plunging into the ocean also indicate feeding fish. Boobies sitting on the surface have lost the main school, and confused, they just pick up leftover scraps. The much heralded, high-flying, frigate bird is not always a good indicator of fish below unless it is flying low, skimming the surface. Frigates soaring high appear to be searching for, or tracking an inactive predator. Expect to find gamefish when they swoop down close to the surface.

Look for any marine animal jumping or spouting. Dolphins are the classic example, but we have found large gamefish around pilot whales and humpback whales. Often these marine mammals are associated with birds; found

together, they almost always guarantee gamefish.

Bait fish are welcome indicators. Bait fish such as anchovetas, sardines and flying fish, driven up and concentrated near the surface, are referred to as "meat balls." They indicate feeding gamefish and dolphin. In the eastern tropical Pacific, the deep-sea lantern fish is an important food in the diet of gamefish, satisfying them so well they frequently refuse a fisherman's bait. Flying fish are also good indicators for dolphin fish, and dolphin fish attract big marlin and yellowfin tuna.

Mature flotsam offers an excellent opportunity for finding big fish. Flotsam becomes mature when it has spent enough time at sea to accumulate fouling organisms such as barnacles. A 30-foot log, for example, collects species from each zone it traverses. Size is not always important. We found large logs barren of fish, and schools of fish surrounding a plastic bucket, a broom or a single coconut.

Rick is fascinated by the mystery of flotsam. "Flotsam acts as a sign post in the sea. We have found literally acres of young tuna and other pelagics surrounding these objects. What holds these fish after the initial attraction? There is not enough food to sustain the entire fish mass. There is certainly not enough shelter from a small log. We have yet to decode the answers to this question."

We do know the inhabitants of the flotsam community are constantly changing. Many species may call it home. Interestingly, they do not all inhabit the area close to the log at the same time. I have seen multiple guard changes, with sea turtles replacing feeding sea snakes, later wahoo, shark and tuna might take over. It is important for the bluewater hunter to appreciate these changes. He may find a log, unproductive

A log like this can harbor acres of marine life.

PHOTO BY RICK ROSENTHAL

Note the presence of birds where currents meet.

PHOTO BY RICK ROSENTHAL

earlier in the day, suddenly loaded with fish a few hours later. Look for the big predators such as marlin and tuna out on the periphery or deep below. Do not expect to find them directly below the object because they cruise the periphery, appearing and disappearing like ghosts. Investigate any flotsam that has roosting sea birds. Swim quietly toward the object and stay alert.

Fixed sign posts exist in the sea as well. With our GPS and depth sounder, we were able to return to the same areas overlying bottom prominence, drop-offs and break points. These places, sometimes 40 to 50 miles from shore, continually held fish.

Gamefish concentrate where currents meet. Look for areas where rippled water and smooth water interface together or for an abrupt change in water color, temperature or both. A sea temperature change of just one or two degrees Fahrenheit may be enough to hold gamefish and their prey. Large fish cruise the bluewater side of the interface, picking off bait fish that inhabit the more nutrient-laden green side. We spent days drifting these areas, finding fish working the edges. Thermoclines, subsurface layers of cold water, resemble current breaks. I find many large pelagic fish cruising the cold water interface, some 40 to 60 feet under the water.

Hunt the edges, advises Rick. Large marlin and sailfish cruise the periphery of bait fish aggregations. Avoid penetrating the center of these bait balls, while diving and especially with your boat. Swim quietly along the edge. Limit the number of hunters to one or two, as more divers will spook the large fish and you may not have another close encounter with camera or spear.

24

Sharks

"SHARK" is one of those words that evokes an emotional response in almost everyone. In terms of evolution, these are simple animals that completed their development a million years ago. Shark researchers readily admit that their knowledge of shark behavior is sketchy. That is what makes shark stories so instructive; we can learn more about sharks from their encounters with bluewater hunters.

Bluewater hunters do not view sharks as game, but rather, recognizing they share the same hunting grounds, treat them with respect. This chapter contains many dramatic stories, but keep in mind that given the many hours divers spend in the bluewater, only a few have ever had serious shark encounters.

GUADALUPE WHITE SHARK

This story is about three members of the Long Beach Neptunes and one great white shark. In my opinion, all three divers are heroes: victim Harry Ingram and rescuers Tom Blandford and Vance Carriere. They were the elite of the 14-member expedition bound for Guadalupe Island, Mexico, in the fall of 1984. This is the same location where, two years earlier, I shot my world-record 398-pound bluefin tuna.

Harry, the owner of a California boat-and-engine repair business, was full of excitement, anticipating his chance at a bluefin. A Vietnam combat veteran, Harry was no stranger to danger. Neither was Tom, a Los Angeles police officer and veteran of high-speed chases. Vance, the youngest and perhaps the hardest charger of the group, was learning his profession as a computer graphics expert. (Vance made the cover and helped with the art direction for this book).

Tom Blandford has my deepest admiration. His selfless aid to fellow diver Harry Ingram in the troubled waters of Guadalupe Island earns my life-long respect. Here is Tom's version:

The 30-hour trip to Guadalupe Island is rough and lumpy—too rough even to cook. An unseasonable hurricane sends powerful waves to hinder us and at the same time drenches the island. Days of rain and run-off dirty the usually crystal waters surrounding Guadalupe. We find a sheltered cove with reasonably clear water. Although we're still shaken from the trip, images of giant bluefin tuna swim through our

minds. These images spur us on. We know very few divers have seen these rare and elusive fish. Only a few have landed one. We each secretly imagine ourselves making a miraculous shot that results in our picture on a magazine cover with a world-record tuna.

We anchor the boat over a 40-foot ledge. Disappointed, I cannot find the tuna, but schools of large yellowtail—our consolation prizes—keep us busy. As we take several of the 30-pound yellows, I switch to my small, more efficient yellowtail gun. Of course, every big game diver can tell you having a gun too small for tuna is a sure-fire method for attracting them. Instead of our usual horizontal dives, I try diving vertically, directly to the rocky bottom, hoping to attract the fish.

It works. Tuna appear. The first really big tuna I have ever seen sends my heart thumping. A school of 100- to 150-pound bluefin material-izes, and their illuminated cobalt blue forms with yellow finlets almost mesmerize me. All of my training, all of the endless nights building gear and this lousy boat ride converge in the nexus of the following moments. I shoot at the closest monster, making a solid shot just behind the gills. The line on my reel races away and I find myself transformed into a human water ski hydroplaning behind my spear line. I'm on. POP! The line snaps from my gun; the fish is gone. Feeling deflated, I think perhaps my only chance at a record is ruined because of my broken line. Will I get a second chance?

My fellow divers go crazy. Bluefin at last. Everyone enters the late afternoon water. My

hand is shaking so badly from the adrenaline rush that I have difficulty reloading my gun. The visibility deteriorates. I'm calmer now, on the bottom again, as another tuna school arrives. These are different because they swim right up to me. I make a perfect shot at the closest fish; it takes off towing me again. The towing force abruptly stops. Confusion clogs my mind, racked by its second adrenaline surge in 10 minutes. What happened? Is he dead already? Following my line down to my spent spear, I find disturbed water where my fish should be. Closer, I find a mass of blood and particles of flesh suspended in a ball. What happened to my fish? The shot was perfect. Disappointed and unaware of danger, I reload my gun.

Harry, 40 feet away, yells, ' Shark!' This particular word really gets my attention. An-other massive, heart-thumping adrenaline release changes my world into slow motion as I look up and spot Harry; he is in the middle of a river of boiling, rippling water. I am amazed by the thunderous noise of the water splashing about him. The back and then the dorsal fin of a huge white shark eclipses my view of Harry as the shark surfaces. Harry tumbles over its back as it submerges. I'm sure only part of Harry remains—the part with his mouth, as Harry is still shouting.

Almost overcome with fear, I swim toward him, certain the shark will return. Reaching Harry, I am relieved to see him intact, except for

A white shark—some experts say they grow to 25 feet and reach an age of 40 years.

PHOTO BY JAMES D. WATT

his eyes, which have been replaced by huge white saucers occupying all the remaining space inside his face mask.

Vance Carriere and John Anderson puncture a pontoon on the inflatable as they rush to our aid. Later, I will laugh at the sight of the two of them paddling furiously in their deflating boat. For the moment, I am relieved. Later, I know I will always remember the empty feeling in the pit of my stomach as I watched Harry boil and churn in the explosive attack of a great white shark.

* * * *

Harry Ingram remembers swimming over to Tom after Tom shot his second tuna. The two had agreed to help each other if one of them shot a fish. Harry noted that the visibility was deteriorating as he watched Tom disappear 30 feet below, looking for his tuna. The two divers drifted about 40 feet apart after Tom explained that his fish was gone. Here is Harry's story. (The following took place in less time than it takes to read about it.)

"I'm pumping up, almost ready to dive, when a white shimmering object appears. It looks just like a shallow reef. Wait a minute! This is no shallow reef. Moving closer, this midwater reef suddenly develops an eye—and a mouth—a big gaping hole. Terrified, I think, 'This is it, I'm going to die.' This is a great white shark, nothing else could possibly grow so big. Its girth is astounding, almost grotesque. It could easily fit the length of a fully finned diver. It is 20 or 25 feet long, so long I cannot see the whole animal.

I yell, 'Shark!' as I position the gun between us. The Australian phrase, 'WHITE DEATH' rockets through my mind. I know an animal this size is going to be making all the next

few decisions. I feel like a minnow ready to be swallowed by a large fish. Just get it over quickly. I hope it doesn't hurt. Now I yell, 'White shark!' because I want my fellow divers to know what killed me. I struggle to settle down. I reason, I know divers who swam with white sharks and survived. Maybe I have a chance.

The great white is 30 feet out when he charges. A loud voice in my mind screams, 'He's coming!' He's on me in an instant. How can an animal so large swim so quickly? Everything goes into slow motion. Reflexively, I shoot my arrow. I watch its slow motion flight, thinking, I shot too soon. The shark hits my spent speargun and drives it into my shoulder. I hear an explosion of sound as he breaches, driving me waist high, six feet through the water. I tumble over his back. I know I am hit. I pull up my damaged arm, amazed to find it still attached. Both of my legs are still there. Tom appears at my side, ducking his head in and out of the water madly, looking for the shark. He yells at me to look too. I put my face mask in the water, but I can't see because my eyes will not open. Defenseless, my eyes refuse to watch him return and eat me.

Harry's instincts and training saved his life, and possibly those of others. His spear did hit the shark. His fellow divers watched a scene straight out of *Jaws* as the big shark towed Harry's buoys toward the inside of the island. Harry attributes the abruptness of his attack to the frenzied state this shark was in after eating two large tuna.

Harry's only visible injury, the shoulder bruise, healed in a week. He says the injury to his psyche took longer.

Earlier that day, Vance had fought a stiff current and had seen several large tuna. While spotting the tuna was encouraging, the struggle against the current was exhausting. Toward afternoon, everyone wanted calmer water. A calm bay seemed inviting. (Apparently, the crew did not realize this was the same bay where Al Schneppershoff was killed nine years earlier.) They anchored there and the divers spread out. Vance remembers:

I'm bone tired. I just finished taking my gear off when I see Tom Blandford hydroplaning across the water. Obviously he has a huge tuna. I think, 'Now I have got to get back into the water.' I finally have my gear back on when I hear Harry yell, 'Shark!' I look up to see Harry doing pirouettes in the water. When he yells, 'White shark!' I think, 'No way am I getting into the water now!'

The shark attacks with an incredible avalanche of water, sounding louder than Shamu the killer whale leaping at Sea World. His fin is 3½ feet tall. The top of his exposed back is 10 feet across and I cannot see his head or tail.

As Harry disappears into the boiling white water, I get sick thinking of what I must tell his wife about his death. I hear Harry hollering and wonder how a man who has just been bitten in half can yell. Harry is alive! I rush to free the inflatable boat from its lashings above the speargun rack. A spear punctures the raft as I free it; no matter, I'm going to get Harry anyway.

Vance remembers how Harry and Tom literally levitated into his deflating boat like winged seals. Vance could understand why Harry was so white—he still thought Harry had been bitten and lost blood—but Tom looked the same shade of white. Back at the boat Harry was in an agitated state, repeatedly exclaiming, "He's big. He's just so damn big!" Harry gratefully accepted a drink from Vance and promptly fell asleep.

WHITE SHARKS

Bluewater hunters encounter the "white death" worldwide, primarily in temperate and subtropical waters. Three to four feet long at birth, some experts think that they can grow to lengths in excess of 25 feet and reach an age of 40 years or more. As youngsters, they eat a variety of marine life including fish and crustaceans. White sharks are opportunistic feeders, eating an expanding variety of marine life as they grow larger.

Once they grow to 9 feet, their primary food source expands to include marine mammals. An examination of the stomach contents of large white sharks reveals that besides mammals they eat quite a variety of fast moving gamefish including yellowtail, skipjack and bonita. One white shark, found dead off Ketchikan, Alaska, had curious white pearl-like balls in its stomach, later identified as the eye lenses of Pacific salmon.

The white shark got its name from its appearance on fishing docks where it was invariably placed upside down, white belly revealed. In the water, its top is dark grey to black, which, when viewed from above, renders it almost invisible against the background of deeper water or rocks. This certainly makes them effective stalkers as they frequently hunt and strike their prey from below. Recent information from Australia proves that whites have better eyesight than previously thought. One shark, 20 feet below the surface, rose to gulp a floating cigarette pack in its mouth, which he quickly spat out. Divers fear them most because of their size and their "bite-first, think-about-it-later" attack behavior.

Ralph S. Collier is the president and founder of The Shark Research Committee located in

Van Nuys, California. He says white sharks live for the sole purpose of procreating and eating. Like human babies, everything goes into their mouths, which appear to be their main sensory apparatus for "viewing" and testing their world. Ralph has investigated 60 of more than 100 white shark attacks on the Pacific coast of North America, 16 of which have involved freedivers. While he would be the first to recognize that it is unscientific to generalize on such a small sample size, he does offer the following data.

White shark attacks were clustered in specific areas year after year since 1926. The largest concentration of attacks occurred within 100 miles of the San Francisco Bay (Farallon Islands, Bodega Bay area and Ano Nuevo Island). Once sighted, the sharks often stayed in a given location for a couple of weeks. Attacks were as likely to occur in clear water (greater than 40-foot visibility) as they were in turbid water. They occurred during all months of the year, although most happened in the summer. Most divers attacked were catching abalone and 80 percent were on the surface, or within 10 feet of the surface. This seems reasonable because most freedivers in this area fish for abalone and the average freediver spends 80 percent of his time near the surface.

Great whites appear to have two attack modes. The more common is a high-velocity attack from below and behind, where victims describe the sensation of being hit by a truck. (Only 20 percent of victims see the shark before it attacks.) These animals do not always bite, preferring instead at times to ram the victim with their snouts. Frequently, the attack ends with the first contact or bite. This is why more than 90 percent of shark-attack victims survive. J.E. McClosker, a marine biologist with the famed Steinhart Aquarium in San Francisco,

termed this phenomenon as the "bite and spit" attack adaptation. His theory suggests that whites, having no protective eye covering (unlike most sharks), bite their prey, spit it out and circle as it succumbs to its initial wounds. This way the shark avoids a fight and possible injury to its vulnerable eyes.

Less common is the slow, deliberate attack, whereby the shark makes multiple passes and attacks on his victim. Frequently, the diver has to fend off the shark with repeated blows to the snout. Many white shark encounters do not result in an attack. Common among these encounters, is the diver's description of a large shark approaching head-on, then turning on its side and sliding by within feet, looking him over with "that great black eye."

Peter Klimley, a marine animal behaviorist with the University of California, has analyzed 131 videotape records of white shark attacks on seals and sea lions off the Farallon Islands in Northern California. His observations led to a hypothesis that I paraphrase as the "bite and taste" attack. Apparently, whites prefer the flesh of mammals with a high fat content (seals, sea lions and whales) to the flesh of humans and other leaner mammals. "White sharks may release people because they find them unpalatable," he says. Whites have been observed leaving sea otters, birds and humans uneaten after the initial attack.

White sharks will explore all manner of floating debris. Their teeth marks have been found in plastic buoys, wooden boxes, surf boards, even boats. They took these items into their jaws for a few seconds, then released them, and swam away. Klimley's observations reveal that whites, after the initial attack on a preferred food source such as a seal, either carried their prey until it stopped bleeding or took a quick bite and

Divers fear white sharks because of their bite-first, think-about-it-later attack behavior.

PHOTO BY JAMES D. WATT

quickly recaptured the prey until it stopped bleeding. In either case, feeding did not occur until after bleeding had ceased. In some instances sharks have waited for two hours after bleeding stopped.

Human attack areas in California were usually associated with pinniped (seal) rookeries and were generally free of the kelp canopy. Some theorize that as the pinniped population increases, so will the shark population. Several victims noted unusual seal activity just prior to their attack. One saw grouped sea lions huddled tightly together in the water in an agitated and distressed state, barking and looking quickly above and below the water. Another victim noted a conspicuous absence of fishes and seals. Some noticed that the nearby fish were very spooked and stayed close to the reef.

"Most white shark encounters do not result in an attack," explains South African bluewater hunter and commercial fisherman Jerry Buirski. Struis Bay, South Africa, well-known for white sharks, is a favorite dive spot for Jerry, who over the years has had enough encounters with whites to categorize them into types.

"The first is when you meet the shark, usually at the surface," he says. "After getting into the boat for a few minutes, you resume diving and never see it again. The second is when the shark stays with you, swimming up and down on one side while you head for the boat. The third is the most disconcerting. This is when you are on the bottom and the shark appears, usually from behind and always from the left side. He follows your ascent, often pointing straight at you and seemingly without swimming at all. This angle to the shark's head makes it impossible to get a kill shot with a banger (powerhead). If the water is dirty, the shark's snout will only be a meter away from your speargun, hopefully pointing toward it. The encounter ends with arrival of the safety boat."

Jerry explains that the white shark population off Struis Bay fluctuates yearly and for no apparent reason. He feels comfortable enough

now with white sharks in the area that he has actually shot and recovered yellowtail right next to a white shark—more than once. (These South Africans are tough!)

"From my experiences with whites, it seems that once you have seen the shark and it knows you have seen it, you are safe," Jerry says. There is one caveat here, a point that Jerry goes on to illustrate with the story of five Australian spearfishermen who were diving together. Four of them saw an approaching white. It did not attack them but did attack the fifth diver, who did not see the shark.

South African Tommy Botha is without a doubt one of the world's best freedivers. At age 37, Tommy has won the South African championships nine times. He has represented his country for 16 years all over the world.

I first met Tommy in 1982. The South African freediving community had graciously invited my team, which placed second in the world spearfishing championships in Chile, to tour their country and compete in several meets. During one of the competitions I was hanging onto a buoy line twisting in a raging current. I arranged for the buoy to float over a good ledge 70 feet below. Suddenly, Tommy swam up to my side kicking mightily, without benefit of the line. We dove together and I leveled off at 70 feet, shooting a small fish. Tommy kept going deeper and a full minute after I surfaced, he appeared still fighting the current and stringing a large fish.

Tommy would have won that contest if he had not had the bad luck to swim straight into a bunch of Portuguese man of wars (stinging jellyfish) which blistered his face. After emergency treatment, he still wanted to finish the contest. (One tough South African!)

Tommy believes now that the white shark is protected in South Africa, the population there is increasing. "The public is told that they are becoming extinct, but I believe quite the opposite," he says. "I have had more encounters with them over the past two years than the previous 10." Tommy has seen at least 30 white sharks and says, "I feel it is impossible to know how they will behave. Most of them just intimidate you while others try to bite you. We always carry power-heads and the first thing I do when I see a white is put one on the spear and shout for the boat. Never turn your back on them and always try to remain calm.

"One thing that amazes me about them is their ability to sneak up on you without being seen. At Struis Bay we normally dive close together when we hunt yellowtail. There will be four guys looking in every direction but when you see one, it is normally already on top of you."

Since sharks behave differently in encounters with humans and humans have different reactions to sharks, I offer the following as examples of meetings between them:

South African Tommy Botha was diving near Anvil Rock at False Bay with three friends. One diver broke his gun, so they took turns driving the boat and diving. The water visibility was 40 feet and there were lots of yellowtail and skipjack around.

"I had just speared a skipjack," recalls Tommy. "I shouted for the boat, and as I pulled in my float line, I looked straight into the mouth of a charging white shark.

"Missing me, its momentum took it straight out of the water. I was kicking hard just to stay on the surface of the whirlpooling water. I pushed with my hands but could not see much in the white foam. Somehow I ended up on the middle of the shark's back. Fortunately, the boat was right next to me and I nearly jumped over the other side of it in my haste to get away." Tommy adds that he still landed the skipjack.

On another day, Tommy was diving over a shallow pinnacle off Eerste River near Port Elisabeth in water with 20 feet of visibility. He had just shot and placed in the boat a 17-kilogram mussel cracker. While he let his arms dangle as he breathed deeply for his next dive, a 2½ meter white came up from behind and grabbed his right hand.

"Fortunately for me, only my gloved hand was in the corner of its mouth with my thumb still outside. My first thought was that I was dreaming and this was not really happening. The shark was pulling me in circles on the surface as I woke up to the fact that I had to get my hand free. I felt no pain but the pressure was intense. I put my other hand against his head and pulled free. I looked at my hand immediately, thinking it was gone. Relieved to see it still there, I held it out of the water screaming for the boat. I was very scared, waiting for the next attack in the dirty water.

"My fellow divers, just 20 feet away, never saw the shark. I kept my glove on all the way to the hospital knowing that it was the best pressure dressing available. The row of puncture marks on the inside of my hand required 20 stitches. My hand recovered completely. I believe that if my hand had been in the front of the shark's mouth, where the teeth are bigger, it would have been bitten off." (Diving physicians recommend that injured divers keep their wetsuits on for hemorrhage control unless there is massive arterial bleeding requiring direct pressure).

Another tough South African diver is Attie Louw. Attie dove in the same competitions with the U.S. team mentioned above and won one of the competitions. Amazingly, just six months before the competition, Attie was up to his waist in the jaws of a great white. Attie remembers:

It was August 1983, and the day dawned with low clouds and that typical Cape winter drizzle. Accompanying me on the 30-minute trip to Seal Island in False Bay was my buddy Peter Strydom and two other divers. I knew whites ate seals and that their number had been increasing at the island, but the abundant fish life there was enough of a lure for the more determined diver to risk meeting this feared denizen of the deep.

Peter and I entered the water first and moved over to a ledge in 40 feet of water. The water was not as clean as we had anticipated, and after two dives I thought the seals on the island became uneasy about our presence as they entered the water in large numbers. The poor visibility and anxious seals made me uneasy so I returned to the boat, unloading my gun on the way.

33

Suddenly, I was violently catapulted out of the water. I supposed it was an angry bull seal that had taken umbrage to my disturbing his harem and settled back in the water. I looked down to see if by any chance I had sustained any damage. Horror! My legs were shredded. It had to be a great white.

I realized I had a very good chance of escape if I directed my next actions to repelling any further attacks. I dove and hastily did a 360-degree scan. Immediately, I spotted him swimming past me on my level at a leisurely pace—eyeing me with that great black eye. Actually, a 5-meter great white is a beautiful creature, but under the circumstances I could not appreciate his splendor. I lined up to give him a shot in the eye (this is where South Africans suggest shooting them) as the boat appeared above me. Apparently, when I was hit, I gave a strange yell, drawing the skipper's attention. He saw the shark, too.

How it happened I cannot recall, but the next instant I was in the boat. In the meantime, Peter had been doing a very good impersonation of a piece of kelp as the shark approached him too, giving him the once-over. We picked him up unharmed. That was the beginning of a very long morning for me.

The worst part for Attie was the thrill-seeking crowd amassed at the dock anxious to get a sight of a shark attack victim. Later that day, surgeons reconstructed his upper leg muscles so well that only a small amount of muscle was lost. They found the femoral artery intact just millimeters from a tooth wound. Five weeks later, Attie was back in the water. There's more…

"Having satisfied myself that the whole episode was history, I was disappointed when I experienced a pain in my knee some time later. Exploratory surgery revealed a tooth imbedded in my kneecap."

After this attack, Attie says shark sightings started to increase rapidly. Some days divers came across as many as five whites at various sites along the southern Cape coast. In September 1992 he was diving in less than ideal conditions when once again it happened. "As before, I was lying on the surface breathing up prior to a dive when I was sent on another flying course," he recalls. "This time the shark hit me in the stomach. I had an agonizing moment as I slowly slid my hand down over my stomach to see what was left. Fortunately, I felt my weight belt intact and realized not much could be missing. I made it to the boat in record time.

"As was the case in the first attack, there was a nervous acting seal close by. Now when I come across a seal in the water, I dive elsewhere—as far away as possible." Note: Attie never mentions quitting diving.

Californian Rod Orr is another "two-time loser." Rod, electrician and former competition diver, spends an average of two days a week diving California's rugged north coast for fish and abalone.

In May 1961, Rod was diving in Tomales Bay (now a recognized white shark haunt) looking for fish and abalone. Finding a large abalone on the 20-foot-deep bottom, he glanced up to see a vague shape at the edge of visibility. Looking back to the abalone, the image of the large gills of a shark registered in his mind. Rod looked up to see the shark moving in fast. He tried to duck behind a nearby rock, but the shark beat him there. Rod instinctively straight-armed the beast as he watched its mouth open and the jaws extend. He successfully deflected the shark's mouth down and to the left as he catapulted over its head. In the process the shark clamped down on his left side for a second.

Released, Rod headed for the surface and reaching it, jumped into his nearby inner tube yelling, "Shark! A shark is trying to get me!"

Is this what Harry Ingram saw just before he was hit by a white shark?

Photo by James D. Watt

Then for Rod came the worst part. A woman standing up in a nearby anchored boat saw the circling white and began screaming hysterically, "It's going to eat him. It's going to eat him!"

"Oh no, it's not," thought Rod as he began paddling furiously away in his inner tube. Another passing fisherman came to Rod's rescue. Leaping over the boat's side, Rod received the most pain of the event as he slammed into the deck of the boat. His wetsuit was ruined and his weights were imprinted by shark teeth, but Rod was just scratched.

In September 1990, Rod was not as lucky. He paddled his board for an hour against heavy winds, going north from Russian Gulch, California. He anchored his paddle board 100 yards offshore by snapping a lanyard to the kelp. As he "breathed up" on the surface of the 12-foot visibility water, gun in hand, the lights suddenly went out. It seemed as if a garage door had slammed down on his head. Rod's head was in the jaws of a great white, which had opened its mouth just wide enough to skin back his mask and wetsuit hood. (The folded hood acted as a cushion, ultimately sparing him deeper neck wounds.)

"He hit me head-on as the lights went out," Rod says.

I heard a grinding noise. My head and neck were solid but my body was being thrown around like a rag doll. I had no idea I was moving south until he crashed me into my board, turning it upside down. Reaching up with my hands, I realized I was in a shark's jaws, and not run over by a boat as I first thought. At that moment the lights came back on, and I could see the ocean surface some three feet below through the surrealistic foreground of pointed shark's teeth. I couldn't find an eye with my hands so I started beating him with my still-loaded gun. (Rod never let go of the gun which had one rubber severed on the shark's teeth.) The shark suddenly let me go and as he angled down, I saw his head was wider than my shoulders.

I made it to my overturned board, which I quickly mounted. Kicking frantically, I tried to break the anchor kelp loose. There was blood all over the board and blocking my vision. I saw my

bailing bucket float by and grabbed it, using it to flush off my eyes. I overturned my board, got a knife and cut my anchor. I paddled straight over a wash rock hoping to lose the shark if he followed. Taking my gloves off and making a quick inventory, I found holes in my nose, cheek, above my eye, into my orbit and in my neck.

Rod made it to the beach without further attack where, in shock, he promptly removed his wetsuit—he didn't want doctors to cut it off and ruin it. The gathering crowd gasped as his shoulders appeared covered with congealed blood. The blood was, thankfully, from his neck wound and not his back, as he had feared. Except for "a little trouble with my eye," Rod made a rapid and complete recovery. He still dives; and in fact he was out diving when I tried to reach him about this story.

Australian Andy Ruddock tells a revealing story about one shark's hunting style. Andy, a commercial and sport diver, has been competing in spearfishing contests for 27 years. He has attended five international contests and won the Australian championships twice. Competition diving in Australia is a two-way contest, diver against diver, and diver against shark.

Andy, diving in the New South Wales 1984 Pacific championships, chose a reef three miles offshore with an average depth of 50 to 70 feet. He shot eight fish weighing about 1 kilo each, which he strung off his trailing float 70 feet behind. Halfway through the competition, he got an eerie sensation as the surrounding fish became uncharacteristically timid. Bait fish disappeared from the open water, choosing to hug the rocks below instead.

"Five minutes later I got that feeling again, and as I looked up to where the bait should have been, I saw a large white pointer, 12 to 14 feet, coming directly toward me," Andy says.

He traveled slowly right up to my up-raised gun tip, which I used to fend him off as he bumped it gently. Fascinated, I trailed my hand over the full length of his body as he passed me. He then continued straight onto the fish on my float, taking them all in his mouth in one monstrous bite. He dove to midwater, circled back to me, and rolling over to his side, spat all the fish out.

He turned toward me again, where he came to within six inches of my outstretched gun, still swimming slowly. Next, he swam directly to the outer edge of visibility, where he commenced a 180-degree circle, staying at the edge of my vision, trying to come at me from behind. He kept repeating this behavior for 15 to 20 minutes as I, continually fending him off, made my way back to the boat.

It was my impression that the shark would have liked to have a feed but didn't particularly want to fight for it. Back at the boat, the shark kept rubbing his nose against the side of the boat for about five minutes. I called to my friend, David Tinsley, warning him about the large shark. Just as David joined me, flipping into the boat, the great white followed him, bumping into the boat. The shark rubbed the boat for several more minutes and disappeared. What impressed me most about this episode was the way he stalked me. I'm sure if I hadn't seen him first, I would have been in serious trouble. It is clear to me how this shark worked, circling at the edge of visibility, maneuvering all the time to get me from behind.

Australian bluewater diver Raymond Short knows a sick shark can be dangerous. It was a fine sunny summer day for a swim at Coledale Beach about 100 kilometers south of Sydney. Thirteen-year-old Ray was swimming about 25 meters from shore in two meters of water when a 2½-meter (8-foot) white shark bit him taking a chunk out of his left thigh. Ray began screaming for help just as the shark clamped down on his right calf. It then let go and swallowed Ray's right leg up to the knee joint. Ray beat at the shark's head with his fists. At one point he even bit the shark's snout, but to no avail. The shark stayed clamped around his leg.

Courageous lifesaver Ray Joyce was the first to reach young Ray. Joyce had difficulty moving him to shore. Exploring the blood-obscured water around Ray's leg, Joyce was astonished to find the shark's head still attached. More men arrived and together they pulled and dragged Ray to the shore. The shark refused to release Ray and after getting Ray onto the beach, the rescuers beat the shark with a surfboard. With a mighty effort, they pried the jaws open and released his leg.

Luckily, Coledale hospital is only 300 meters from the beach and the men, not wanting to wait for an ambulance, laid Ray in a station wagon and raced to the hospital. Ray, conscious throughout the whole ordeal, remembers "drifting in and out" on the short seven-minute ride to the hospital, where surgeons saved his life and repaired his wounds.

The shark did not fare so well. It died on the beach and souvenir seekers quickly removed its jaws and fins. A biologist, examining the remains, found infected bites (probably mating wounds) on this female white shark. He theorized that the shark, crazed with disease, swam into shallow water and attacked the first easy opportunity she found.

Ray still appreciates the ocean's beauty and bounty. Over the years since his attack he has become a bona fide bluewater hunter. His son is an avid surfer. Ray, acting on a tip, found the jaws of that same shark 25 years later in a brine solution languishing in a farmer's garage. Having soaked too long in the solution, the jaws had dissolved. When reflecting on his shark attack, Ray muses, "You know I'm probably the only white shark attack victim in the world who can prove that my shark was indeed a white shark."

TIGER SHARKS

You know you have to be wary of a beast that eats several of its litter mates—in the womb! Tiger sharks, found in tropical and subtropical waters, are respected by bluewater divers because of their man-eating reputation, their immense size and their stealth.

When we first proposed the idea of spearfishing for the giant tuna around the Mexican Rivillagigedo Archipelago, experienced sportfishing boat captains told us it was impossible. Tiger sharks, they said, would eat us. They based their theory on sightings of these huge fish attacking angled fish next to their boats. In those waters it is not uncommon for fishermen to reel in the head of a 200-to 300-pound tuna with a semicircular wound behind the gills, where the body should be.

Undaunted we went anyway, and our first trips were successful. However, on one trip several years later, I discovered a 14-foot tiger at my fin-tips, on the surface. I was in my hunting mode, and I thought my eyes were covering the surrounding area well, looking above, below and side to side. Apparently, I missed this huge animal, which stealthily approached me from my blind spot—the area directly behind me on the surface. When I finally spotted it there, I practically leaped out of my skin. The shark, frightened by my convulsion, shuddered too, and then swam off. As it swam by, I estimated that two of me could have fit easily in its stomach.

It is patently dangerous to make generalizations about shark behavior because there is always the unpredictable individual or circumstance, as Australian Ray Short can attest. With this caveat aside, most tiger sharks do appear to behave consistently. Having been implicated in shark attacks on surfers in the Hawaiian Islands, they are considered to be the most dangerous in shallow, dirty water. In deeper water the tiger,

unlike the white shark, generally circles its prey and "thinks about it for a while" before attacking. Hopefully, this interlude before an attack, will allow you enough time to exit the water.

Australian "spearo" Greg Pickering has had plenty of experience with tiger sharks. He explains that tigers, members of the requiem shark family, are found virtually everywhere in Northern Australia, from close to shore in mangroves, around coral reefs and estuaries, to the deeper offshore waters. Much more common than white sharks, they are veritable garbage cans, frequenting prawn trawlers as they sort their catch.

"They have a habit of turning up without the diver knowing that they are present," Greg says. "Often quite docile, they do not race around like bronze whalers. However, there are exceptions. They can move quickly when necessary and behave in an aggressive manner. While they have attacked floats, bitten spears and rushed divers, they mostly cruise around on the bottom eating diver's burley (chum).

"Their habits seem to vary with the water visibility, boldly circling closer to divers at the edge of the visibility in dirty water, but becoming

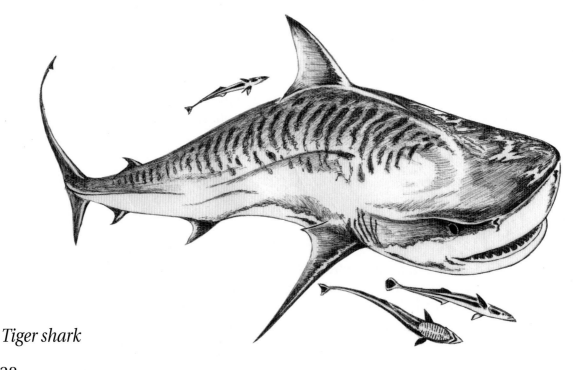

Tiger shark

more wary in clean water." Greg contends that tigers can be tolerated if they remain on the bottom, but when they start coming up toward the diver, they cannot be trusted.

Many close encounters with tiger sharks have made Greg and his friends particularly wary. In one instance Greg temporarily attached his float line to his weight belt and dove to 40 feet. A surface-swimming tiger shark grabbed the fish strung to his float and as it swam off with them, dragged an attached Greg backward. Another seized his fish, floating just four feet behind him—too close to get his gun between the shark and himself. Yet another, attempting to eat Greg's just-speared fish, chomped his spearshaft instead. When this big shark returned, Greg's buddy, accomplished diver Barry Paxman, hit it squarely in the head with a powerhead. The shark, appearing dead, settled to the bottom. It "revived" an hour later and swam off.

Once a big tiger swam off with a 6-foot bronze whaler shark the divers were forced to kill in self defense. Grabbing the whaler by the back, it picked it off the bottom and brought it to the surface where it grabbed its head and swam off. "The dead whaler looked small hanging out of the tiger's mouth as it swam away," Greg remembers.

Greg can attest to the tiger's stealth as well. He and Barry Paxman were diving at Leeander Reef 250 miles north of Perth, West Australia. Two tiger sharks circled lazily on the bottom, probably drawn in by the divers gutting their fish. "After a few minutes, several samson fish, about 40 pounds, came through the area attracted by the burley in the water. Since the tigers were on the bottom, about 60 feet down, I decided to have a go at one of the fish. I dove and shot one of the samson; the fish took off but quickly became stuck in a rocky ledge. Ascending, I let line play out of my reel. When I hit the surface, Barry said, 'Did you see the big tiger next to you?' I said I had not.

"Apparently a third, 14-foot tiger had appeared on the surface when I dove, and as I peeled over for the descent, it went for me. Barry immediately swam down and rammed his gun into its side. All this happened and I never saw the shark. Barry said it had its mouth open and was less than three feet from me when he pushed it away."

Generally seeking the diver's fish, sharks could mistake the diver for food as well. One of Greg's good friends had his legs badly lacerated by a tiger shark, presumably going after the diver's fish, which were strung around his waist. Greg says that the tiger shark's typical hunting style is to circle its victim during the day and attack at night. "This has happened in Australia when boats have capsized," Greg says. "On one occasion, a tiger shark followed three people, who were hanging onto driftwood, for three days. They repeatedly tried to drive the shark away, but it eventually grabbed one of the crew. The remaining two tried, unsuccessfully, to save their friend who had disappeared under the waves into the shark's great jaws."

While tiger sharks generally do not attack immediately, other kinds of sharks do. The following segment explains why even smaller sharks must be watched carefully.

OTHER SHARKS

Despite their relatively small size, grey reef sharks are very dangerous. This shark's aggressive territorial defense of its coral reef or atoll has caused divers serious injuries and death. Uniformly dark grey with whitish stomachs, they average five feet in length with some reaching eight feet. While bluewater hunters generally dive beyond the grey reef shark's local territory, they can expect to encounter these sharks when hunting for pelagic species along a deep coral drop-off.

Active competitors for food, even among their fellows, grey reefs fiercely defend their territory on the reef. They display a characteristic physical posturing with their pectoral fins

Terry Maas and the tiger shark.

I admit to becoming somewhat complacent about the large tigers frequenting San Benedicto Island, Mexico. Most sightings involve a solitary pass, with the curious shark keeping its distance and then swimming away. After such sightings, we'd call the divers back to the boat and move to another spot. I should have remembered Greg's words: "When tiger sharks start coming up toward the diver, they can't be trusted."

On November 5, 1997, my attitude toward tigers changed. I swam up-current from the boat and located the pinnacle I was looking for, hazing it out 100 feet below. I wanted to be on the deep-water side, where I knew tuna swam and where I'd photographed Ron Mullins with a 200-pound tuna two years earlier. About 30 feet down, ahead of the pinnacle, I sighted something 80 feet below.

Something was swimming up to me. A shark. Big shark. Boxy face—must be a tiger. Coming straight up. Keep my gun between us. No time to put on my powerhead. It will surely veer off soon, then I'll call for the skiff and leave. Closer. Veer. Closer—veer off! Closer still—it's not veering away. Four feet away, it's going too fast to change course. Its mouth is opening!

My gun fired. I watched my shaft bend as the shark's massive body lurched to the right. I went to the left and jumped into the nearby panga holding onto my float and line. I expected to lose my gear. Luckily, I was able to pull up the beast in about 15 minutes; its body was as long as the 14-foot skiff.

After bending two flying gaffs at the stern of the Polaris Supreme, we finally hoisted the 1,000-pound shark on deck, its jaws snapping in defiance, my spearhead imbedded deeply in its head, between the eyes. Examination of its abdomen revealed an empty stomach save for a fist-sized fish head and two liver lobes, each of which weighed more than me. Regardless of the dramatic story and photos I have as reminders, I wish the episode had never happened.

Agonistic display of the grey reef shark.

lowered and their backs arched, just before they attack—not for food, but to defend their territory. Experts advise against any aggressive display on the part of the diver when confronted with a posturing grey reef shark.

Jim Stewart knows how dangerous a posturing grey reef shark can be. A member of the famed Bottom Scratchers Club of San Diego, Jim started diving in 1941 and was probably the first diver to encounter the giant bluefin tuna of Guadalupe Island, Mexico. Always the bluewater hunter, he also enjoyed a flourishing professional diving career. It was on one of his commercial trips that he encountered a life-threatening attack from a grey reef shark.

In March 1961, Jim and his buddy Ron Church were installing tsunami warning equipment close to coral-bound Wake Island in the Pacific. The two freedivers took pictures of an underwater cable they had just anchored to the bottom. Finished, they swam for shore, intending to climb out of the water at the end of a channel 150 feet long and 35 feet wide. The ocean side of the sand-bottomed channel was 60 feet deep, gradually shallowing to 20 feet near shore. Because of the heavy surge, the visibility was poor, five to six feet on the surface, 10 to 15 feet below. Fighting the surge, the two separated, each going up a side of the channel.

Reaching the surf break near shore, Jim spotted a grey reef shark, which turned into the middle of the channel. Having become familiar with grey reefs during the atomic tests at Bikini Atoll, he wasn't too concerned when it made a turn back toward him. With nothing in his hands, Jim swam directly toward it. The shark veered away toward Ron, who took its picture, just before it disappeared into the channel below.

"My next dive, including the attack, took just 40 seconds," Jim recalls.

Following the shark into clearer, deeper water, I sighted it heading out of the channel toward the open ocean. It dropped its pectoral fins in a posture I'd seen other sharks use. Next, it pulled its head up high and undulated like a corkscrew—something I'd never seen before. Quickly changing postures, it made several quick, jerky turns while snapping its jaws. It then swam in a straight line for a few feet before going into a full-body lateral shaking, much like a dog with a bone. After that, 10 feet below and 25 feet in front of me, it suddenly rolled into a loop, reversed direction and charged at my left shoulder. It was quickly in my face as I defensively rolled away and threw up my right arm. Grabbing my elbow, it made two quick bites and disappeared, leaving me with a dangling fist-sized chunk of flesh torn from my elbow, an exposed glistening joint capsule and several bleeding arteries. Splinting the joint with my other arm, I used my hand to apply pressure to my brachial artery, under my arm pit, which effectively stemmed the flow of blood. I remember being impressed with how white and glistening my joint appeared. After three surgeries and several years of healing I have regained full use of my arm.

Tiger sharks are known to eat their litter mates—in the womb!

PHOTOS ON PREVIOUS PAGE BY A.J. BERNSTEIN

Jim's advice is to respect the territorial nature of the grey reef shark. In his later work, he has seen this territorial posturing several times. He feels that his shark was not reacting in self defense because it was on the open-ocean side of the pair of divers, free to exit at will; rather, it was defending its feeding territory. "Since the attack, I'm much more alert when grey reef sharks are near," he says.

Hammerhead sharks are known man-eaters. They seem to have two separate modes: a mating mode and a feeding mode. They appear quite docile and even shy when they group in circles over a pinnacle or seamount. Famed underwater photographer Howard Hall, wearing a silent rebreathing apparatus, documented their mating behavior. Males would select a female high in the swirling column of sharks, and grasp her around the neck, and together they would drift down through their companions to the ocean floor.

I have never had problems with schooling hammerhead sharks, but I have had trouble with solitary individuals, especially some that were grey colored—unlike the brown schoolers. One shark tried to eat a barracuda I shot during a national spearfishing championship in Florida. As I yelled for help, I kept pulling my fish, 15 feet below, from the jaws of the 7-foot shark. Before help arrived, the shark tired of this game and approached me directly, swimming tight, fast circles around me on the surface. My teammate John Ernst finally arrived and made a strategic shot with a barbless, lineless shaft that sent the shark scurrying away. Another time, a lone 8-foot hammerhead made repeated passes to my fin-tips, again on the surface. One sharp blow from my speartip to its snout finally discouraged it.

Barry Wagner, a seasoned bluewater diver from San Diego, had a terrifying encounter with a hammerhead shark off La Jolla Cove, San Diego. It was August 1968, and Barry had just competed in the National Spearfishing Championships; he was in prime physical condition. One evening, having shot three, 20-pound yellowtail, he started back for the beach. Encountering a strong current, he decided to swim with his arms to add power to his kick. He released his reel, which was supposed to allow his gun to follow three feet behind, leaving his hands free.

After about 30 seconds of freestyle swimming, he felt one of his yellowtail come alive and thrash on his back, where he had them secured with his stringer. Reaching behind himself to subdue the fish, he grabbed not its tail as he expected, but the head-horn of an 8-foot hammerhead shark. The shark, with the yellowtail in its mouth, began shaking Barry. He remembers:

> I thought, 'This can't be happening.' He shook me like a dog shaking a rag. I reached for my gun, finding to my terror that it had unreeled to the bottom, 30 feet below me. I reached for my weight belt buckle, but it too was gone, sucked into the black hole of my panic! In desperation, I sucked in my gut and attempted to wiggle free from the weight belt.

> With the belt at my knees, the big shark came around for another bite. He bit at my reel, which I quickly pulled from his mouth. He grabbed another yellowtail and ripped it in two, engulfing me in an explosion of the reddest blood I'd ever seen.

> Finally, free of the belt, I quickly pulled up my gun in anticipation of a standoff. He circled me once and then swam to the bottom. The last image I remember was his belly flashing upward as he chewed on the remaining fish on my belt. That was the last shark I have ever seen in La Jolla.

A tiger shark. It is patently dangerous to make generalizations about shark behavior.

Photo by James D. Watt

43

Australian Andy Ruddock considers hammerhead sharks a nuisance. "They are mostly interested in our fish, and once they show up, they are hard to discourage," Andy says.

I remember one incident that exemplifies their persistence. My friend John Powell and I had shot some coral trout when a 12- to 14-foot hammerhead appeared. It circled in and out of the visibility and bumped a fish in my hand. John and I pulled our fish floats closer to us, but this did not dissuade the shark, which kept coming at us. John shot its side with a headless shaft. The hammerhead merely turned, snapped at the shaft and pulled it free.

During the next four to five dives, while I was looking for John's spear, it circled and bumped me twice. I found the spear, John reloaded and shot it in the gills. The hammerhead disappeared in a profusion of blood only to reappear four minutes later. I tried shooting it on the top of the head, but my shot was too far forward. It swam off and returned in two minutes. That's when we decided to leave the area.

Sharks in packs can be unnerving. Imagine yourself in the forest surrounded by wolves attacking from the earth below and from the sky above and from all sides. It is almost impossible to defend oneself against this kind of three-dimensional attack. North American yellowtail record holder René Rojas and I found ourselves in trouble off San Benedicto Island, Mexico where we were hunting tuna and wahoo in deep water. Thousands of small skipjack tuna blanketed the ocean about 80 feet below us.

René shot a wahoo that raced off on the surface. Suddenly, a torpedo streaked straight up through the skipjacks and circled us. It was quickly followed by another. Soon there were five whitetip sharks dancing around René and me as we instinctively formed a back-to-back defense. We dodged these excited and hungry sharks which were attracted by the wahoo's escape run. They came at us from every direction. I kept wondering why they were bothering us when the wounded wahoo was just 100 feet away on the surface kicking and thrashing about. Finally,

sensing the wahoo, they streaked off in its direction. Seconds later, we watched René's empty spearshaft sinking to the bottom. Instantly, the sharks were back, following the now limp trailing line. For a few seconds more, they danced before us before disappearing into the blue below. I could not imagine how a solitary diver would fare in similar circumstances.

According to Andy Ruddock, whitetip reef sharks are a problem in Australia. It's not their size—they average 4 to 6 feet in length, but rather their aggressive nature that poses danger to the bluewater diver. As they try to take fish from divers' spears, floats and hands, their behavior excites the more dangerous bronze whaler and silver-fringed whaler sharks. Usually cautiously cruising the periphery, whalers can be enticed into a full-blown feeding frenzy by the frantic actions of the smaller whitetip sharks as they attack divers' fish.

Spearing coral trout on the Great Barrier Reef, Andy once lost all of his fish in a whaler shark feeding frenzy. He had a good-sized stringer of fish tied to his float when he aimed at another 20-pound coral trout. Once shot, the fish fought vigorously. A 9- to 10-foot blacktip whaler took his fish in its mouth. "As I tried to pull my line and wrestle my fish from the shark's jaws, others became interested," he said. "Soon 15 to 20 sharks attacked my float, each taking a fish and tearing it apart. It was a full-blown feeding frenzy and I was caught in the middle. One shark charged me and took my gun from my hands as I shoved the gun's butt end into its face. Another started chewing on my float. Luckily, I was not injured, and after a few minutes, once all of my fish were consumed, the sharks settled down and resumed their normal pattern of swimming slowly on the bottom."

A good friend once told Andy a generalization that seems to have been borne out in his experiences with sharks. "Slow-moving sharks act the most benign, but when they start moving quickly—watch out!"

Australian Greg Pickering had a very close encounter with a silvertip shark that almost ended in disaster. Greg, Robert Torelli, Peter Herbert (Herb) of New Zealand and others organized a dream bluewater trip to Rowley Shoals, 170 miles off Broome, Northwest Australia, on the charter boat *Wave Spirit*. Swimming along the drop-off over 400 feet of deep blue water, Greg saw sailfish, wahoo and yellowfin tuna, all accompanied by sharks. Diving with his friend Herb and keen to shoot his first wahoo, Greg came across a school of small wahoo accompanied by 30 to 40 sharks, mainly from the silvertip and grey reef species. Dodging tuna and sharks, he shot a wahoo. Even though his good spine shot killed the wahoo, he had a difficult time getting it into the boat because the sharks wanted it as much as he did.

Greg recalls the rest of the story:

A short time after dropping off the wahoo, Herb and I, swimming along the edge of the drop-off, came across a dozen more silvertip sharks. Even with no fish in our possession, they became very aggressive, circling 30 feet below. The biggest, about 7-feet long and scarred along its back with apparent mating wounds, broke from the pack. Swimming upward in a spiral fashion, it came close to Herb with its mouth opened slightly. It charged. Herb had no choice but to spear the brute. It was knocked senseless for 10 seconds before it started thrashing wildly. It rushed me next, and I, too, fired.

It kept thrashing and rolling, eventually becoming tangled in both of our float lines. Before I knew what was happening, the shark had rolled its body up in my line, its head tangled around my right leg. My line had caught on my leg-mounted knife sheath, allowing the shark to roll up in the line against my body. Frantically, I pushed its head away with my gun, trying desperately to prevent it from biting me. It was only after the rubber strap broke on my knife sheath that I could free myself from this Siamese tangle. Miraculously, I remained uninjured. Our tender finally showed up after this ordeal—he had been busy helping a fellow diver land a sailfish. Regaining his composure, Herb took a quick photo using the Nikonos hanging from his neck.

Greg loves to tell the story of his friend and mentor Wally Gibbins, one of Australia's respected fathers of spearfishing. It was Wally who explored most of the offshore bluewater locations popular today. Wally was salvage diving in the Solomon Islands where some sections of the rocky cliffs drop into 3,000 feet of water.

"Many silvertip sharks inhabit these edges, and on one occasion Wally found himself rushed by a number of sharks at once," Greg says. "Unfortunately he didn't have a gun in his hand so he improvised. He bunched himself into a tight ball and as the sharks came closer, he quickly thrust out his legs and arms and spooked them all. Wal is a very cool customer when it comes to sharks!"

In South Africa, next to the white shark, the zambezi shark is the most feared. Tim Condon writing in *Underwater Special Edition No. 17 - Great White Shark* says this about the zambezi: "You can scream in the face of a zambezi shark, bash him severely on the nose, and all he'll do is stare blankly back at you, almost like a punch-drunk fighter—a vicious and dangerous one at that."

Their unpredictability is aptly displayed in an incident Tim recalls while spearfishing on the Little Coral Reef at Leven Point, Zululand. Swimming on the surface almost shoulder-to-shoulder with his friend, the late Noel Galli, a 2-meter zambezi shark approached very slowly, snaking along the reef 10 to 12 meters below. At no stage did it appear agitated or excited, and no one had yet speared any fish so the divers weren't particularly concerned. When it was directly beneath them, it made a dramatic lightning back flip and tore at incredible speed straight up at Noel, whose gun was pointing in the shark's direction. With a terrific impact, the shark impaled itself on Noel's loaded spear and knocked him inches out of the water. "I was a frightened spectator with the shark thrashing only a few feet away," Tom remembers. "With a vicious shake the shark freed itself and sped to the bottom, where, to our amazement, it continued its slow snakelike progress across the top of the reef as if nothing had happened."

Herb's picture of the end of the shark incident at Rowley Shoals.

PHOTO BY PETER HERBERT

Tim says the best defense to these sharks is to keep circling, using your speargun to make a buffer zone between you and the shark, and if necessary, using it as a shark-billie to prod it away. "Should you encounter this shark," he suggests, "do not shoot fish in its presence, and if possible, move to an alternate reef."

A close relative to the zambezi, and just as mean, is the bull shark which inhabits Florida and Caribbean waters. One big bull almost swam off with the son of my friend Ron Schlusemeyer. While we were scouting for the 1966 Miami National Spearfishing Championships, my teammate Carl Krupansky and I traveled to Jupiter, Florida accepting Ron's kind invitation to introduce us to subtropical spearfishing. It was not too long before we saw bull sharks gathering on the reef. Ron and his buddies, used to diving with big bulls, just laughed at our obvious neophytes' discomfort.

"Terry, it was that lax attitude toward bull sharks, developed over years of diving with them, that got me and my son in trouble," Ron said. Ron and Kevin, his 11-year-old son, had

46

found a good reef off the Bahamas in their usual fashion—by towing a diver behind the boat on the surface. They stopped to check it out. When Ron spotted a bull shark he told Kevin to stay on the surface while he examined the reef further.

"The shark was acting kind of jerky as if to tell me that this was his part of the ocean and I was not welcome," Ron recalls. "I made one last dive to see if the shark was gone. I was down about 25 feet when the shark charged me, and to my surprise raced by me and grabbed my son who, without my knowledge, had followed me down. In defense Kevin threw up his left arm, which the shark grabbed. I had underestimated the size of the shark—it was 7- to 8-feet long and weighed 300 to 400 pounds. Kevin beat at it furiously with his free hand while I jabbed at its head repeatedly with my spear. Reacting purely by instinct, we countered the attack for at least 30 seconds, but we were losing ground. Finally, one of my spear-jabs to its eye caused it to release Kevin."

Kevin survived the ordeal, initially receiving 500 sutures during five and one-half hours of surgery in the Bahamas and later a skin graft in Florida. Kevin even returned to diving. It took a little push at first, but he soon became relaxed and comfortable in the water again, and he still dives with his dad today. His weight lifting hobby has built up the muscles around the shark's wound, helping to mask the 2- by 3-inch scar on his left forearm.

"Looking back now, what impressed me most about this shark was its robotic action exemplified by its large eye devoid of life, devoid of care, as it grabbed and held my son—like the *Terminator*," Ron says. "This incident obviously changed my whole outlook on sharks. I suggest that divers always pay attention in the presence of sharks because anything can happen. It is easy to make the mistake of overconfidence."

The zambezi or bull shark.

Even sharks are subject to shark attack. The shark above was injured in a shark feeding frenzy similar to the one at the left, where whaler sharks attacked and vaporized a speared dogtooth tuna.

Physiology and the bluewater hunter

This chapter, written in two sections, covers physiologic principles important to your success and well-being as a bluewater hunter. The first half deals with the specter of shallow-water blackout, its causes and prevention. In the second half, I discuss selected topics aimed at enhancing your performance in the bluewater environment.

SHALLOW-WATER BLACKOUT

Every year we lose too many divers to shallow-water blackout. Almost everyone I interviewed for this book has a story to tell about this frightening but all too common occurrence. Shallow-water blackout (SWB) is the sudden loss of consciousness caused by oxygen starvation. Unconsciousness strikes most commonly within 15 feet (five meters) of the surface, where expanding, oxygen-hungry lungs literally suck oxygen from the diver's blood.

SWB conjures up images from the movie *Invasion of the Body Snatchers.* Once you lose consciousness you die. The blackout occurs quickly, insidiously and without warning. Mercifully, the victims of this condition die without any idea of their impending death. Beginning breath-hold divers, because of their lack of adaptation, are not generally subject to this condition. It is the intermediate diver who is most at risk. He is in an accelerated phase of training, and his physical and mental adaptations allow him to dive deeper and longer with each new diving day—sometimes too deep or too long. *Advanced divers are not immune.*

I blacked out once and had two near misses before the age of 22. Jerry Stugen, my early mentor, remembers me at age 16 coming up from a dive with purple lips. Unaware of my oxygen depleted state, I was rapidly preparing to dive again to remove a large fish holed up below. Jerry yanked the snorkel from my mouth and commanded me to stop diving for the day. When I was 18 years old, I passed out in a swimming pool during an underwater endurance test for my physical education class. The second I stopped swimming my coach jumped into the water and brought me to the pool deck where I regained consciousness. Aside from being frightened, the only other problem I had was painful legs lasting two days. My last near miss happened at age 22. I entered a Florida spearfishing contest with a borrowed gun. Ascending after a 70-foot dive, I shot a large jack which took off in a blur. Not wanting to lose the gun, I remember fighting the fish to within a few feet of the surface. The next thing I remember was being awakened by bumping my head against our anchored boat.

* * * *

Skip Hellen's story is typical of many shallow-water blackout incidents. Skip and I were diving at Ship's Rock, one-half mile off of Catalina Island, California. We were hunting for the largest white seabass, competing in the Long Beach Neptunes' annual Blue Water Meet. Ship's Rock is shaped like a pyramid. Its sides consist of large boulders cascading to the sea floor 120 feet below. White seabass cruise near the boulders. Earlier in the day I shot a 50-pound white seabass. Skip, a fierce competitor, saw my fish and he was pumped! I'll never forget what happened next.

Skip dives to a boulder 50 feet below. He orients himself in the open water and waits…and waits…and waits. I am anxious to take my turn on the rock. Finally, Skip starts his ascent and I keep his image in the corner of my eye as I start down. Fifteen feet from the surface, he suddenly arches his back, his gun fires and his arms shoot out from his sides. He sinks backward as if impaled on a cross. I drop my gun and angle my dive to intercept Skip. I release his weight belt and, holding Skip around the shoulders, we ascend together.

On the surface, I hold Skip's head clear of the waves. His face is blue-black. I feel he is close to death. His jaws are clenched on his snorkel. With effort, I rip the snorkel from his

mouth, and strike him on the chest. 'Breathe!' I yell. Skip takes one ragged breath. His next breath returns him to consciousness and he exclaims, 'Hey! Where's my weight belt? Where's my gun?'

Lucky for Skip, he recovered that day without permanent injury, and 16 years later he realized his goal, spearing a world-record 80-pound white seabass.

THE PHYSIOLOGY OF SHALLOW-WATER BLACKOUT

The human body is capable of remarkable adaptations to the underwater environment. Even untrained divers will show a dramatic slowing of the heart when immersed. This is commonly referred to as the "diving reflex." Immersion of the face in cold water causes the heart to slow automatically. Chest compression can also slow the heart. Emergency-room physicians use this phenomenon to their advantage when they need to slow the heart. They might apply ice water to the patient's face and eyes, or they might have the patient take a deep breath and then tighten his abdominal and chest muscles. The result is often a dramatic slowing of the heart. Untrained divers can experience up to a 40 percent drop in heart rate. Trained divers can produce an even lower heart rate—some can slow to an incredible 20 beats per minute.

Trained freedivers develop several other physiological adaptations that lead to deeper and longer dives. The spleen, acting as a blood reservoir, assists trained divers in increasing their performance. Apparently their spleen shrinks while diving, causing a release of extra blood cells.

According to William E. Hurford M.D., and coauthors writing in *The Journal of Applied Physiology*, the spleens of the Japanese ama divers (professional women shellfish freedivers) they studied decreased in size by 20 percent when they dove. At the same time their hemoglobin concentration increased by 10 percent (*Volume 69, pages 932-936, 1990*).

This adaptation, similar to one observed in marine mammals (the Weddell seal's blood cell concentration increases by up to 65 percent), could increase the diver's ability to take up oxygen at the surface. It could also increase oxygen delivery to critical tissues during the dive.

Interestingly, the spleen's contraction and the resultant release of hemoglobin is not immediate—it starts taking effect after a quarter-hour of sustained diving. This spleen adaptation, as well as other physiologic changes, probably take a half-hour for full effect. This might account for the increased performance trained freedivers notice after their first half-hour of diving.

There are other known adaptations: blood vessels in the skin contract under conditions of low oxygen in order to leave more blood available for important organs, namely the heart, brain and muscles. Changes in blood chemistry allow the body to carry and use oxygen more efficiently. These changes, in effect, squeeze the last molecule of available oxygen from nonessential organs. Most importantly, the diver's mind adapts to longer periods of apnea (no breathing). He can ignore, for longer periods of time, his internal voice that begins as a whisper but soon screams—*BREATHE.*

These adaptations, taken together, allow trained divers to dive deeper and longer, but mind control and the following techniques and factors also bring divers closer to oxygen starvation.

Hyperventilation provides yet another mechanism that the trained diver can use to bypass his need to breathe. Hyperventilation is the practice of excessive breathing with an increase in the rate of respiration or an increase in the depth of respiration, or both. This will not store extra oxygen. On the contrary, if practiced too vigorously, it will actually rob the body of oxygen. The magical benefit of hyperventilation is what it does to carbon dioxide levels in the blood. Rapid or deep breathing reduces carbon dioxide levels rapidly. It is high levels of carbon dioxide, not low levels of oxygen, that stimulate the need to breathe.

The beginning diver is very sensitive to carbon dioxide levels. These levels build even with a breath-hold of 15 seconds, causing the lungs to feel "on fire." The trained diver has "blown off" massive amounts of carbon dioxide with hyperventilation, thus outsmarting the brain's breathing center. Normally metabolizing body tissues, producing carbon dioxide at a regular rate, do not replace enough carbon dioxide to stimulate this breathing center until the body is seriously short of oxygen. Trained divers can also short-circuit the desire to breathe by sheer willpower.

Hyperventilation causes some central nervous system changes as well. Practiced to excess, it causes decreased cerebral blood flow, dizziness and muscle cramping in the arms and legs. But moderate degrees of hyperventilation can cause a state of euphoria and well-being. This can lead to overconfidence and the dramatic consequence of a body performing too long without a breath: blackout.

Pressure changes in the freediver's descent-ascent cycle conspire to rob him of oxygen as he nears the surface by a mechanism I call the "vacuum effect." Gas levels, namely oxygen and carbon dioxide, are continuously balancing themselves in the body. Gases balance between the lungs and body tissues. The body draws oxygen from the lungs as it requires. The oxygen concentration in the lungs of a descending diver *increases* because of the increasing water pressure. As the brain and tissues use oxygen, more oxygen is available from the lungs while he is still descending. This all works well as long as there is oxygen in the lungs and the diver remains at his descended level.

The problem is in ascent. The reexpanding lungs of the ascending diver increase in volume as the water pressure decreases, and this results in a rapid *decrease* of oxygen in the lungs to critical levels. The balance that forced oxygen into the body is now reversed. This vacuum effect is really a net flow of oxygen from the body to the lungs. It is most pronounced in the last 10 to 15 feet below the surface, where the greatest relative lung expansion occurs. This is where unconsciousness frequently happens. The blackout is instantaneous and without warning. It is the result of a critically low level of oxygen, which in effect, switches off the brain.

* * * *

Jack Prodonovich and Wally Potts, fathers of California spearfishing, were diving the virgin waters of the La Jolla Cove in the mid-1940s. Jack was on his paddle board removing a spear point from a grouper. Wally, stalking five large yellowtail made two dives in quick succession. He shot a large one on his third dive. Underwater, he pursued the escaping fish. Each time its tail came within his grasp, it burst ahead, tantalizingly just out of reach.

Finally grabbing the fish, he headed for the surface. Dodging a clump of kelp, he aimed for clear water above. Realizing he was not going to make it, Wally remembers dropping his fish but does not remember dropping his pole spear. "The last thing I remember was seeing a cloud of little white stars before my eyes," Wally recalls. Wally was totally focused on his pursuit and capture of that fish. Jack remembers:

> I couldn't find Wally—he should have come up. I yelled to friends in a boat close by for help. Shortly, Wally surfaced, lifeless, arms dangling. His spear was gone. I grabbed him by the head and pulled him face down onto my surfboard. I knew he was dead for sure. In desperation, I pounded him on the back. Wally woke up mid-sentence saying, 'Gol darn, I just about had him.'

Wally never had a clue he was out. Jack accounts for Wally's good fortune because of his tendency to float. "We didn't have weight belts or wetsuits in those days," Jack says (nor did they have CPR). This story illustrates two important points, one about the usefulness of positive buoyancy and the other about how a freediver's extreme focus on a goal gets him into trouble. The diver rendered unconscious by shallow-water blackout might make one convulsive spasm, but then he becomes inanimate. He either sinks or floats, depending on his buoyancy at the depth he ceases to swim. This is why divers should weight themselves for positive buoyancy at 15 feet.

Underwater exercise is a deadly problem for the freediver. Researchers have discovered that exercise also fools the breathing center, resetting it at a dangerously low level. Simply stated, heavy exercise decreases the diver's perceived need to breathe, spending valuable oxygen in the process.

The unconscious diver is now a potential drowning victim. If he floats, the vacuum effect will cease, and there might be enough residual oxygen to allow for consciousness to return. Sinking divers, while they have lost voluntary control, still have protective reflexes. The laryngospasm reflex causes the vocal cords to close, preventing water from entering the lungs. Rescuing a diver at this stage might require yanking his snorkel from his clenched jaw muscles and administering forceful mouth-to-mouth breathing pressure to overcome the spasmed vocal cords. Some recommend mouth-to-snorkel breathing as another way to get emergency oxygen into the diver. An unconscious diver may be so deprived of oxygen that his face is deep blue or black.

As oxygen starvation continues, death is so near that even the protective laryngospasm reflex relaxes and, within seconds, water enters the lungs. It is still possible to revive him at this stage. He will, however, require hospitalization and intensive treatment. When water enters the lungs, it causes a dramatic swelling of the delicate lung tissues, which leads to acute respiratory distress several hours after the incident. This is why medical evaluation is essential even if the diver appears not to have suffered any injury immediately after apparent revival.

Brothers Mike and Howard Benedict of San Diego were diving in a thick California kelp forest on a warm sunny day in the mid-1970s. Fish were everywhere. The brothers discovered a new untouched reef. They knew it was a virgin reef because of the 10-inch abalone perched prominently ontop. Soon, each had a belt stringer with 50 pounds of fish attached, hula-skirt fashion, around their waists. They separated, which is not unusual for them. Howard remembers:

I am out of breath, coming up from a dive. Curiously, I see a 10-inch abalone drifting down from the surface. My unconscious brother follows the abalone, his back is arched, his arms are straight out pointing backwards. Desperate for air myself, I still manage to reason out a plan as I swim to intercept him. I discard both of our weight belts and holding him, we both float up to the surface. I do not kick in order to conserve what little oxygen I have left.

We surface. There are no boats in sight. Mike is deep blue. He won't breathe. I cannot get his snorkel out of his clenched jaws. Finally, I free the snorkel and start mouth-to-mouth ventilation. I experience a horror you cannot believe as I force air into my dead brother's mouth. What will I tell Mom? Just then, Mike spasms. I hold him at arms length, facing me. His eyes are rolling around. When his eyes stop rolling and focus on me, he says, "Did you see that abalone?!" Mike drifts back in and out of consciousness several times as I swim him back to the beach.

Mike spent three days in the hospital intensive care unit while his swollen lungs responded to therapy. He remembers expending a great deal of energy pulling that abalone free from the rock. His heavy load of fish impeded his ascent. Both the exertion and load caused him to consume too much oxygen.

After six to eight minutes without oxygen, the brain suffers permanent damage. The heart often continues to beat after brain damage occurs. Cardiopulmonary resuscitation (CPR) at this point frequently revives victims to a vegetative state. CPR should always be administered to the drowning victim, no matter how long he has spent underwater because the diving reflex and a cold environment offer the brain additional protection. Victims resuscitated in the field often experience an unusual recovery. They wake up screaming and then lapse back into unconsciousness, repeating this behavior over and over again.

Hyperbaric oxygen treatments, a new technique, offer limited hope to the comatose diver. Oxygen is administered in a decompression chamber identical to the one used to rescue scuba divers from the bends. Theoretically, the oxygen, under pressure, penetrates the brain tissues and wakes up the damaged nerve cells. Some think the oxygen reactivates nerve cells forced into involuntary hibernation by the prolonged lack of oxygen. This technique is controversial—not all neurologists believe it is effective—and it is expensive ($400 to $800 per hour). Patients undergo 60- to 90-minute treatments from three to five times a week, sometimes for years. Many patients do not recover completely, suffering mental and physical deficits. For example, they might experience difficulty in speech and walking. Some recover to the point where they can take limited care of themselves.

PREVENTION OF SHALLOW-WATER BLACKOUT

Shallow-water blackout was a hot research topic for diving physicians in the 1960s, when they worked out the basic physiology described above. They also studied the case histories of SWB victims, identifying several factors that can contribute to this condition.

These include hyperventilation, exercise, a competitive personality, a focused mind-set and youth.

The use of hyperventilation in preparation for freediving is controversial. No one disagrees that prolonged hyperventilation, after minutes of vigorous breathing accompanied by dizziness and tingling in the arms and legs, is dangerous. Some diving physicians believe that *any* hyperventilation is deadly because of the variation in effects among individuals and on one person, from one time to another. Other physicians, studying professional freedivers such as the ama divers of Japan, found that they routinely hyperventilated mildly and took a deep breath before descending. Their hyperventilation is very mild; they limit it by pursed lip breathing before a dive.

Probably the best approach can be found in the *U.S. Navy Diving Manual (Volume 1, Air Diving)*, which states, "Hyperventilation with air before a skindive is almost standard procedure and is reasonably safe if it is not carried too far. Hyperventilation with air should not be continued beyond three to four breaths, and the diver should start to surface as soon as he notices a definite urge to resume breathing."

Learn the deadly effects of exercise underwater and plan to deal with this situation. Freedivers learn to prolong their dives by profoundly relaxing their muscles (see the section on deep diving). Most divers make minimal use of their muscles except when they fight a fish or free an anchor. A physician writing in an Australian medical journal found, "A common scenario for diving deaths in Australia is the experienced diver with weight belt on, speargun fired." Long Beach Neptune Ted Heesen chronicles the mistakes he made that could have resulted in the above scenario:

I made a shallow dive to about 25 feet, where I spotted some whites (white seabass). The largest one seemed to be about 20 pounds (my first mistake—the fish was nearly twice that size). My shot was good, and I thought I should grab this dead little 20-pound fish and swim it to the surface before it got tangled in the kelp (my second mistake). Before I could reach the fish, it came to life and started to head toward the bottom as my line tangled in my reel. I could have simply let go of the gun at this point, but I surely would never have seen it again. I spent a lot of time making that gun and was not about ready to part with it.

At this point I was probably 70 to 80 feet deep, trying to untangle my line, when one of my ears hurt painfully (I had forgotten to clear during the chase), and this woke me up to the fact that I was in trouble. The correct thing to do would have been to drop my weight belt and gun, but I was so wasted that I didn't have the brains to do that (my third mistake). Somehow I made it to the surface, still conscious but seeing stars from distant galaxies. After a few minutes of recovery, I recalled that I had shot a fish.

Ted recovered his fish, but to this day he is afraid to dive Ship's Rock on Catalina Island where this incident occurred. Ted was lucky. Too many divers have not recognized that preoccupation and excessive exercise can be lethal.

Researchers have found that the typical victim is young and highly competitive. Many SWB victims are young (teens through early thirties).

Brian Yoshikawa mimics a shallow-water blackout.

I don't know if this is because they lack experience or if some other unrecognized factor comes into play. The point is that young freedivers must be wary. Any diver who surfaces with the shakes, tunnel vision, starry vision or momentary memory loss has missed blackout by the narrowest of margins—just seconds. This should be considered a near-death experience and the dive should be examined for mistakes. There is more than one story about divers, rescued once from SWB, drowning on subsequent diving trips.

Focusing on a goal is dangerous. The stories in this chapter show how the divers, preoccupied with a goal, got into trouble. Skip remembers his last thoughts before his blackout. "My lungs were burning. I looked up and I saw the surface was near. I lengthened my kicking stride. I knew I was going to make it." Skip was focused on one thing—getting to the surface. Wally, Mike and Ted were intent on stalking or fighting a fish. You must prepare yourself to recognize when you are focusing on a goal. An internal warning should say, "I'm focusing too much. It's time to leave, drop my weight belt, drop my gun."

Medical researchers feel that many pool deaths, classified as drownings, are really the result of shallow-water blackout. Most occur in male adolescents and young adults attempting competitive endurance breath-holding, frequently "on a dare." Drowning victims, especially children, have been resuscitated from long periods of immersion in *cold* water—30 minutes or more. The same is not true for victims blacking out in warm-water swimming pools. Warm water hastens death by allowing tissues, especially brain tissues, to continue metabolizing rapidly; without oxygen, irreversible cell damage occurs in minutes.

James Warnock, the 31-year-old son of champion Ted Warnock, drowned in a warm swimming pool, chest deep. The Warnock family, hoping to prevent such deaths in other young athletes, has graciously allowed me to discuss the events surrounding their son's death. No strangers to shallow-water blackout,

the Warnocks discussed this danger many times, especially after James had a near blackout years before.

Studying mariculture in Florida, James was excited to hear that the National Spearfishing Championships would be held in an area he knew well. A three-time North Atlantic Spearfishing Champion, James was eager to start training. He purchased a new stop watch and was practicing breath-hold diving in a medical-therapy pool. A concerned paraplegic patient spotted James' inanimate body and summoned help. Rescuers saw James' new watch fall from his hand as they pulled him from the water. Sadly, attempts at CPR were unsuccessful.

SUMMARY

This section is so important that I want to summarize ways to avoid shallow-water blackout:

• Do not hyperventilate to excess—no more than three or four breaths.

• Recognize that any strenuous exercise will limit your bottom time drastically; when you exercise, head for the surface much sooner than usual.

• Recognize a dangerous situation when your mind starts to focus on a goal, and drop your weight belt.

• Treat your weight belt as a disposable item; if in doubt, drop it. Bring a spare weight belt to decrease your hesitancy to drop it.

• Avoid endurance dives. If you must make a long or deep dive, make sure you have a buddy standing by on the surface.

• Adjust your weight belt so that you will float at 15 feet.

• Consider a swimming pool a dangerous place to practice endurance breath-holding. Always have an observer standing by to assist.

• Learn the basics of CPR and think about adapting them to your diving arena, whether diving from shore, board or boat.

PREPARING YOUR BODY FOR THE HUNT

The most important asset you have as a bluewater diver is your body. As a freediver you have demonstrated the uncommon ability to overcome major mental and physical barriers to the sport. Mental impediments include feelings of claustrophobia, the fear of swimming in the open ocean and the fear of sharks. Physical difficulties include ear clearing (pressure equalization) problems, cold intolerance, wetsuit intolerance and inadequate physical conditioning. Because the sport is so demanding, it's crucial to take care of your body—to give yourself enough nutrients and training and to beware of potential problems such as dehydration and hypothermia. Below, I'll explain how to equip your body for the rigors of bluewater hunting.

How to train your body. Surprisingly, youth and daily training sessions are not prerequisites for success. Since most of our diving is done in slow motion, we do not require sprinting skills. Many hours spent in the bluewater environment bring familiarity, and with that familiarity comes the ability to relax—a crucial adaptation for breath-hold diving. The experience gained by the older diver, through repeated dives and hunts, tends to offset the younger diver's physical advantages. Many divers excel through their fifth and sixth decades.

The best physical conditioning exercise for freediving is freediving. You can stay in excellent shape by diving just once a week. When I am unable to dive, I put on fins and swim in a 75-foot (23-meter) pool, alternating one lap on the surface with one lap underwater. A 30-minute workout three times a week is adequate to retain my skills.

Target shooting in a swimming pool or in a calm sea is excellent practice for spearfishing. You will learn more about your aim in one hour with a target than you will in a whole spearfishing season. There are simply too many variables involved in spearing fish for you to figure out why a shot failed. Was the aim incorrect? Did the fish move? Was the fish further away than I thought? (For target construction, see the chapter on equipment.)

What to eat before and during the hunt. Even relaxed freediving requires an astounding amount of energy, much of which is allocated for heat production. Freediving burns more calories per minute than any activity other that fast axe-chopping, according to scientists at the University of California at Berkeley. They estimate the average 175-pound diver burns 20 calories per minute, or a whopping 1,200 calories per hour. And since divers often spend six to eight hours per day in the water, this means only one thing: *you've got to eat.*

I recommend loading up on carbohydrates the night before and the morning of diving. A thousand to 2,000 calories of such foods as cereals, breads, pancakes, fruits eaten with syrups or jellies will sustain you for up to three hours. After that, you must renourish yourself. We experimented with all sorts of liquid formulas, such as honey dissolved in orange juice. Unfortunately, while these liquids did supply us with energy, they also burned our throats when we inverted for a dive.

There are two diet supplements that provide energy but do not cause heartburn. "Ensure" and "Sustagen," both available in drugstores, are medically complete liquid diet preparations designed for patients who cannot eat (fractured-jaw foods). "Nutrament" is a body-building food supplement packaged as a high-caloric liquid. Both kinds of drinks work very well. These foods are much easier to tolerate when consumed cold, and their liquid nature helps to resist dehydration.

How to prevent dehydration. Dehydration leads to fatigue, headache and a general decrease in athletic performance. Divers dehydrate for two reasons. The first is due to breathing through a snorkel. Air breathed through a snorkel bypasses the sinuses and nasal cavities. These cavities act as humidifiers, capturing moisture from exhaled air. Bypassing these water traps allows extra water to escape the body. The second cause of water loss is a condition called "immersion diuresis." Bodily immersion stimulates the kidneys to increase urine output. Compensate for your water loss by drinking extra water.

How to clear your ears in special circumstances. Ear clearing can present problems for even the most accomplished divers troubled with colds or allergies. These conditions cause swelling of the eustachian tubes leading from the throat to the ears. Swelling prevents the passage of air, a necessity for ear clearing. To enhance your ability to clear your ears, you can use chemical and/or mechanical aids as well as a specially designed mask.

Chemical agents include antihistamines and decongestants. "Seldane" (terfenadine) is a new antihistamine that shrinks tissue swelling due to allergies. Unlike most antihistamines, it causes little drowsiness. Take one the night before diving and one the day of diving. This drug lasts 12 hours. "Sudafed," another decongestant, works differently. The regular dose lasts three to four hours (there is a 12-hour preparation available). Sudafed works well for up to two days, but the body quickly adjusts to this medicine. Chronic use of this drug can produce a rebound effect, which when it wears off, can lead to swelling greater than the original swelling you treated. **DO NOT USE ANY OF THESE DRUGS WITHOUT YOUR PHYSICIAN'S ADVICE.**

Preinflation of your eustachian tube is a good mechanical method for enhancing ear clearing. The day before diving, just pinch your nose and clear your ears. Maintain pressure for 30 seconds. This will probably make you dizzy. Repeat this exercise several times and do it again the day you dive. Wait for an hour or so after waking to prevent forcing morning mucous into these tubes. Pre-inflate again on the surface before you dive. Keep constant clearing pressure against your ears throughout the descent.

Mask design influences clearing. My home-made plastic mask has two little elevations that fit into my nasal openings. As I descend, these little bumps seal my nose so efficiently that I do not need to touch my mask. Commercial masks can be modified by the addition of Silicone Seal into the nasal pocket. Let the silicone set for several minutes, then put clear plastic wrap over it. Wear the mask, with your snorkel in place. Spend several minutes molding the silicone to fit your nasal openings.

Experienced divers learn to clear their ears by tensing the throat muscles responsible for opening their eustachian tubes. You can discover these muscles by protruding your lower jaw and swallowing. Sometimes one ear will clear quickly, while the other won't. As you increase pressure on the reluctant ear, the eardrum in the cleared ear expands painfully. A temporary remedy is to plug the outside opening of the good ear (with finger pressure) while continuing internal clearing pressure against the problem one.

Remember, frequent small clearings are better than several large ones. I have scared more than one school of gamefish with an untimely, noisy, ear clearing.

Do not descend with uncleared ears; a burst eardrum is not worth the risk. Dale Cote, a senior member of the Long Beach Neptunes and North American record-holder for yellowtail, explains what happens if you wait too long to clear:

I was chasing a 150-pound black seabass that almost drowned me earlier when my hand got caught in the spear line. Rested from that episode, I needed to collect my fish stuck on the bottom 70 feet below. I took a second gun and descended. I was overweighted as I swam straight for the bottom. I shot the fish just as an explosion occurred in each ear, explosions only I could hear. I tried clearing on the surface. Air bubbled out from both of my ears! My eardrums were ruptured. I had descended too quickly with too much weight and without sufficient clearing. Luckily, no water entered my ears, which could have caused sickening vertigo and confusion. My ears drained for two weeks and healed in four.

Dale Cote blew both eardrums.

How to prevent hypothermia. Bluewater hunters are especially vulnerable to hypothermia and the consequences can be serious. Prolonged exposure to water, even tropical water, will suck off body heat faster than you can regenerate it. As a bluewater hunter you are especially vulnerable. In order to dive long and deep, you conserve energy by slowing your metabolism—you relax your muscles and your heart slows. Your economy of movement provides little muscular exercise. As a result, you produce little muscular heat.

Lowering your body temperature one degree centigrade, from 37 to 36 degrees, will cause you to shiver and your heart to speed. Muscular power and dexterity suffer. Your oxygen consumption increases—not a good thing for breath-hold divers. Another one-degree drop, from 36 to 35 degrees, causes mental confusion, difficulty with speech and memory loss. I remember getting so cold, scouting for a contest in Northern California, that I simply forgot all my shore bearings. I wasted my eight hours in the water because hypothermia destroyed my short-term memory.

Progressive hypothermia often occurs on multiday trips. It is common to experience a gradual cooling of your central body temperature (core temperature) without being aware of it. Upon returning to warm surface water after a dive into a thermocline, you will experience superficial skin rewarming that masks your slow heat loss. Long, slow cooling of your body does not initiate shivering. Each successive day increases your "thermal debt." Progressive hypothermia results in fatigue and loss of enthusiasm. Finding yourself too tired to care for your equipment or becoming excessively sleepy after diving are indicators of hypothermia.

Avoid hypothermia with good thermal protection. Make sure you wear enough "rubber" and patch those holes. A good hood is essential because the vessels in your scalp cannot constrict, preventing a surprising amount of body heat from radiating away.

Treatment for hypothermia is rewarming by immersion in comfortably hot water. It is important that the water circulates; studies have shown that a shower or still bath is not as effective. Most marine engines, including outboards, have a hot water plumbing take-off. It is possible to use this hot water, mixed properly with cooler sea water, for rewarming. It's a great feeling to have a hot-water hose pushed down the back of your wetsuit after a period of cold-water diving.

Mark Barville hunting at Guadalupe Island, his floats in tow.

PHOTO BY TERRY MAAS

Spearguns and freediving gear

The best bluewater gear is both safe and efficient. The chapter on survival in the bluewater explains why you need to look at every piece of your equipment with a view toward safety.

For example, when you evaluate a float line ask, "Is there a potential for this material to throw a knot around me?" Or a fin: "Will my foot come loose from the pocket deep into my dive?" Or a weight belt: "Does the release mechanism work smoothly and dependably?"

The chapter on ethics explains why every shot you take is important. Once speared, an escaping bluewater fish is unlikely to survive. Every shot you take and every piece of your gear should guarantee your catch. This chapter first covers spearguns and terminal gear (lines and floats attached to the speargun), and ends with a discussion on special modifications bluewater hunters make to their freediving gear, including masks, fins and weight belts.

SPEARGUNS

No other item provokes as much controversy among bluewater hunters as the speargun. Speargun design brings out the staunchly independent nature of many spearfishermen. Imagine the most accurate and advanced speargun, researched and developed by NASA. Give this ultimate speargun to five bluewater hunters. I guarantee, in one month's time, these guns will be modified—or, rather, "improved," in the eyes of their owners.

Southern California freedivers Harry Davis, Steve Alexander and I have a combined 82 years experience in the design, construction and use of spearguns. Both Harry and Steve bring a scientific approach to their craft. Harry built a 32-foot test tank to examine spearhead dynamics. The tank is equipped with a video camera capable of capturing a spearshaft in midflight. Steve tests different spearheads for their relative ability to penetrate fish, and they both test the power potential of different batches of speargun band material.

Despite our attempts at science, most of what we know about spearguns is empirical in nature. Speargun design will continue to improve, but I am confident that our current guns have reached the point where they are adequate for any bluewater fish. Use the best gun possible to help fulfill your ethical obligation to make every shot count.

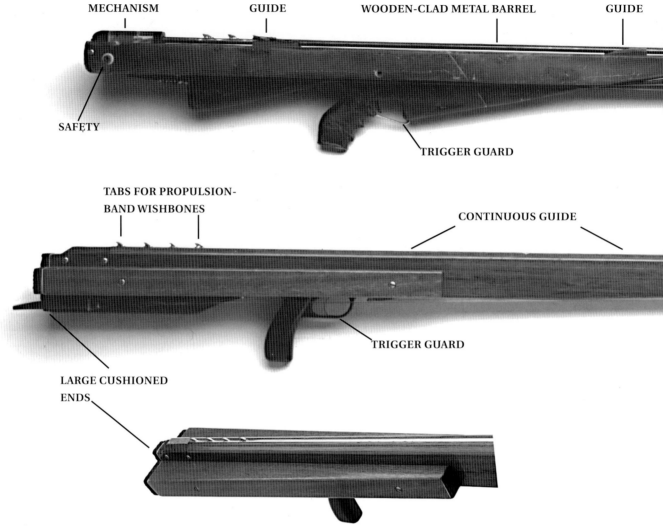

MECHANISM GUIDE WOODEN-CLAD METAL BARREL GUIDE

SAFETY

TRIGGER GUARD

TABS FOR PROPULSION-
BAND WISHBONES

CONTINUOUS GUIDE

TRIGGER GUARD

LARGE CUSHIONED
ENDS

Basic speargun parts.

The ideal speargun is powerful, accurate, durable and safe. These valuable characteristics are affected by the interplay of the gun's parts. Let's first take a look at each component. Later, we will discuss how these parts work together to provide accuracy and power. Note: this chapter is written for divers with a basic understanding of spearguns and how they work. The novice should be able to understand most of the terminology by studying the appropriate illustrations.

Your choice of a spear is essentially a compromise between speed and weight. A speedy, light shaft will not have sufficient impact at 20 feet to stop a large bluewater fish. A heavy shaft will have enough momentum for impact at 20 feet, but it will be too slow. A ⅜-inch (9½-millimeter) diameter shaft is the best compromise.

The most suitable shaft material available is 17-4 PH stainless steel. The high-tensile strength provided by this heat-treatable material prevents most permanent bends. Fish weighing more than 100 pounds (45 kilograms) are capable, however, of bending even this superior material. 17-4 PH stainless is expensive, and you must first machine it and weld it in its annealed (soft) state. The treatment process requires heat at 900 degrees Fahrenheit for one hour followed by gradual cooling. Six feet (1.8 meters) is a good

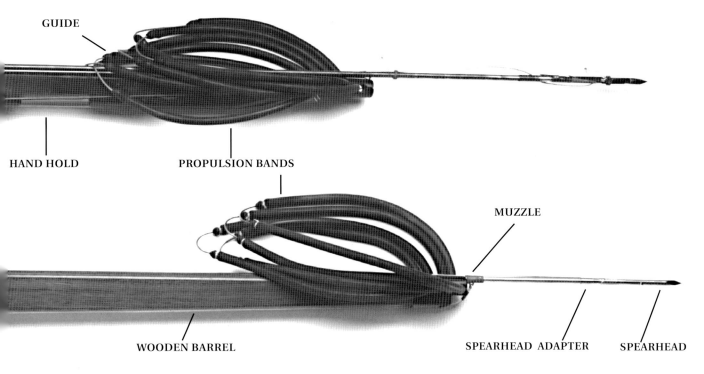

GUIDE

HAND HOLD

PROPULSION BANDS

MUZZLE

WOODEN BARREL

SPEARHEAD ADAPTER

SPEARHEAD

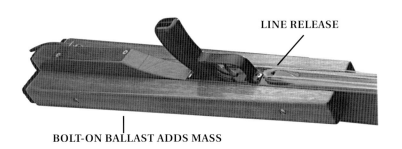

LINE RELEASE

BOLT-ON BALLAST ADDS MASS

length. The spearhead end of the shaft is machined with a thread pattern 5/16 inches by 24 threads per inch. These threads should end in a butt shoulder with the spear tip adaptor bottoming on this shoulder. Welded tabs serve as attachment points for the propulsion bands. Select a shaft with the front tab drilled to receive the spearshaft cable; the hole needs to be high enough to clear the spearshaft guides. The rear of the shaft is machined to match the trigger mechanism.

Barrels are made of metal or wood. Teak is the best choice for a wooden gun because its high oil content resists water absorption. Wood grain absorbs water irregularly, which leads to unequal swelling and, ultimately, to warping. Steve splits a piece of teakwood and laminates the two pieces together in a mirror-image relationship. He reasons that any tendency of the wood to warp in one direction is countered by its mate warping in the opposite direction.

I prefer a metal barrel, made from stainless steel tubing, with a wall thickness of .035 inches and a diameter of 1¼ inches (3.2 centimeters). I fill the barrel with a closely fitted plastic rod, cemented with polyurethane foam (the same foam we use to fill our floats). The added weight is no problem; the solid core provides good anchorage for spear guides and the barrel cannot leak.

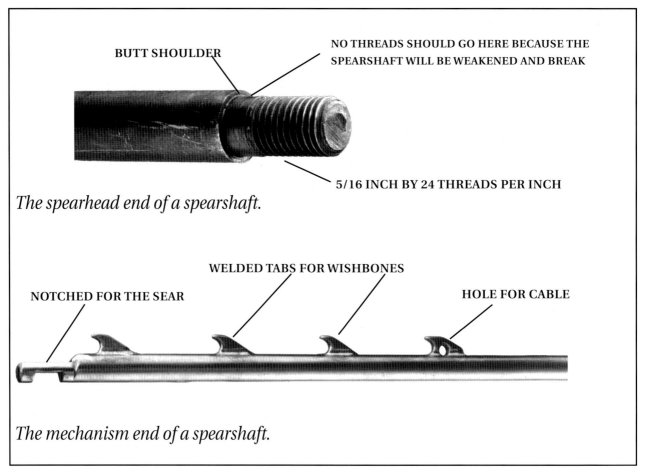

BUTT SHOULDER

NO THREADS SHOULD GO HERE BECAUSE THE
SPEARSHAFT WILL BE WEAKENED AND BREAK

5/16 INCH BY 24 THREADS PER INCH

The spearhead end of a spearshaft.

WELDED TABS FOR WISHBONES

NOTCHED FOR THE SEAR

HOLE FOR CABLE

The mechanism end of a spearshaft.

"Gun barrels should be absolutely straight and symmetrical," Steve suggests. "They must be of adequate thickness and stiffness to maintain a straight configuration after the power bands are loaded. The muzzle should not extend more than ½ inch past the band slot as this only creates extra lateral drag." A good length for the barrel, measured end to end, is 56 inches (142 centimeters). While a longer barrel provides more reach and additional band stretch, it is more difficult to load and maneuver.

A shaft guidance system is required to stabilize the shaft the instant the trigger is pulled. Steve likes an enclosed track for shaft control. Harry and I prefer our so-called "capture guides," which encircle three quarters of the shaft's circumference, preventing it from jumping up or sideways. These guides are slotted at the top to allow the passage of

the spearshaft tabs, and they should be tapered on each side to help direct a slightly rotated spear tab into the slot. The opening is 13/32 inches (0.4 millimeters), slightly wider than the shaft diameter to prevent binding. Three guides, with the middle and rear guides equally spaced between the front guide and the trigger mechanism, are sufficient to stabilize and guide the shaft.

Front guide position is important. Once the wishbones release, the shaft is free to rotate. This could allow the tabs to strike the front guide if it were positioned too far forward. The tabs must not strike any projection on the barrel. Doing so will produce inconsistent results. Fifteen inches back from the end of the muzzle is a safe distance to locate the front guide. Another good addition to the barrel is a notched grip near the front of the gun. You can carry the gun by hold-

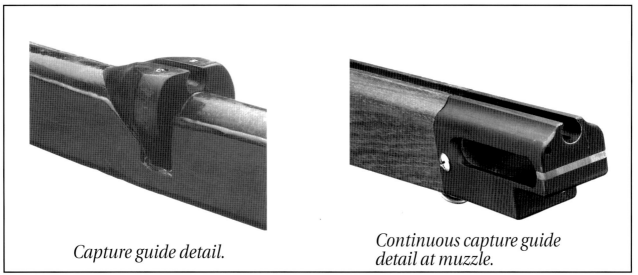

Capture guide detail.

Continuous capture guide detail at muzzle.

ing it here when in transit, fighting a current or swimming over barren ground.

The gun handle should be positioned at least 13 inches (33 centimeters) from the rear of the gun. Eighteen inches (46 centimeters) is better for aiming, but this distance brings the rear of the gun closer to your face, and gun recoil can produce broken masks, bent noses, fat lips and other serious injury. With a 56-inch (1.42-meter) barrel and a 72-inch (1.82-meter) shaft, the spear tip will be about 18 inches beyond the muzzle, providing good tip visibility. This geometry is excellent for maneuvering and aiming because most divers sight by superimposing their spear tip onto the target.

Eighteen pounds (8 kilos) is a good weight for the assembled gun, including the spear and spearhead. This weight reduces both horizontal and vertical gun recoil. (See the section on accuracy.) The front two-thirds of the gun should be streamlined so that you can move the gun easily through the water. In the water, the gun should be balanced at the handle with a slight tendency to sink at the spear tip end, and it should float after the spear is discharged. You can modify the weight and balance of your gun by attaching weighted, streamlined wooden blocks to the rear third. Adjust the weight of these blocks by drilling holes in them and inserting enough lead to

achieve neutral buoyancy and balance. Generally, you need to add flotation ahead of the handle and weight behind it.

The spear release mechanism is the heart of the gun. It should be a two-stage device. One lever, activated by the trigger, releases the second lever, which in turn releases the shaft. Do not experiment here; select a gun with a reliable, tested spear release mechanism. This mechanism must have an effective safety that positively engages the primary lever (the lever actuated by the trigger push-rod). Safeties that engage the trigger are not reliable and may allow accidental release. Test the safety by loading the gun in the water, placing it on safety and pulling the trigger. Afterward, be careful when you release the safety because sometimes faulty safety mechanisms release the spear when they are disengaged. A trigger guard is necessary to prevent accidental discharge caused by an unintentional blow to the trigger. The spear line release mechanism should be timed to release the line just *before* the shaft is fired. A delayed line release will pull the shaft off its course or break the line.

A push-rod is required to transmit finger pressure, backward, to the mechanism. Select a gun using lightweight push-rod material to reduce the possibility of accidental discharge if you bump or drop the gun. Make sure the

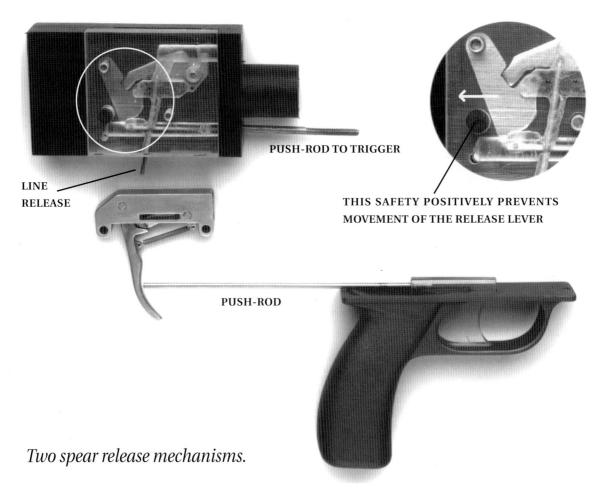

LINE RELEASE

PUSH-ROD TO TRIGGER

THIS SAFETY POSITIVELY PREVENTS MOVEMENT OF THE RELEASE LEVER

PUSH-ROD

Two spear release mechanisms.

push-rod is strong enough to resist the sear's pressure to release; a weak push-rod will bend and then affect the position and operation of the trigger. This might allow the mechanism to discharge prematurely.

Power bands vary greatly in their elasticity and energy storage. Bands with a high modulus of elasticity will, for a given diameter, provide more tension (energy) and will maintain that tension over a period of time better than a band with a low modulus of elasticity. The best bands have a high power-to-volume ratio, which maximizes power and reduces bulk. Minimal bulk means less friction and more speed. Spearfishing legend Jack Prodonovich provides a great service to Southern California divers by offering special black rubber specifically formulated to possess a high modulus of elasticity.

Commercial rubber varies in diameter by as much as 12 percent between manufacturers. A ⅝-inch band has 25 percent more area than a 9/16-inch band and therefore 25 percent more power. Test a sample of rubber before you invest in it. Harry and Steve use a simple apparatus to test rubber from various suppliers. Perhaps an interested club member could build one and make it available to other members.

Take a 6-inch (15-centimeter) piece of rubber sling material and secure metal hooks to both ends. Make a white mark, with a fingernail whitener pencil, one inch from each end so that you have four inches (10 centimeters) between each mark. Find the elastic limit by stretching the band material. The elastic limit is reached when an additional increase in length no longer produces a corresponding increase on the tension

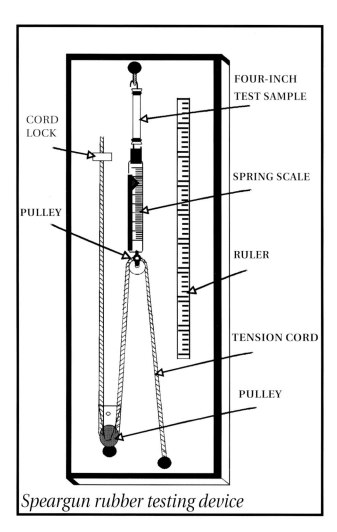

Speargun rubber testing device

9/16 INCH	GOOD		POOR	
PERCENT STRETCH	INITIAL (POUNDS)	ONE HOUR	INITIAL (POUNDS)	ONE HOUR
200	52	42	40	34
300	88	69	62	48
400	99	89	72	62

5/8 INCH	GOOD		POOR	
PERCENT STRETCH	INITIAL (POUNDS)	ONE HOUR	INITIAL (POUNDS)	ONE HOUR
200	71	60	53	42
300	111	97	79	60
400	132	122	89	77

scale. An excellent result is a stretch of four times the original length, or from four inches to 16 inches (40 centimeters) on the ruler scale. A 3 ½ times stretch, or 14 inches (35.5 centimeter), indicates rubber of lesser but acceptable quality. Any extra band stretch is a bonus because it pulls the shaft longer, giving it more momentum and speed.

It is important to have rubber material capable of retaining power for long periods of time. The gun should deliver nearly full power an hour or more after loading. On the scale, measure power retention after 20 minutes by slowly releasing the stretch on the band until the white mark again corresponds with its initial stretch at the elastic limit. Read the scale. The following tables compare good and bad samples, which may vary as much as 60 percent in strength (the numbers are in pounds).

Use nylon line wishbones. Metal wishbones break after several hundred loadings. They weaken with each cycle of loading and firing. A weak metal wishbone is difficult to detect since it looks as good as new. The sharp edge of a broken wishbone is dangerous and can cause lacerations. Hard braid stiff nylon line inch (3 millimeters) works well (# 72 gangen line). It will not break after many loading cycles. Nylon gives an excellent visual warning of impending failure, although I have yet to have these wishbones fail before the rubber band material.

Securing the bands to the nylon wishbone material is easy. Cut the nylon 9½ inches (24 centimeters) and tie a double overhand knot around each end. Keep the knot as small as possible to avoid stressing the rubber, which leads to early cracking and failure. Force these knots into the rubber ½ inch (1.25 centimeters). Place a small piece of electrical tape over the band and tie a tight knot with heavy fishing line or lacing line. Be sure to test the results in a vise because wishbones pull loose at the most inconvenient times.

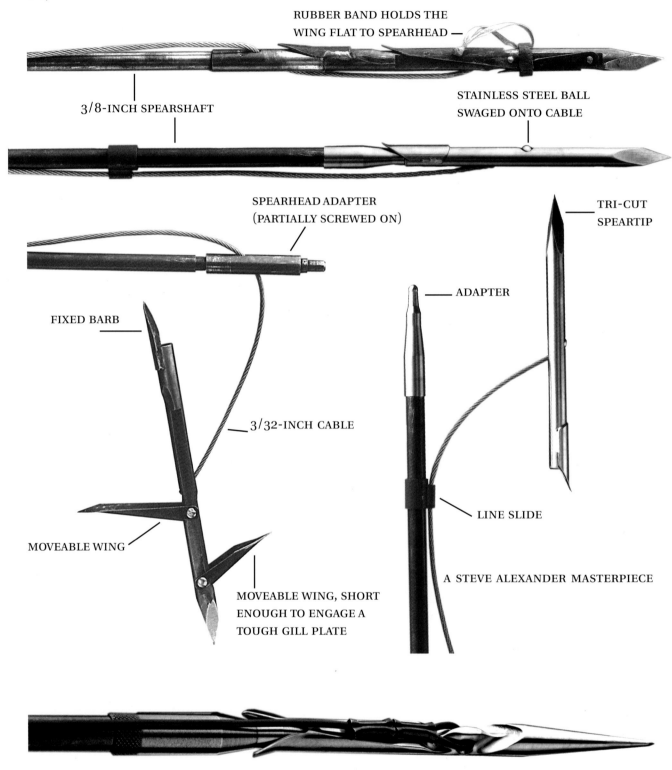

RUBBER BAND HOLDS THE
WING FLAT TO SPEARHEAD —

3/8-INCH SPEARSHAFT

STAINLESS STEEL BALL
SWAGED ONTO CABLE

SPEARHEAD ADAPTER
(PARTIALLY SCREWED ON)

TRI-CUT
SPEARTIP

ADAPTER

FIXED BARB

3/32-INCH CABLE

LINE SLIDE

MOVEABLE WING

MOVEABLE WING, SHORT
ENOUGH TO ENGAGE A
TOUGH GILL PLATE

A STEVE ALEXANDER MASTERPIECE

A JAY RIFFE MASTERPIECE

Three excellent detachable spearhead designs.

SPEARHEADS

The best spearhead for large fish detaches from the spearshaft. The most secure way to hold a fish is to drive one of these heads completely through it, allowing the spearhead to toggle on the other side. It is free to play the fish independently of the huge lever arm of an attached shaft, which is capable of gouging a large hole in your fish and could lead to its escape. The head should not wobble when seated on its adapter, and there should be no frictional interference to disengagement. A good test is to turn the shaft, spearhead side down. The head should fall off under its own weight. The head must disengage easily inside the fish as well. Test this by applying side pressure to the spearhead tip; it should slide off easily from the adapter. Now, disengage the tip about ⅛ of an inch. It should have plenty of wobble, which aids in its deployment inside the fish.

You have two basic detachable head (slip-tip) designs to choose from. Steve and Harry prefer the sleek design of a head without folding wings. They stress that the one or two small barbs at the end of the head must be small and symmetrical. While I prefer a design incorporating folding wings, Harry's tests show these wings slow the shaft significantly.

The minimum length for the tip is 5 inches, but 8 inches is not too long. Reduce friction by carefully selecting your tip line type and its method of attachment. Stainless steel, 49-strand 7 x 7 wire with a diameter of 0.1 inches (2½ millimeters), is good. Do not double the line backward or tuck it under the power bands as this will cause the spear to veer off course. Use elastic bands, made by cutting off small pieces of surgical rubber, to hold the head onto the adapter and to hold the folding wings against the head. Be sure that if you use a slide ring, it is totally free so it will not interfere with tip disengagement. Steve tested speartips and found that it took half as much energy for a tri-cut tip to penetrate a fish as it took for a pencil-shaped tip.

Two stories illustrate the development and use of my own detachable head.

In 1983, warm water El Niño conditions sent Mexican tuna hundreds of miles north to the Channel Islands of California. National champion Bill Ernst and I were diving for gamefish near Santa Barbara Island when we were surprised by giant tuna.

'I see four huge tuna!' yells Bill. Just two dives later, four monster bluefin tuna move into my view, swimming in typical tuna formation: bunched close together and speedy. Suddenly, they break formation and swim toward me like tame rockfish. Their atypical behavior astonishes me. One comes within range, then another. I find myself getting 'schooled,' frantically switching my aim from one fish to another as they trade places getting closer. They are huge! I aim at a 400-pound fish and fire at the gill plates, expecting its forward speed to cause the arrow to land somewhere behind its head on the lateral line.

This fish is swimming so slowly that the spear actually hits his gill plate. He shakes the spear off quickly as the spearhead pulls free from the 1-inch thick armored gill cover. A few dives later, the original four tuna swim by me again, just out of range. One of them has a white divot on his gill plate.

This incident caused me to develop a detachable spearhead with a variable penetration design. I lost this fish because my 1½ inch wings did not penetrate deeply enough to deploy and engage. While my goal is a shot that completely penetrates the fish with the head toggling on the opposite side, the above example explains why I wanted a spearhead capable of functioning under a variety of circumstances.

This spearhead, when viewed straight on, looks like an ice pick. Two staggered and recessed wings fold out of sight. The gill plate shot, described above, illustrates the need for the wings to function when the fish cannot be completely penetrated. The first wing is short and stout. It is near the tri-cut spear point so it need only penetrate the fish 3½ inches to engage. Compare this to the five or six inches required with a more conventional design. The second wing opens opposite the first, further down the head. The end of the head, opposite the point, is fitted with a fixed barb. These three parts work together like a great retentive claw under the fish's skin.

This combination saved my first yellowfin tuna record, a 225-pound beauty. I was diving near an underwater pinnacle in the crystal clear waters off of Clarion Island, Mexico.

I have been diving for hours. Just one other diver remains in the water with me. Spotting the largest yellowfin either of us has ever seen, Loc Vetter dives toward the fish 40 feet below. The fish angles away from Loc, toward me. I dive. The fish swims between me and the pinnacle. What good luck! I use the pinnacle to my advantage as I swim toward the blue and yellow spangled fish. My path 'pinches' him between me and the rock, allowing me to get much closer than I would have been able to in open water. I shoot.

The fish quivers once, then vanishes into the depths. My two buoys follow him, twisting and turning furiously, as they trail bubbles 80 feet below. Soon, they, too, vanish into 300 feet of water. Why didn't I have three buoys?!

Dejected, I swim back to the boat. Luckily this vessel is equipped with a crow's nest. I climb it and scan the horizon. One half hour later a buoy appears a quarter mile away, bobbing, half sinking, riding the waves. We race out in the inflatable boat. Relieved, I find

sharks have not eaten this beautiful fish. I am especially grateful that my buddy, Loc, did not take a desperation shot, frightening this record catch.

My spearhead saved that day for me. The midbody shot missed vital structures, but the head did penetrate eight inches, just enough to allow all three barbs to engage. We found a small entry hole, and as my spearhead pulled through the soft flesh, it ended up just under the skin. It turned sideways, expanding into a great claw, allowing the fish's tough skin to resist the pull of one hundred feet of trail line and two buoys.

Use stainless steel cable for the spear line. It's best to use 1/16-inch, 7 x 7-strand bare cable, or 1/16 inch cable coated to a diameter of 3/32 inch with PVC. Do not use monofilament or Kevlar for gamefish over 50 pounds (22 kilograms). Synthetic line material slips from crimps and fails due to crushing and abrasion. Harry tested various types of lines and cable crimps and found that both a single stainless steel crimp and dual copper crimps did not fail at 500 pounds (230 kilograms), which is very close to the cable's strength.

For best results, use the crimping tool specified by the crimp manufacturer. Test your crimping technique with a levered dead weight. An improperly crimped cable will fail at a surprisingly low tension (200 pounds). Correct cable braiding actually produces a loop stronger than the cable it's made from; crimp the resulting end to control it. So, for the strongest connections, braid or double crimp the cable as illustrated on the facing page.

Try using two-and-one half line wraps, front to back, around the barrel. This allows five lengths of cable to play out before the spear line pulls the float line. This length is about 30 feet, longer than the longest shot. A long line also gives you a few seconds to get out of the way of your speeding float line and floats as your big fish rockets away. You can avoid line tangles by routing the line on alternate sides of the barrel

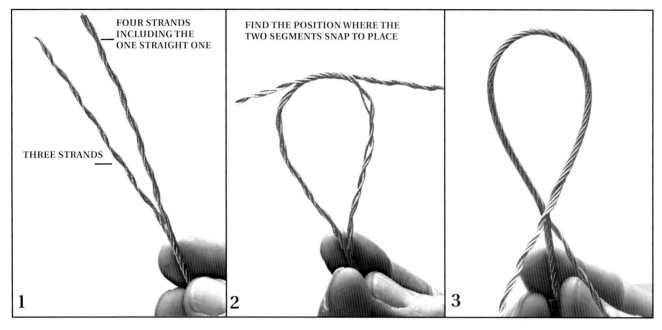

FOUR STRANDS INCLUDING THE ONE STRAIGHT ONE

THREE STRANDS

1

FIND THE POSITION WHERE THE TWO SEGMENTS SNAP TO PLACE

2

3

Separate the 7 x 7 strand cable into two sections. One contains three twisted groups of seven, the other contains four groups of seven including the one straight group.

Bring the two segments together and form a loop. The cable will snap to place at several locations. Be sure you plan for enough excess for the whole loop and crimp.

Finish the loop by twisting each side into its mate.

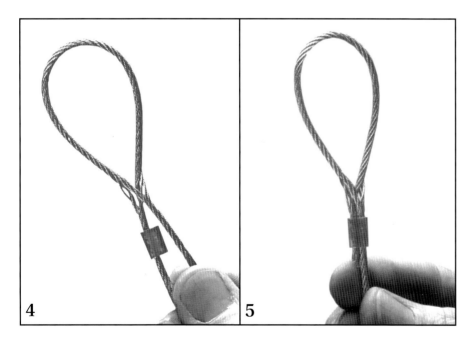

4

5

Fit a crimp. Its primary use is to finish the ends.

Compress the crimp and trim the excess.

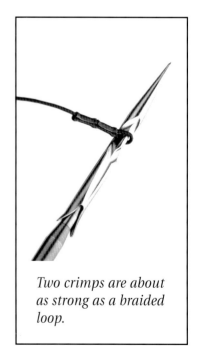

Two crimps are about as strong as a braided loop.

The Yoshikawa braided loop.

or by wrapping it backward so that line wraps come off in the right sequence—top wrap first.

Make sure the spear line separates from the gun stock because you may need that barrel to defend yourself. South African champion Tommy Botha knows what it feels like to be left without a gun. Tommy recalls spearfishing with two friends off Struisbay, South Africa.

Eric, Sean and I were spearing yellowtail. Apart from a couple of small sharks, the diving was uneventful. A shoal of yellowtail came by and we each got one. I followed the shoal down 50 feet, where I speared mine. The fish pulled the gun out of my hand. I held onto my float and just before ascending, a 4-meter (13-foot) white shark moved in. It seemed to be interested in my fish so I let out a bit more line. The white suddenly turned away from my fish and swam straight for me. Not having anything in my hand, I realized I was in trouble. I swam toward the surface, not too fast, but strong.

Looking up, I saw the other two divers. I angled toward them. The shark was getting closer—all I saw was his nose and mouth. My buddy Eric had just strung his fish and was reloading. Sean was still fighting his fish as I swam up, looking down, not wanting to take my eyes off the shark. I swam straight into Eric's gun, knocking it from his grasp. Now none of us had a weapon in our hands and we had a 4-meter shark in our company. A lot of white water and screaming followed. Sean won the struggle to the boat. Sometime during the fracas a big flap of fabric tore from his wetsuit. He still does not know how that happened or where it went. Safe in the boat, we each collected our float lines and landed our fish.

Bluewater gamefish are gear busters. Evaluate every part of your gear for strength. The illustrations below show gear broken by large tuna.

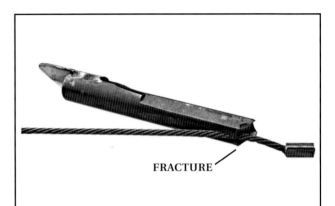

FRACTURE

This detachable head was fractured at its weakest point.

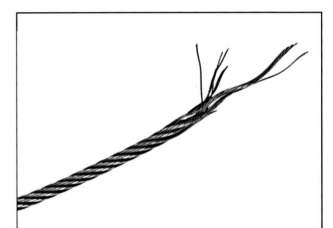

The initial run of a tuna, estimated to weigh 300 pounds, shredded this 1/16-inch, 500-pound test cable. Interestingly, the braided and crimped end remained intact.

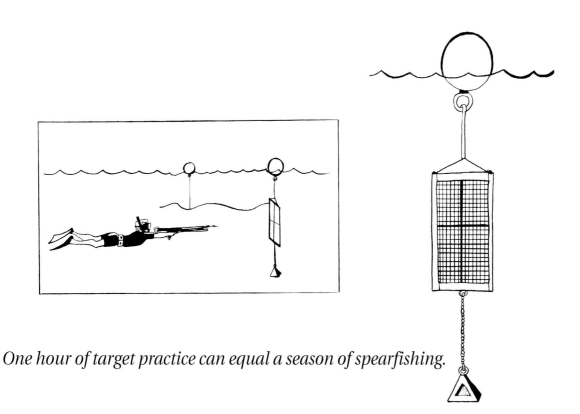

One hour of target practice can equal a season of spearfishing.

ACCURACY

Accuracy with your speargun requires a good aim and design control over dynamic reactions such as recoil and shaft whip.

Use a target to perfect your aim. Target practice is also an excellent way to test the effects of changes in your speargun configuration. Harry suggests constructing a target out of one-inch square fish net stretched over a wooden frame 2 feet wide and 3 feet tall (0.6 x 1.0 meters). Make crosshairs with yellow polypropylene rope. Suspend the target from a float and anchor it to the bottom with a weight. Mark a line at 10 feet (3 meters), 15 feet (4½ meters) and 20 feet (6 meters). Suspend this line from another smaller buoy, which should drift straight away in a slight current. Practice making shots from these distances. It is easy to tell where the shot landed because the spear line will pass through one of the squares. Your aim is good if you can maintain a 2-inch circle at 15 to 20 feet. Learn how to compensate for the shaft as it drops at greater distances. Expect a relatively flat shot up to 15 feet and a drop of 4 to 6 inches at 20 feet.

Steve uses another target unaffected by the sea surface. He floats a fish-shaped piece of neoprene wetsuit material, tied to a soft-wood stick, from two weights resting on a sandy bottom. His range line is marked every five feet with ribbons and is weighted to the bottom. He suggests weighting yourself heavily and inching over the bottom until you reach your desired range. Once shot, the spear is easily removed from the neoprene.

For accurate aiming, the muzzle end of the barrel should be free from visual obstructions. The shaft should protrude past the end of the barrel by at least 8 to 10 inches. This places the spear tip about 18 inches beyond the muzzle. I aim by sighting straight down the barrel with the butt of the gun low and placing my speartip directly over the spot I expect to hit. A shorter shaft extension cannot be seen very well past the muzzle and the bands.

73

Steve aims by sighting down the side of the gun turned 90 degrees. He reasons that since spearguns are most inaccurate in the vertical plane and that most fish present a horizontal target, he should turn the gun on its side. He claims the dual advantages of better visibility, with two-eye sighting, and more safety, because the gun butt is not lined up with his face.

Do not forget to practice the "hip shot" because sometimes bluewater fish can appear within a few feet of you, seemingly out of nowhere. Extending your gun would spook them. Instead, shoot from your waist and aim low because your natural tendency will be to shoot too high.

The mystery of the wayward spearshaft was solved when we realized that spears bend under conditions of high stress. They bend the instant they are released. Two observations led to this conclusion. First, our speargun barrels, without lateral guidance of the shaft, displayed abrasion marks several millimeters off center. Second, an accurate speargun would suddenly become wildly erratic with the addition of just one more power band.

A shaft resists bending until overwhelming power is applied. On release, the back end of the shaft literally tries to catch up with the front, turning the straight shaft into spaghetti. The solution to this problem came with the development of "capture" guides and channels.

Your shaft must be perfectly straight. A bent shaft will deform quickly as it is launched. "Find a small piece of straight wire," says Steve. "Put it between your fingers and apply end-to-end pressure along its long axis. Note how much pressure is required to bend it. Now, take another piece of wire and bend it slightly. Repeat the pressure test. It will bend quite easily. This test shows how even the slightest bend makes a starting point for a bow to start."

Thicker shafts resist bending better than thin ones. Check all new production shafts, as many of them are not straight.

There are two good methods for straightening a bent spearshaft. Steve's method requires a heavy hammer (brass will not mar the metal) and a metal straight edge, ½-inch wide and 6-feet long. The straight edge needs to be machined or ground perfectly straight, within a tolerance of a couple thousandths of an inch (this costs about $150). You also need metal support blocks, ½ inch or taller, and a hard working surface such as a metal table or a concrete floor.

To illustrate, let us straighten a heat-treated 17-4 PH shaft, 6 feet long, with a bend in the middle. Place the shaft against the straight edge and mark the beginning and the end of the bend. Position the spear on the table under the blocks at these marks. Support the best end of the shaft with a block. Hold the other end of the shaft with vise grips. The vise grips prevent the shaft from turning. Swing the hammer at the midpoint. Using your eyes as a guide, repeat this process until the shaft is reasonably straight.

Next, use the straight edge again. Hang the metal straight edge vertically from rafters. Hold the shaft against the straight edge and use a bright backlight to highlight the bend. Look for the light space. Mark the bend and go back to the hard work surface. Reposition the two blocks closer and hit the shaft again. Repeat this process using smaller support blocks and smaller strikes until the shaft is straight.

Try not to strike the shaft too hard, causing it to bend in the wrong direction. This process takes 10 to 15 minutes for a simple bend. It takes Steve 45 minutes to an hour to straighten a shaft someone else has already tried to straighten. They have invariably induced extra bends into the shaft in their efforts to straighten it. Heat-treated shafts become softer when straightened. You can straighten a heat-treated shaft no more than three times before it becomes unreliable and requires another heat treatment.

Harry uses a light box and a 12-inch metal straight edge to straighten shafts. He suggests constructing a light box by encasing a 6-foot florescent bulb in a three-sided wooden box.

Cover the box with frosted plastic and place two parallel pieces of black electrical tape ½-inch apart down the center. Blacken the rest of the plastic, leaving a slit of light. Use two V-blocks, low to the plastic, to support the shaft as you rotate it. Start by placing the blocks on each side of the middle third of the shaft. Viewing from above, slowly rotate the shaft over the slit light and identify the greatest irregularity. Now take the straight edge and move it horizontally to locate the center, and the greatest concavity, of the bend (most shafts have just one major bend). After marking the center of the bend, take it to a vise. Place the center of the bend in the end of the vise, and clamp it with the bend oriented in the horizontal plane.

Now comes the tricky part. Take the free end of the shaft and bend it several inches against the bent direction, and strike it with a 1-pound hammer six to eight inches from the bend. Harry recommends practicing on an old shaft first. Judging how far to overcorrect and how hard to strike the shaft is a skill gained by experience. Once the center is corrected, work on the ends by orienting the blocks two-thirds on one end and two-thirds on the other. (Exclude any welded tab areas, as these are frequently bent and are best treated last.) Check the final results on the slit lamp with V-blocks supporting each end of the shaft.

Make sure the barrel is perfectly straight. It should not bend excessively when fully loaded. You can test the amount of bending by measuring the straightness of the loaded shaft. Load the gun *in the water* and run a string along the top of the shaft. For safety, never take the loaded gun out of the water, and make sure that the gun is equipped with a safety that positively jams the sear lever in place. Any bow producing less than ⅛ inch (3 millimeters) of daylight between the string and the shaft is acceptable, but the less bend the better.

The amount of trigger pull effects accuracy. Surprisingly, trigger pull (the amount of finger pressure on the trigger required to discharge the spear) has a great effect on accuracy. "Too little pull may cause premature firing before your aim is completed," Harry says. "Too much pull causes jerking, which ruins your aim. A delayed release may result in a missed shot. The pull should be light enough that there is no recollection of it after the shot. It should be firm enough to provide some finger resistance when test firing (six pounds is a good pressure). The pull distance should be long enough to prevent accidental firing (¼ to ⅜ inches, or 6 to 10 millimeters)."

Managing speargun recoil is important for two reasons: safety and accuracy. Horizontal recoil is so powerful that in some cases, it leads to wrist injury. A lightly weighted gun (about 5 pounds), heavily loaded with power bands, is unsafe. Decrease wrist impact by selecting a gun with the handle angled back 120 degrees from the horizontal orientation of the barrel.

Also, recoil against an unlocked elbow can allow the barrel to smash into a diver's face. Many divers have bruised or cut their heads. Recoil from one gun shattered a diver's face mask and almost completely severed his nose. Fortunately, quick transportation to a plastic surgeon saved his nose. Another diver fractured a rib when he tried to control recoil with his chest.

Control recoil by shooting your gun with both arms. Extend your trigger arm enough to lock your elbow joint. Use the other arm to hold and stabilize the back of the barrel. This hand-arm configuration is excellent for aim adjustment. The arm at the gun's rear easily pivots the gun around the trigger hand. See Gerald Lim's profile photograph in Chapter 2, *Bluewater Hunting*.

Adding mass (weight) to the gun barrel helps to control horizontal recoil by providing a very stable launch platform for your spear. More of the available energy is imparted directly into the shaft, with less going into useless recoil. A heavy gun, weighted for neutral buoyancy in the water, is quite easy to aim. Make sure your gun floats after the spear is fired.

Vertical recoil drives the shaft downward. Stop-action video imaging of the shaft leaving a hand-held gun reveals that the muzzle end kicks upward. This upward motion of the barrel moves the back end of the escaping shaft up, directing the spearshaft in a downward path. The shaft shoots lower and lower as both band pressure and the resulting vertical recoil increase. Harry's 32-foot video tank tests confirm that firmly mounted guns, unable to recoil, shoot true.

The offset relationship of the power bands pulling from their origin, below the shaft, to their wishbone position above the shaft induces this recoil, pivoting the gun around the handle. You can minimize vertical recoil by keeping the plane of thrust bands as nearly parallel to the shaft as possible and increasing the weight of your gun to at least 18 pounds. Also, designing the handle to fit as closely to the shaft as possible will lessen the tendency of the gun to rotate at the handle. One problem with welded wishbone tabs is that the wishbones sitting on top of the shaft tend to increase vertical recoil. This tendency to shoot low can be offset by aiming techniques. I hold the gun butt just below my chin, which compensates for about three inches vertically at a range of 15 feet.

Speartip design greatly influences accuracy. Any asymmetry in the head can cause the shaft to veer. The tip must be concentrically centered on the adapter, as any offset will also veer the shaft. Two wings or barbs are generally better than one because one wing may induce asymmetrical drag. One barb kept small, however, should not cause too much symmetrical drag and has the advantage of more efficient toggling inside the fish. The turned-up tips of the spearhead wings will also steer the shaft; make sure they are small and sharp. Use two wings, or barbs, on opposite sides of the head to cancel their tendency to veer or twist; excessive twisting slows the shaft and induces inaccuracies.

Test for shaft twist by carefully marking the top of your shooting line, avoiding twisting it as you load. Fire the gun over a sandy bottom and count the number of line twists to the resting shaft. You may be surprised; anywhere from zero to 10 twists are common (five twists in 25 feet would be almost one twist per shaft length.)

Harry's 500-gallon, 32-foot test tank yielded some interesting data regarding shaft dynamics, power and accuracy:

1. While the initial muzzle velocity of a typical spear measured 60-plus miles (96 kilometers) per hour, the spear averaged 45 miles (72 kilometers) per hour over a distance of 15 feet. This translates to less than a quarter of a second between spear release and impact at 15 feet. Many divers have seen fish react fast enough to dodge the shaft!

2. Spearhead design had a great effect in accuracy and drag. Large break-away spearheads with multiple wings had significant drag. Smooth break-away spearheads with small fixed barbs had minimal drag. Spearheads with lines attached to one side caused the spear to veer slightly to that side.

3. The methods of attaching the 1/16-inch (1½-millimeter) spearline made little difference. Whether the line was attached to the shaft with a slip ring or directly at one of the wishbone tabs did not significantly affect the performance of the spear.

4. A small amount of barrel bending is acceptable and has little or no effect on accuracy.

5. Wishbone termination, whether in notches or on tabs, made no difference in speed or accuracy.

Your bluewater gun should be capable of launching a spear with enough force to pass through a large gamefish at a distance of 15 feet or more. Basically, your design should maximize thrust and minimize drag. A 6-foot (1.8-meter), ⅜-inch (1-centimeter) shaft will need at least four 9/16-inch (14-millimeter) bands with a high modulus of elasticity to supply sufficient thrust. Reduce friction by using straight guides. Use thin shooting line and avoid loops in the cable as much as possible. Make sure the spearhead is streamlined, with its wings hidden in recesses behind the speartip.

A large-diameter shaft system, developed by Gerald Lim, incorporates a 7/16-inch-diameter spearshaft 62½ inches long. Along with Ben Wolfe's Norprene bungee system (described in the next section), Gerald successfully landed three tackle-busting yellowfin tuna weighing over 100 pounds, including his 260-pound pending record. He uses seven 80-pound pull bands, to power the spearshaft. Two advantages of the large-diameter shaft include its resistance to flexing and whipping (requiring no capture guides) and its high-impact delivery.

While the previous discussion concentrated on large, heavy guns, many bluewater species can be taken with a small-diameter shaft (7 millimeters) launched from a two-banded gun. South African Jimmy Uys took his 242-kilogram (533-pound) black marlin with a long, thin-shafted gun. Advocates of this system argue that the thin shaft bends and conforms to the fleeing fish's profile, thereby reducing drag on the shaft that might otherwise work a hole in its flesh. Bluewater hunters using this lightweight system usually attempt a kill shot to prevent excessive stress on their gear.

The following lists review safety suggestions for the design, care and use of spearguns.

Design

• Your gun must be equipped with a safety that positively engages one of the mechanism release levers—do not trust safeties placed elsewhere (trigger, push-rod).

• Make sure your trigger is protected with a trigger guard.

• The push-rod of a remote-handled gun should be both light and strong—it must not bend under the influence of the loaded sear lever.

• Do not overpower any barrel, as this will lead to collapse of the barrel under a load exceeding its strength.

• Avoid wooden barrels with unreinforced horizontal laminations that might split at the laminations with age or overpowering.

• Consider nylon wishbones to prevent lacerations—a possibility with broken metal wishbones.

Care

• Inspect your gun before each use. Look for rust and corrosion in metal barrels, and cracks and delaminations in wooden barrels.

• Wash your gun with freshwater after each use.

• For enhanced life, store rubber slings in a sealed plastic bag and keep them in the refrigerator.

• Periodically check the attachment security of the handle. If the handle fails when firing, the gun butt can cause serious facial injuries.

Use

• Always treat a speargun as though it were loaded.

• Be sure that the spear is positively locked into the trigger mechanism and that the safety is engaged before loading your gun.

• Keep the tip pointed in a safe direction at all times—be constantly aware of where your gun is pointed.

• Never rely on a mechanical safety alone.

• Never load a speargun out of water, or remove a loaded gun from the water.

• When shooting your gun, never allow the butt end of the gun near your face, and back up the end of the gun with your free hand.

• Remove detachable spearheads when not in use. Cover fixed spearheads with tip protectors.

FREEDIVING GEAR

Terminal gear begins at the speargun and ends at the float(s). It includes the float line, floats and connectors. I have successfully used a clear-vinyl plastic floating tube, ⅜ inch in diameter, containing 400-pound nylon test line. A 75-foot length works well; shorter lines cause the float to submerge during deep dives, while longer lines create extra drag.

FLOAT LINES

Inserting the heavy nylon into the tube used to be problematic. I tried blowing a cloth wad, attached to thin fishing line, through the tube with compressed air. Terry Lentz suspended the tube from the top of a two-story building and dropped a machined weight through it. Bluewater diver Jim Mabry, drawing on his electrician's skills, found the easiest method. Using a helper to straighten the tube and a vacuum cleaner hose, he suctioned half a cotton swab tied to fishing line through the tube—in 30 seconds. Tie the heavy line to the fishing line and pull it through.

Knot the line securely to a 5/16-inch, stainless-steel plug designed to seal each end of the tube. Because the tube may be subject to great pressures—for example, following a bluewater fish sounding into 300 feet of water—it must be sealed with care. Squirt Silicone Seal into the warmed ends of the tube and push the plug in place. Wrap thin nylon line or stainless steel wire around the tube, compressing it into the plug's machined grooves.

South Africans employ a short heavy-rubber bungee, tied to their float line, as a shock absorber. The bungee helps to prevent the flesh-tearing shock when the fish reaches the end of the line, and it also plays the fish with a constant-pressure pull toward the float.

Agile-minded bluewater diver Ben Wolfe, of the Los Angeles Fathomiers diving club, has developed what I consider to be the ultimate float line. It combines the benefits of the floating plastic line with the shock-absorbing quality of rubber. His bungee float line consists of a 50-foot section of elastic Norprene tubing filled with 150 feet of parachute cord, sealed as described above. Norprene, an elastomeric tube, resistant to ozone and ultraviolet light, seems to be the perfect float line material. It breaks at a stretch of four times its length—that's why you use 150 feet of cord for 50 feet of Norprene (a three times stretch).

Once a speared fish reaches the end of the line, the line begins to stretch, applying a steadily increasing force against the fish, equaling the buoyancy of the float(s). The float line prevents sudden shock, tires the fish and automatically retrieves it. An additional advantage of the full-stretch float line is that it may be possible to use just one float instead of the multiple floats we currently employ.

Ben prefers parachute cord because it compresses inside the tube without kinking, and it, too, stretches. To gather the cord into the tube, first insert the cord as described, secure one end and anchor it to the tube. Then stretch the Norprene over the 150 feet of parachute cord and secure the other end. For big fish, Ben recommends the ½-inch outside-diameter tube with a ¼-inch inside diameter. Norprene is manufactured by the Norton Company, Akron, Ohio.

FLOATS

Bluewater divers are constantly developing new floats. While everyone agrees we need them, few agree on a common design. On our first record-breaking trip to Guadalupe Island in 1982, 14 bluewater divers brought along 14 different floats. We soon discovered that high-profile floats created too much wind drag which prevented easy towing. Small floats had inadequate flotation and large floats, such as

red-eye buoys, caused speared fish to rip free when they hit the end of the line.

Streamlined lifeguard floats were the ideal compromise because of their low profile, streamlined shape and low drag. Using several floats produces a graduated pull against fleeing fish, not a sudden shock.

Three lifeguard floats are sufficient for the biggest fish. They must be filled with high-density foam. Hollow floats implode, popping like a balloon at 40 feet, while buoys filled with low-density (two-pound) foam, crush at 80 feet. (Foam density and strength is measured by weighing a cubic foot of expanded, cured foam.)

Use eight-pound polyurethane closed-cell foam, cured with equal parts of liquid. Make sure the liquids in this two-part system are heated to 70 degrees Fahrenheit. Mix small batches (paper cup size) with a whisk bent from a clothes hanger and turned with an electric drill. Mixing larger quantities risks overexpansion of the curing mass, up and out of the buoy and onto your floor.

Make ballast for the last buoy, the one that supports the diver's flag, by pouring foam around a four-pound lead weight centered inside the bottom of the float. Position and then pour foam around a plastic or metal flag receiver. Place a small fish net buoy on top of the fiberglass flag mast to help it bob upright when it overturns in large swells.

Equip each of the two buoys closest to your gun with an 1˘-inch-diameter ABS plastic tube, running down the center of the float and exiting toward the rear. Pour foam around it and later fill it with 100 feet of nylon line. Contain the line in the tube with a compressible foam plug, fashioned from lobster-buoy foam. Make a hole in the end-arm of the float and insert a length of speargun rubber band material. Tie the band to the line packed inside the buoy and to the float line leading to the gun. The rubber band acts as a release—when the fish dives and pulls the first float about 90 percent under, the rubber band shrinks free from its hole releasing the line and plug packed inside the buoy.

My rig consists of 25 feet of shooting cable, strung on the gun, connected to 75 feet of floating tube-line, which connects to three buoys. The first two buoys contain 100 feet of 400-pound nylon test line, held in place in rough seas by the rubber, release mechanism just described. Connect the buoy line close to the handle of the gun so that any surface swell or wake, pulling on the line, will have minimal effect on your aim. Connecting it at the butt end of a mid-handled gun creates a larger lever arm, making your aim unstable.

Many divers, particularly beginners, make the mistake of using inadequate clips or snaps to connect their lines to their spears and to their floats. Too many fish have been lost by inattention to this detail. Never use a spring-loaded snap (harness snaps, eye snaps), as they all eventually fail. I recommend a heavy swivel, rated to at least 500 pounds, attached to the buoy with 3/32-inch, stainless-steel cable, braided or double crimped. Use stainless steel D-rings to make all your other connections.

I like a multiple-buoy system because of its gradual deployment of resistance, which tires the fish. One buoy releases 100 feet of line, the next releases another 100 feet of line. The Europeans, diving in the relatively calm Mediterranean, use a different small-float system. They mount a large reel to their gun and connect to it up to 600 feet of trail line. Starting 75 feet back from the gun, they attach as many as 15 to 20 equally-spaced, coconut-sized buoys. While the pull is guaranteed to be gradual with this system, I believe so many buoys could cause too much drag in the stronger waves and currents prevailing in most of the world's oceans.

Ben Wolfe's bungee system, in combination with three lifeguard buoys, may be the ultimate terminal gear combination. The bungee by itself may prove to be so effective that bluewater divers might be able to abandon multiple buoys in favor of a larger, simpler, single buoy. The cost savings in fabrication time and money would be welcome, but this system might still apply too

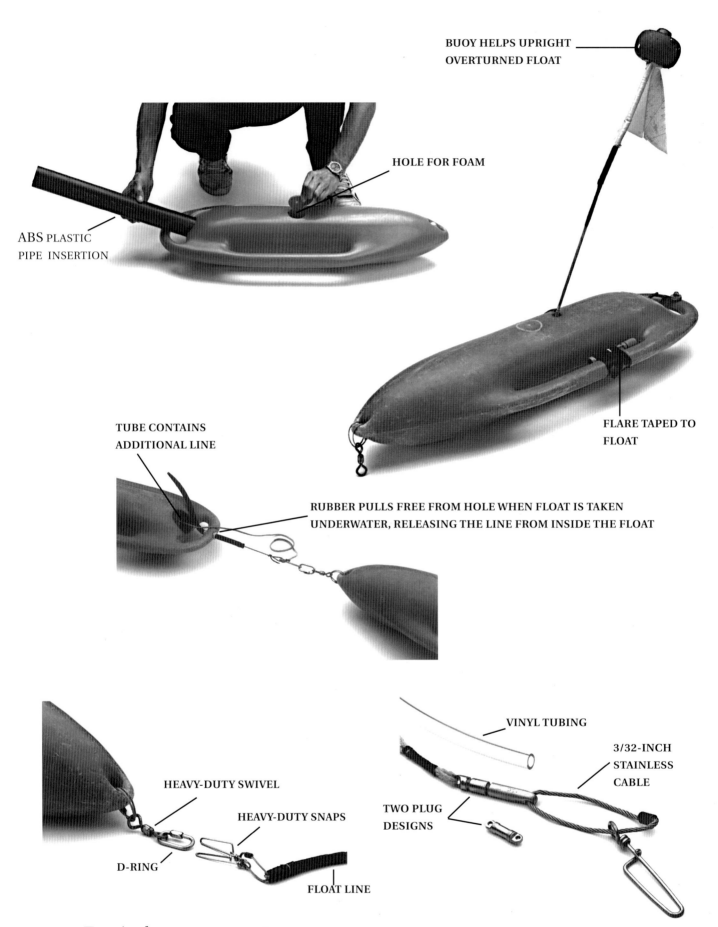

BUOY HELPS UPRIGHT
OVERTURNED FLOAT

HOLE FOR FOAM

ABS PLASTIC
PIPE INSERTION

FLARE TAPED TO
FLOAT

TUBE CONTAINS
ADDITIONAL LINE

RUBBER PULLS FREE FROM HOLE WHEN FLOAT IS TAKEN
UNDERWATER, RELEASING THE LINE FROM INSIDE THE FLOAT

VINYL TUBING

3/32-INCH
STAINLESS
CABLE

HEAVY-DUTY SWIVEL

HEAVY-DUTY SNAPS

TWO PLUG
DESIGNS

D-RING

FLOAT LINE

Terminal gear components.

I am currently developing a single float for use with Norprene tube. Shaped somewhat like a surfboard, it's fashioned from a block of space-age Divinycell foam (four-pound) and measures 54 inches long, 14 inches wide and 3 inches thick. These dimensions are sufficient to displace 2,300 cubic inches or 80 pounds of water. Subtracting 20 pounds of fiberglass and attachments, it should float 60 pounds, enough to manage any bluewater fish.

For easy transportation in a suitcase, it breaks down into two equal 27-inch pieces. Plastic dowels and metal straps keep it rigid. There is a handle at the back for use both in transportation and for playing fish. A flag receiver holds the weighted end of the mast of a float-off flag. The flag, attached to the float by a lanyard, is free to deploy and float upright in case the float overturns or is taken underwater.

Several attachment points on the top will accommodate food, flares, whistles and other gear. A heavy nylon lanyard wraps around and through the nose of the board, and exits below the float. This keeps towing pressure below the board, thereby lessening its tendency to flip over.

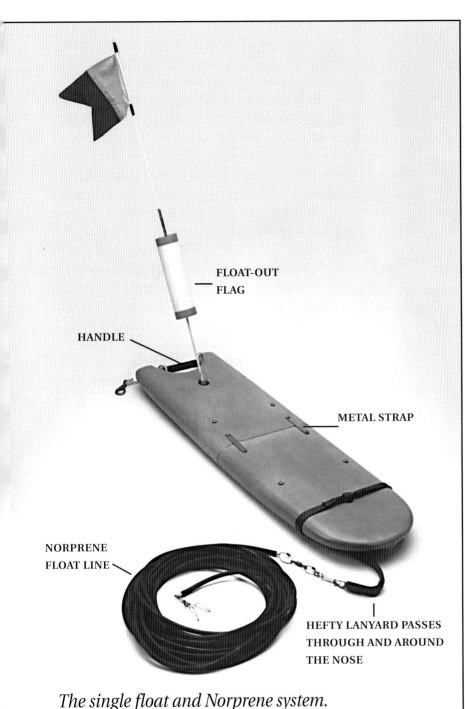

FLOAT-OUT FLAG

HANDLE

METAL STRAP

NORPRENE FLOAT LINE

HEFTY LANYARD PASSES THROUGH AND AROUND THE NOSE

The single float and Norprene system.

much back pressure to a fish strong enough to stretch the bungee to its maximum length. Depending on the size of the single buoy, the shock of the fish reaching the end of the line, could rip the shaft free.

MASKS

I made my own mask, complete with corrective lenses. The mask is fabricated on a facial-duplication mold made from hard-set

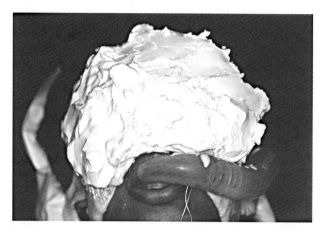

A plaster impression with snorkel in place.

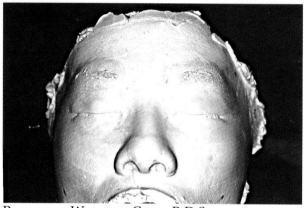

PHOTOS BY WINSTON CHEE, B.D.S.

A plaster facial mold.

plaster poured into a softer plaster impression of my face. Even though the mask is made from hard plastic, it feels comfortable, with its custom fit and low volume. If you try this technique, be sure to remove all facial hair, as coverage with Vaseline is not enough to protect it from getting stuck in impression plaster. I remember reducing one of our toughest divers to tears while I cut his mustache hairs loose from the plaster impression fused to his face. If you can talk your dentist out of some alginate impression material, do it. Its gelatin-like consistency is much kinder to your face and doesn't pull hair. For correct upper lip contour, keep a snorkel in your mouth when the impression sets on your face.

I use two small elevations in the nasal pocket to occlude my nasal openings. This allows me to clear my ears hands free. You can modify a production mask with silicone cement, built up in small layers. Place clear-plastic wrap over the last layer, and wear the mask for a short time while the silicone sets.

The technique for clearing your ears with a firm mask goes as follows: as you descend, water pressure will force the nasal pads into your nose, allowing you to clear easily. After you have cleared, prevent "mask squeeze" by pursing your upper lip slightly. This deformation will temporarily pull away the nasal pads, allowing you to add pressure-equalizing air.

Finding or building a low-volume mask is important because it reduces the amount of precious air lost to mask pressure equalization. Achieve this by bringing the lens as close to your eyes as possible; a close lens also greatly enhances your peripheral vision. Keep adding plastic or silicone to the inside of your mask until you have filled all the space not required for vision.

SNORKELS

A short snorkel with the large bore is best—it provides plenty of air with the least respiratory effort. Make it as short as possible, but still long enough to prevent water entry in rough seas. Occasionally, water will make its way into your snorkel. With experience, you will develop the ability to detect the increased resistance in breathing effort caused by this water and abort further breathing efforts until it's cleared.

Several snorkel designs help prevent surface water entry. These designs make use of assorted intake and exhaust valves. These designs are fine, provided they do not restrict air movement, thereby increasing the diver's respiration effort. Be sure the attachment point of the snorkel to the mask strap is squeak-free.

FINS

Because of their efficiency and recoil, long flexible fins work better than short, stout ones. Any of the currently produced long fins are excellent. Water-test them for sound; make sure they do not make squeaking noises at the foot pocket.

It is possible to widen the top of the foot pocket to fit an unusual foot form. Draw out a shoelace pattern and add a line where you plan to split the top of the fin. Make the lacing holes with a red-hot bolt (3 millimeters). Sear a hole for each lace (usually one or two pair) and add another hole at the end of the proposed release cut. This hole prevents further ripping of the pocket after you cut it with a razor blade. For a comfortable fit, lace up the holes with permanently knotted, heavy nylon string.

WEIGHT BELTS

The best weight belts are made from rubber or elastic webbing, which expands and contracts with abdominal breathing. It does not slip on your waist, even when deep dives cause your chest diameter to decrease. Use 1½-pound (0.67- kilogram) weights, and space them evenly. Avoid large knives or other attachments that might catch a float line. Keep it streamlined.

The stretchable quality of the rubber belt helped save veteran bluewater hunter John Yantis from a dangerous situation while diving with friends for abalone off the Northern California coast. Returning to the surface with an abalone, John was mysteriously halted just two feet short of the surface. He could see the surface, but no matter how hard he kicked, he couldn't reach it. Dropping the abalone and kicking in near panic, John "No Buns" Yantis made it to the surface as his elastic weight belt slipped from his waist. Another diver, retrieving John's weight belt, was also stopped short of the surface. Close examination of the belt revealed that one end of a near-invisible, stout monofilament

fishing line had tangled in the weights, while the other end was firmly anchored to the bottom with a fishing lure.

When you invert for a dive, your weight belt might have a tendency to slip up your waist onto the small of your back. For those of you with a bad back, the pressure can be painful. A Velcro nylon crotch strap, running from the mid-back and fastened to the front of the weight belt, prevents slipping. Be very sure it's not fastened over your belt release mechanism, and test your weight belt for easy release with the strap in place.

Probably the most important quality of a weight belt is *your* attitude toward it. It must be considered as a lifesaver for the prevention of shallow-water blackout. On deep endurance dives, California diver Gerald Lim releases his belt and holds it in his clasped hand. He hopes the weight belt will fall away should he lose consciousness. Consider your belt totally expendable. No matter the time or money lost, at the first sign of trouble—dump it! (Trouble signs are covered in the section on shallow-water blackout.) You must determine and practice your actions *in advance* of a breath-hold emergency. Releasing your weight belt should be an automatic response. Bring along an extra belt so you have no hesitancy about dropping it.

KNIVES

Knives are indispensable. We use knives to cut up bait fish for chum, dispatch fish and in emergencies, to cut line tangles. Because they have themselves been implicated in dangerous line tangles, take special care when attaching knives to your body. A quick-release knife pouch is a good idea; use Velcro or light rubber bands, or anything that pulls away quickly if tangled. Bluewater diver and U.S. national spearfishing champion Bill Ernst uses a knife with a self-retaining sheath, attached to his chest with Velcro, handle-side down. Located on the left side of his chest in an out-of-the-way location, it is easily accessible to his right hand. Another good location for right-handed divers is the left, upper arm.

WETSUITS

Using a wetsuit in all but the warmest waters helps prevent mind-numbing: hypothermia. It also offers good protection against jellyfish and helps avoid abrasions. I watched world champion Massimo Scarpati take a rare Mediterranean yellowtail while scouting for a contest. He claimed his blue wetsuit helped him get close to that fish. Since then, I've worn a blue, nylon-out, skin-in, wetsuit. It works well for me; my fellow divers say I blend in with the surrounding water.

Use Vaseline or silicone grease behind your legs and ankles to prevent rub abrasions. Unlike less expensive Vaseline, silicone grease does not dissolve wetsuit glue. For ease of entry into your wetsuit, use a lubrication spray bottle. Find a body lotion or hair conditioner containing organic ingredients only—no chemicals or fragrances. Dilute the lotion, half-and-half with water, and spray it into your suit.

For protection against Portuguese man of wars and jellyfish, South Africans wear panty hose over their faces with openings cut for their eyes and mouth. Yes, they look every bit as funny as you imagine, but with this protection, they are able to dive in inhospitable seas where mats of these stinging creatures cover the surface.

POWERHEADS

Designed to protect against sharks, powerheads are probably as dangerous to divers as the sharks (see the chapter on survival). Legal considerations prevent me from detailing the fabrication of powerheads. However, I suggest that you avoid designs actuated with a separate firing pin. Currently, the most popular powerheads are disposable, and the speartip acts as the firing pin. Designed for a onetime use, they consist basically of a metal tube containing a sealed-in cartridge. A rubber tube adapter helps hold the powerhead onto the spearhead prior to firing. The powerhead is fired at the shark. The spearhead ignites the shell when the powerhead strikes the shark, and the resulting impact drives the speartip through the primer. The cartridge need not contain a slug, as it is the explosive gases that cause the damage.

To defend against sharks, some California abalone divers use a plastic pistol, the Glock. This weapon is relatively water resistant. For reliability, divers seal and change their ammunition regularly. Because slugs fired from the pistol have such a short range, just a few feet, these divers claim it is the noise from the rapidly discharging shells that drive sharks away.

TAPE MEASURES AND SCALES

Don't forget these—they may be important for documenting your catch, especially on multiday trips.

Some tuna are simply too large to weigh on a boat. Using the following formula, a tape measure and a calculator, you can accurately gauge the weight of both yellowfin and bluefin tuna. Measure, in inches, the girth of the widest part of the fish, and measure its length from the tip of its closed mouth to the fork in its tail. Square the girth and multiply it by the length. For the "tuna weight," divide the product by 800. For example, calculate the weight of a tuna 87 inches long with a girth of 57 inches. The product of 57 x 57 x 87 divided by 800 is 353 pounds.

ATTITUDES

Bluewater hunting and freediving are demanding sports. The gear, relatively simple when compared to scuba gear, is still very important. The best divers learn how to fabricate or modify their own equipment. Most important, they evaluate every piece of gear, and every modification, with a view toward safety.

Survival in the bluewater environment

"The word 'safety' doesn't cut it. Think about *survival* every time you plan for bluewater diving," says champion Terry Lentz, the only individual world spearfishing champion from the northern hemisphere. His many years as a competitor, bluewater and commercial black coral diver make him a respected expert in survival. As I reflected on his thoughts, I realized Terry was right. Bluewater diving has the potential for so many accidents and misadventures that at every phase of a dive trip, you need to think about survival.

Most bluewater adventures start and finish with a boat trip. Because this phase is merely a means to an end, many divers do not treat it seriously. On a recent boating trip on the Ambar III (a superbly equipped 73-foot dive yacht), we interrupted our travels to Socorro Island, Mexico, to join the unsuccessful hunt for a scuba instructor lost overboard from another boat the night before. He had fallen off without his life vest during a shift change, and apparently his disappearance went unnoticed for several hours. Even falling off the boat during the day is dangerous, especially if the event goes unrealized for a short period. Your best defense is a lifejacket equipped with an emergency locator, whistle and strobe light.

If you feel the equipment on the lifejacket is too expensive (it will cost several hundred dollars), at least follow these basic precautions: insist on two pilots at the helm for night operations. Keep a constant head count of all members of the crew. Do not go near the edge of the boat unobserved. (Guys, this includes trips to the side for urination because this is when most of you fall over.)

Begin your boat trip by reviewing the location of emergency equipment and discussing emergency plans. Learn the location of life vests, life rafts and emergency locators—lights and signal generators. Discuss safety procedures for the dive. Appoint someone to observe from the boat, and agree on hand signals for both routine and emergency pickup. Decide on how to get to an injured diver quickly. Use a small chase-boat or, if one is not available, make sure your boat is equipped with a quick-release anchor. Outfit the chase-boat with a handheld VHF radio, two pairs of gloves, an extra speargun and a flying gaff.

Don't forget a tourniquet—its application to an arm or leg might be life-saving. In an emergency, make one with a speargun band. Twist it tightly with a knife sheath or spear.

Adequate preparation does not guarantee success, as the events surrounding Al Schneppershoff's death show. Al traveled to Guadalupe Island, Mexico, in September 1973 with three other divers and his 9-year-old son, Little Al. Seeking calm water for the night, they anchored the boat in a protected bay over water about 40-feet deep. Al was excited about seeing 300-pound tuna earlier that day. True to his style, he was the last one to remain in the 40-foot visibility water, while Little Al watched from the bow.

Suddenly, Little Al (now an active bluewater diver himself) yelled, "Something's wrong with my dad." Struggling violently with only his head visible above the water, Al screamed, "Shark! Tourniquet!" Gone was all his gear, including his mask, gun, fins and weight belt. Rescuers swiftly unleashed the anchor with a quick-release and immediately backed the boat to Al. They hauled him onto the swimstep, where he died just five minutes after the attack. A great bluewater diver had passed on. The autopsy confirmed the cause of death was exsanguination from a bite to the right calf, severing a major artery. White shark teeth were found imbedded in the wounds. While the rescuers probably should have applied a tourniquet during their efforts at CPR, they reported Al did not bleed once he was removed from the water.

Bluewater divers should consider boats as dangerous as sharks. Many of us have stories of near-misses and actual encounters with boats and limb-severing boat propellers. Surprisingly, several of the boatmen involved in these accidents were divers themselves. During one Bluewater Meet at Catalina Island, one diver racing to a spot ran over another's fins, severing both fin blades in half.

Another time, during a contest sponsored by the Long Beach Neptunes, one contestant ran over another diver in the kelp, severing his jaw and just missing his carotid artery. Boat drivers should approach divers cautiously, coming from the direction of deep water, if practical. Use slow speed and anticipate finding bluewater divers great distances from their own boats, sometimes 1/2 mile or more. Bluewater divers should carry a diver's flag, either on their person, or better, on their float. Hopefully the flag will warn off boatmen.

A flagged buoy makes divers easier to locate. "You only need to lose one diver before you insist that all divers in your party carry a flag," Hawaiian Brian Yosikawa says. In addition to holding the North American record for wahoo, Brian is one of Hawaii's most enthusiastic bluewater hunters. He recalls one day off the island of Maui when his group lost a diver.

Mo'olepo Point, known for its turbulent seas and strong currents, holds large fish and sharks. Rough weather makes it accessible just 10 days a year. Brian, Wendell Ko, Myles Yoshikawa, Paul Brown and Terrence Takahata ventured out to the killer point on a marginal day. Due to the heavy current, their plan was to drift-dive in pairs, alternating one member of a pair with the boat driver. In two hours, they had landed several large ulua and they had seen big tuna. In spite of the increasing wind and current, they decided to make one last pass through the area.

Brian dropped off four divers in the four-knot current. Three divers quickly became occupied with a 70-pound ulua, while the fourth drifted away. Landing the fish, the three divers and Brian became aware of their missing friend. During their initial 45-minute search, they passed over large tiger sharks and began to wonder if they would find body parts, or nothing at all. With the sea building to six feet and whitecaps everywhere, they summoned Marine Rescue for an aerial search. Leaving the hazardous seas outside to the helicopter, the divers took half-an-hour in their return to the point.

Bone-chilling water breaking over the bow and building winds magnified the stony silence among them. Two hours later, they finally recognized Paul's float and pulled an exhausted, but uninjured, Paul aboard.

"I saw you guys pick up Terrence, and I tried calling you," Paul told the group. "The problem was that the sun was behind me, and you could not see me through the chop and glare. The current was really taking me fast—the bottom was whizzing by like I was looking through a glass-bottom boat! In desperation, I shot my spear into the rocks and rode out the current hanging onto my gun line. The current was so strong that it kept pulling both me and my float underwater during some of the surges. When the current finally slackened a little, I freed my speartip and angled in for shore."

Brian says the group learned some hard lessons from that near-catastrophic dive. "First, always respect Mother Nature. She is fickle, full of sass and changing moods. Second, I recommend the following safety equipment. A large buoyant float and a diver's flag are essential. Consider carrying several waterproof aerial flares and smoke flares. A signal mirror and a whistle are also good ideas. Last, spearfishing is a rugged sport that puts us in extreme situations. Respect the elements, put safety above glory and dive to stay alive."

It is possible to lose a diver at night. Sometimes huge yellowfin tuna show up at dusk. This was the case one evening at Socorro Island, Mexico. Six of us were diving on a current-swept point as the sun dropped below the horizon. Five of us made it into the safety boat; we lost the sixth. The first items we found a half hour later, in the pitch-black night were our lost diver's floats and loaded speargun floating offshore. One terrifying hour later we found him calling from the wave-washed rocky shore. Now we always have a plan about where to meet in cases such as these. This situation presents another good argument for the use of waterproof flares.

Consider trailing a current line behind your anchored boat. Use it to get back to the boat if the current increases or when a fish takes you down-current. I use 300 feet of 1/4-inch polypropylene line with a red-eye buoy at the end. This system though helpful, is not foolproof. One day three of us found ourselves hanging onto the red-eye buoy, 300 feet behind the boat in a raging current. We were 50 miles from the closest land. Suddenly, that 1/4-inch line looked pretty weak. Since there were only three of us on the trip, no one would have been available to rescue us if the line had snapped. An alternative to this technique is the "live boat" technique described by Brian above.

Bluewater fish have enough strength to overcome a diver. While researching this section, I was impressed with the number of near drownings caused by comparatively small fish, in the 30- to 50-pound range. Florida freediver Dee Wesley, formerly of the U.S. Virgin Islands, tells of the shocking results when he was towed behind his 52-pound, world-record barracuda. Dee stalked the old "moss back" from one reef patch to another. The crafty fish finally made a mistake and offered Dee a good shot with his short-lined arbalete. His shot, however, did not kill the fish, which took off at lightning speed, leaving Dee twisting and turning in its wake. The first thing to go was Dee's mask, which wound up around his neck. Second to go was his Speedo swimsuit, which caught on his knees. Dee was in no danger of drowning because he could have released his gun at any time. Others have not been so lucky.

Beware of your spear line; it is a potential killer. A giant black seabass almost drowned veteran Long Beach Neptune Dale Cote. Dale, once the men's North American record holder for yellowtail (62 pounds) and now in his 70s, is still one of the most active and enthusiastic divers in the club. He remembers Anacapa Island, California, in the mid 60s, when hunting giant black seabass was allowed.

Never having shot a black seabass or seen one, for that matter, I was instructed to look for a large black fish. No problem—the water visibility was

Dee Wesley loses his suit to a barracuda.

clear to the bottom 60 feet below. After about 20 minutes, I saw movement near the reef. Excited and pumped up with air and adrenaline, I dove to the 150-pound fish 50 feet below. I circled in behind a kelp stalk and slammed my shaft into its side just as it turned away. I swam full speed to the surface for air as it stripped 150 feet of line from my reel.

On the surface, I held my gun with a fierce grip as the big fish towed me about two blocks to another kelp bed. Abruptly, the fish stopped and I pulled hand-over-hand style until I was on top of him. I had hoped for an easy recovery, but I was unlucky. The fish took off again and somehow some of the line I recovered formed a deadly clove hitch knot around my left wrist. Suddenly I was 18 feet underwater thinking I was in deep trouble.

As I tried to keep cool, my mind churned furiously for ideas. I remembered the small knife I carried on my weight belt. Very, very carefully, I inched it from its sheath, knowing I was a dead man if I dropped it. Incredibly, at that moment the fish stopped, tangled on the bottom. Looking up, I judged that if I swam forward I could reach the surface. On the surface I used the knife to pry the knot from my wrist, and was ready to cut it if the fish took off again.

(Note, the remainder of this story appears in the section on ear-clearing. Later this same bad-luck day, Dale blew both of his eardrums when he recovered this fish from the bottom!)

You would expect a problem with a big fish like Dale's, but spearing a smaller fish can quickly lead to disaster. Bil Wagner of San Diego, a bluewater diver with 30 years experience, was diving his favorite spot, the Coronado Islands of Mexico, when he almost drowned.

"We'd had some serious problems with sea lions taking our fish once we shot them," Bil recalls.

One big 500- to 600-pound bull Steller sea lion had become quite aggressive. We recognized him by the big fish hook stuck through his lower lip. On this day I dove down to investigate a school of bonito while my partners rested in the boat. I found a 30-pound yellowtail swimming below the bonito and made a good shot midway through it. It acted stoned, hardly quivering, when I took it to the surface. On the surface, I released the stringer, which I carry across my weight belt, and let it dangle as I hand-lined the fish toward me.

Just as I got hold of my shaft, the yellowtail came to life and went berserk as it headed for the bottom. Fearing a line wrap, I let the fish go. Suddenly the big sea lion appeared and grabbed my yellowtail. Next, I found myself 15 feet down and going fast toward the bottom. I released my reel but nothing happened and I kept descending. As I got my feet under me to start kicking upward, I saw that my stringer was tangled around the end of my gun. I reached for my knife on my leg, only to find that the stringer had wrapped around the knife's release mechanism, preventing me from getting it free.

Still headed down and kicking as hard as I could, I decided that I was going to die. My last effort was devoted to ripping the knife free from my wetsuit which I did, tearing it from its sheath, straps and snaps. Luckily, having the knife off my leg changed the angle of my stringer line enough to allow it to untangle from my gun. I pulled the reel release on the gun, and I made it to the surface just before I thought I would pass out. I managed two quick breaths before the sea lion, reaching the end of my 150-foot reel line, pulled me under again. This time my decision was easy and I released the gun. This would be the fifth and last time I lost that gun. When I meet that sea lion again, I wonder if it will be sporting a spear-shaft from its upper lip.

Your line can tangle on almost anything, including you or the bottom. South African Tommy Botha tells a chilling story about diving on the wreck *Produce* in Durbin, South Africa, in 30 meters of water.

When the current slackens enough to allow us to dive, we usually can count on large schools of kob from 15 to 40 kilos. The boat dropped us off up-current from the wreck and we drifted down toward it. The visibility was good and I managed to shoot a 6-kilogram rock salmon. When I surfaced from my next dive I heard one of the guys yelling, 'Nick's down! Nick's down!'

With my heart pumping wildly as I swam up-current, I tried to relax for the 30-meter dive I knew I had to make. I was down about 20 meters before I could see the bottom. I swam about 30 meters, just staying high enough to make out the bottom, thus extending my dive time and vision. But I could not see him. Then on my way back to the surface, still swimming up-current, I saw Nick behind a big piece of wreckage. Nobody was watching me, and I knew I would black out if I went down again.

I called for Gyula Plagiani, who was up-current, and told him to dive. I grabbed another weight belt from the boat to 'bomb down' after them, but decided to let Gyula return first. I spotted him coming up with Nick in his arms and dove down to help. About 10 meters from the surface, Gyula blacked out. I grabbed both divers and

swam them to the surface. When we reached the surface, Gyula started convulsing and came to. We loaded Nick on the boat, but in spite of our best efforts to revive him, he never regained consciousness.

Gyula found him at the end of his breath. He was in about 80 feet of water. When Gyula started toward the surface with him, he noticed that Nick's float line was caught in his weight belt and that the quick-release buckle had turned around on his waist, winding up on his back. Apparently, he had shot something on the bottom that became tangled, and when Nick swam up about 30 feet, he became caught in his float line. The line pulled the buckle, now on his back, so tight that he could not loosen it. When we recovered his equipment, we found his 7-millimeter spear badly bent and stuck in the wreck.

Nick was a young diver—-just 21 years old— with a lot of potential. He was also aware of his limitations in deep water. I believe he died not because he stayed down too long, but because he was unable to free himself from his float line. Had I tried to bring him up on the first dive, I would definitely have blacked out. Had I not seen Gyula come up with Nick, two people would have died.

While 1/16-inch cable is the best line for the first 20 feet of your spearline, be wary because it cuts. Joe Felicione, or "Jewfish Joe" as he is known on the west coast of Florida, lost a finger to his cable line. Joe liked to hunt large jewfish near the pilings that make up the channel markers off Tarpon Springs, Florida. One day he was diving next to a five-pole marker in visibility less than one foot. Hunting only by sound, he made two unsuccessful shots out into the gloom at large fish. His third shot earned him a ride. When the fish tired, Joe returned to the pilings, as was his custom, and started to the surface with the 150-pound fish. The fish made one last run, pulling the cable tightly against Joe's little finger and the wooden piling.

The cable instantly cut through his glove and finger. Raising his gloved hand inches before his face and seeing his missing finger, Joe became even more determined to land that fish. He succeeded, and his finger stub has long since healed. "I sometimes wonder what would have happened if the cable had wrapped my head instead of my finger," Joe said. "You know, we were just kids then, not really looking ahead for danger."

Veteran bluewater hunter Doug Ulmer has legs that tell stories. His left leg has multiple punctate scars where a "dead" yellowtail came alive at his side. Its wild thrashing drove Doug's spearhead into his thigh several times in rapid succession before he could subdue the wild fish.

Doug's right thigh sports a thin circular scar completely around it. Doug, others and I were diving San Benedicto Island, Mexico, for yellowfin tuna. I shot a monster and yelled for the chase-boat. Doug, a deckhand, and Doug's friend Steve Smith raced the small panga (a narrow 12-foot Mexican skiff) to my aid. Our adrenaline flowed as the four of us pulled the big beast in, leaving the line in a haphazard coil on the deck. Leaning over the side and shocked at the size of this tuna, I yelled, "Look how big he is!" That command brought everyone to my side of the boat, nearly swamping it. I had no choice but to release the fish. Three hundred pounds of angry tuna dove for the bottom, several hundred feet below.

Doug almost followed it as he stepped into the spear line coil. Only the quick action of Doug's friend, Steve, saved him from a severe leg laceration or worse, drowning. Doug remembers the terror as Steve quickly untangled his leg, now half way over the side. But Doug was not daunted; just two days later he shot and landed his first large tuna, a 200-pound beauty, the largest of the trip.

Avoid loading spearguns out of the water; the lack of water friction can cause the gun to get away from you. I know of one person who slipped while loading a small gun, sending the shaft under his lower jaw and into his mouth. A single tooth stopped it from exiting his cheek. Another diver was not so lucky. His gun slipped, sending the shaft through his lower jaw and into his brain, killing him instantly.

The potential energy stored in a four- or five-banded loaded speargun is enormous. I remember watching when a gun accidentally discharged as its owner loaded the final band. The launched shaft quickly took the attached gun in tow, and together they sailed through the air 100 yards (100 meters) across a kelp forest.

Powerheads (bangers) are dangerous; designed as a defense against sharks, they frequently injure humans. When it comes to harm inflicted, the score is sharks one and divers four. Powerheads, popular in Florida, have resulted in blown-off fingers and hands. One diver sunk his boat when a powerhead accidentally discharged against the hull while another lost part of his thigh in a separate incident.

Do not use powerheads with a built-in firing pin. They tend to discharge accidentally when dropped or when treated roughly. It is simply too easy for the firing pin to set off the cartridge, as U.S. national team champion Don Evers knows. Don, whose first love is competitive freediving, makes a living by commercial diving. One day while diving for abalone, Don's buddy, decompressing in midwater, loaded their 12-gauge powerhead to deter large predators. When he reached the surface, mindful of the powerhead's potential danger, he handed it up to Don in the horizontal plane, aimed away from Don into open space.

"When I turned the powerhead to point upwards in order to grasp the business end and disarm the mechanism, the powerhead discharged in a deafening roar," Don remembers. "Made of heavy stainless steel, the top part had enough weight to slam down on the firing pin. My friend, certain my head was blown away, did not want to look up." Don's knowledge of how dangerous this weapon was and his consequent angling of the powerhead away from his body, prevented this calamity. Don's hearing quickly returned and he has since redesigned his powerhead with a lighter-weight aluminum barrel to help prevent inadvertent discharge.

Some divers find it convenient to carry their powerheads tucked under a wetsuit sleeve or in an attached wetsuit pouch. Many times, a tired diver will forget this, and the powerhead will go flying when his suit is pulled off. The powerhead could be jarred with enough force to discharge; this is how the Florida diver injured his thigh.

New Zealander Ron Johnson provided an article from *Dive Log Magazine* of New Zealand that recounted six similar accidents. In one case an experienced diver, preparing his equipment for the next day's dive, placed a loaded powerhead on his workbench. Unattended, it rolled off the table and discharged on the floor. The resulting explosion "surgically" removed his left testicle!

Never shoot any powerhead at a solid object because the resulting explosion will rebound the shaft back to you. Australian "spearo" Bob Sands was bored one day as he swam into a shallow beach waiting for a friend to pick him up. Wading through the 2-foot deep water, he spied a submerged log. Curious as to the effect his powerhead might have on the log, he took aim and fired. The spear hit the log, discharged the powerhead and fired the shaft back toward Bob. "The force was incredible. Luckily for me the shaft came directly back to my outstretched gun, hitting the muzzle precisely at its end," Bob said.

"The resultant force drove the gun into my chin, pitching me over onto my back. I had a good view of the ricocheting shaft as it spun in the air, landing 100 meters behind me."

There is another story of the Bahamian scuba diver with a reputation for hard drinking and hard diving. A friend had commissioned him to retrieve a particularly beautiful piece of coral to decorate a living room table. (Obviously this was in the days before we thought about protecting the corals.) Underwater, a diving buddy happened to notice him take aim, with his powerhead-equipped speargun, at the base of a coral tree. The resulting explosion and recoil sent the shaft back, striking him in the forehead. Horrified, the buddy retrieved his friend, now twitching on the bottom like a stoned fish, with the spear still protruding from his head.

The story has a miraculous ending. His buddy got him to the surface, where fellow divers extracted the spear. He regained consciousness and, as the story goes, he slunk up to his cabin like a run-over-alley cat, then medicated himself with red-eye and penicillin. Three days later, he emerged from his cabin no worse for the accident. A medical examination revealed that the spear end had entered his frontal sinus, through its outer wall, stopping just short of the inner wall and his brain.

Never shoot a powerhead at a solid object.

Ethics, conservation and public relations

For a number of reasons, spearfishing has gotten a bad rap. In the early 70s, the sport was rocked by the anti-spearfishing proclamations of two famous scuba divers. In 1972, biologist Dr Hans Hass, underwater photographer and author, wrote his *Manifesto #1*, calling for a legislative ban on the manufacture and use of spearguns. The editor of the influential *Skin Diver Magazine* and other noted divers quickly joined his ranks.

Two years later, film maker Jacques Cousteau resigned his presidency of the world underwater federation cmas, stating, "I cannot chair an organization that is mainly supporting spearfishing contests." In 1975, during a day-long visit to the governor and legislature of California, he recommended that the state ban spearfishing. For a while it seemed that the whole diving community, frustrated by the effects of pollution, overfishing and overpopulation, focused on the one issue *they* felt they could control: spearfishing.

Adding fuel to the flame were tales of rotting fish, speared and forgotten, and legions of European spearfishermen catching huge numbers of reef fish. Beach divers haven't helped the cause, either, dragging their catches through gasping crowds. But the fact is, bluewater hunters are the least productive hunters of the oceans, garnering an extremely limited catch compared to sportfishermen and commercial fishing fleets. And they are acutely aware of the vulnerability of

This giant black seabass, while a trophy, is probably over 75 years old. In the 1970s, California divers joined other sportsmen in supporting a ban on the take of these fish. Left to right, John Yantis, Larry Kimble and friend hoist this fish aboard.

PHOTO BY JOE SCHREINER

near-shore ecosystems. This chapter details the ways that responsible divers conserve fish and explains how we in the spearfishing community can improve our public relations.

The freediver has a powerful advantage over the fisherman: the ability to accurately select his prey. He may choose to shoot, or not to shoot. This conscious decision, made before every shot, makes spearfishing the most selective form of fish harvesting. The diver has total discretion over the species, size and sometimes even sex of his catch. While responsible game anglers practice "catch and release," responsible spearfishermen practice "release and catch." They "release" all of the fish that swim by, that don't meet their criteria, and they "catch" the specific fish they want.

Fish and game studies in the United States and Australia prove how little spearfishermen take in comparison to other forms of fishing. For example, Dan Miller in his California Department of Fish and Game study, *Ocean Sportfishing Catch and Effort, Oregon to Point Arguello, 1965,* found that California spearfishermen are the least impactful hunters of the oceans, taking 0.5 percent of the state's sport catch.

The comparison of sport catch to the vast numbers of fish taken by commercial fishermen is astounding. During the period 1984 through 1989, according to the Marine Recreational Fisheries Survey and the California Department of Fish and Game annual commercial landings bulletins, commercial fishermen averaged landings of 442 million pounds of fish compared to sportfishermen who landed just 29.8 million pounds, or 6.7 percent. Viewed another way, for every 3,000 fish taken from Caliornia waters, commercial fishermen account for 2,769, sportfishermen 201 and skindivers one!

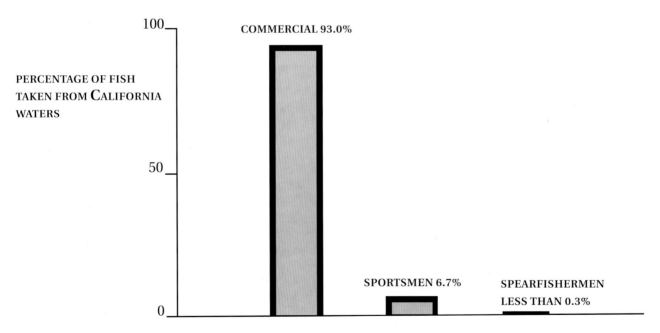

Fish taken from California waters by group.

Extrapolated from data in the California Department of Fish and Game study, *Ocean Sportfishing Catch and Effort, Oregon to Point Arguello,* 1965 contained in *Fish Bulletin Number 130;* from the Department's annual commercial landings bulletin; and from data received from the Marine Recreational Fisheries Survey (1984-1989).

Spearfishing is the most fuel-efficient method of harvesting. When compared to anglers and commercial fishermen, it produces less pollution (because of the decreased dependence on trolling boats) and the so-called *bycatch* is eliminated. Bycatch is all of the unwanted or undersized fish that are caught and killed along with the intended fish in other forms of fishing, such as gill netting. This bycatch is often simply shoveled back overboard, dead. For example, the shrimping industry discards 10 pounds of bycatch for every one pound of shrimp.

As they improve their skills, most divers establish more restrictive personal minimums of size and quantity. With experience and success, they tend to hunt larger but fewer fish. Many dive trips yield few or no fish because those available did not meet the diver's new criteria. This same diver will continuously refine his equipment, through countless hours of rigging and rerigging, in an effort to create the gun best suited for his quarry. His goal is to minimize, or eliminate, the loss of speared fish. His speargun is powered only by muscle, and powerheads are reserved for defense. The diver will study textbooks and magazines and talk to others to make sure that his skills, knowledge and equipment are the best available.

I believe that man's interaction with his fellow man and all living creatures requires a fine balance. This balance is in constant flux. Man is neither the overlord of nature nor its servant. We are part of the whole. No man should be responsible for, or allow, the extinction of a species. Everyone agrees that endangered species should be protected. The question is, how do we maintain a balance for nonendangered species?

Fish populations left alone will reach an equilibrium with their environment. The population will expand to the limits of the available space and food supply. There is a fisheries-management concept called the *maximum sustainable yield* which allows for the pruning of a fish population, while still leaving enough breeding members to restore the population to sustainable levels. In most cases, this maximum yield, with judicious pruning, will result in the maximum productivity of a stock in terms of catch. Predators and man can eliminate unhealthy fish, freeing up natural resources for those remaining, helping the strong to survive and protecting a healthy gene pool for future generations.

Maintaining fish populations at the maximum sustainable yield is the ideal. Unfortunately, according to the National Marine Fisheries Service, we are facing a serious decline in almost all commercially important species. This decline is the result of overfishing, degradation of the environment, pollution, overpopulation and other variables. Continued overfishing of a species can reduce populations to the point where collapse of the species is inevitable.

Today, we find ourselves fishing species below the maximum sustainable yield but above the collapse level. I believe there is a place for the hunter in our time, but we must be constantly mindful that our efforts do not leave any fish population near the critical level, and we must make every effort to bring all populations up to their maximum sustainable yield. We must also be active in the legislation of commercial fisheries because they represent the greatest potential threat for overfishing.

Divers should support fish science. Marine reserves, providing reservoirs for breeding populations and opportunities for fish research, need to be established and nurtured. Science will reveal the mysteries of the ocean's fishes and guide us in our selection of the appropriate species for hunting. Scientists found that my 400-pound bluefin tuna was only 11 years old, while a 430-pound, slow-growing California giant black seabass, was 75 years old. Obviously tuna, with their rapid growth, can replace large adults in their population in one-seventh the time it takes black seabass populations to replace a similarly sized fish. Because tuna grow so quickly, bluewater hunters should consider targeting tuna in greater numbers than black seabass.

We must be active in all phases of fisheries management. California divers supported a moratorium on the take of the giant black seabass, which were close to being wiped out. Today divers do not target them, and sportfishermen puncture the air bladders of any black seabass they catch, releasing them unharmed. Black seabass populations would make a quicker come back were it not for a loophole in the commercial fishing laws, which allow for an "incidental catch," permitting the landing of one black seabass per boat. This encourages the unethical practice of culling. It is possible for a net boat to capture many black seabass, on multiple net sets, and each time discard little fish for bigger ones. Wouldn't it make sense to entirely outlaw the commercial catch to conform with the sport-take of black seabass?

In New South Wales, Australia, similar species such as the giant grouper, black cod and estuary cod, are protected from all forms of fishing.

The California ban on near-shore gill netting will help restore the balance of many species that frequent the coastal region. White seabass, yellowtail, black seabass and halibut are a few of the beneficiaries of this law. California sportsmen, in conjunction with the state's utilities and research centers, are now taking a proactive approach. They have established breeding and grow-out facilities for both white seabass and halibut.

Bluewater divers in the northeastern United States helped to develop local laws with respect to striped bass. Some, like Mike Laptew (see the chapter on striped bass), use their bluewater skills to photograph and video striped bass, making this fish's behavior available to the surface fisherman and the naturalist. Florida divers have taken an active lead in preserving the corals and designating certain areas as fish sanctuaries.

Bluewater divers must be careful to develop a good relationship with the inhabitants of the countries they visit. The Mexican waters off Cabo San Lucas, at the tip of Baja California, are prime bluewater fishing grounds, coveted by local fishermen and tourists alike. Some spearfishermen from the United States have caused the local Mexican fishermen problems, barging into their best locations, their floats and lines scattered everywhere, and making it difficult for the locals to fish. Some have sold their fish to the local markets, creating ill will among the local fishermen, who rely on the ocean for a living.

Brothers Ian and Peter McGonagle, having worked both on sportfishing boats and construction sites in the area, are known by the local fishermen better than most "gringos." Avid bluewater hunters themselves (see the chapters on dolphin fish and marlin), they have worked out a successful strategy with the local fishermen. First, they never shoot more fish than they can use themselves. Second, they avoid the popular fishing grounds during early morning and midday, when the Mexicans are fishing. Instead, they limit their diving to the evening hours, after 3 p.m. When they dive earlier, they find remote locations or drift in the bait, away from other fishermen. Third, they stay in constant dialogue with the locals, helping them to understand how few fish they take and how selective they are. More divers with attitudes like this will help assure a friendly reception in any foreign country.

Australian bluewater hunters Rob Torelli and Adam Smith, writing in a personal communication, report the current conservation ethic in Australia. Rob is a national competitor and editor of *Freediving and Spearfishing News* and Adam, a keen spearfisherman and marine biologist, works for the government as a fisheries manager.

"In the early days a spearfisherman's catch was dominated by large cod and grouper, but now some species are protected and we observe these fish, preferring instead to hunt pelagics," they say. "Even with pelagics, we generally select the good eating fish such as mackerel, and allow barracuda and trevally to swim past."

96

They add that many of the current Australian conservation laws were prompted by divers, who through their familiarity with local reef fish and habitats were the first to acknowledge adverse trends in fish populations and bring the problem to the attention of legislators.

Australians adhere to laws and rules that they hope will help sustain their resources. Most localities limit spearfishing to the breath-holding diver. Many species are now protected, and spearfishing contest rules allow for just one fish per species, and edible fish only. Current fisheries management practices are aimed at resource sharing, conservation and the control of black marketing.

According to Rob and Adam, Australian fisheries biologists have embraced a new concept that they feel is more appropriate than the maximum sustainable yield idea. They prefer the broader approach of *ecologically sustainable development*, viewing fish populations not as individuals, but as parts of a greater whole. Management of spearfishermen in Australia may involve gear and area restrictions (marine parks and closed zones). Spearfishermen are limited by maximum and minimum size limits, bag limits and protected species.

Rob and Adam are proud of their country's spearfishermen ("spearos") and defend spearfishing by stating, "We are very restricted by rules and regulations and the physical limitations of our breath-holding ability. We catch relatively few fish compared to anglers and commercial fishers, and most spearfishing pressure is limited to metropolitan areas. We feel this method of hunting is the most environmentally acceptable because it is selective and does not indiscriminately kill nontargeted species."

Some bluewater hunters conserve current fish by reviewing past hunts and documenting their catch in diaries or on film. These records remind them of their successful hunts, and they often find enough satisfaction in them that they limit their efforts to larger fish of that species, or turn their efforts to different species.

Members of the Bottom Scratchers, the California fathers of spearfishing, have developed a method for making the most of their hunts: they record each catch. Jack Prodonovich, one of California's spearfishing legends, carefully chronicled each dive in a small red diary; he reads the cryptic notes up close with one eye—the other eye was blinded when a powerhead-equipped spear bounced back from a swimming pool wall. These notes conjure up images of the hunt, and in effect, enable him to relive it. Jack maintains a picture book diary with frequent contributions from divers all over the Pacific coast.

The Bottom Scratchers made their own personal progression to ever higher standards. These men—six of the original 15 are 80 years old now—remain keepers of the flame. While they lament the passing of the times when legions of 100-pound black seabass swam nose-to-tail through kelp-shrouded canopies, and a 10-minute swim offshore could yield a 30-pound white seabass, they do revel in our expansion into the deep blue. They encourage others to continue where they left off.

Many spearfishing contests preserve fish. The explanation to this apparent paradox lies in the numbers of fish taken per hour of effort. A good example is the Long Beach Neptunes' annual Catalina Bluewater Meet, where divers are allowed to enter *one* fish from a selected list of bluewater species. Hunting is limited to one day, from dawn until noon. Trophies are awarded for the six largest fish. A typical meet yields 20 fish taken by 130 divers. Most contestants make at least one scouting dive trip to the island during the weeks immediately preceding the contest. They generally avoid shooting fish, preferring instead to leave them for the contest.

Adding the scouting time of about four hours to the contest time of six hours yields 10 hours, which works out to 0.015 fish per hour of effort. My survey of sportsfishing boats working the same area finds that the average catch rate is one fish per hour, or 66 times the rate of the

High-ranking contestants in the first Australian Open Bluewater Freediving Classic, and major contributors to this book. Holding spanish mackerel, from left to right, are Rob Torelli, Greg Pickering, Andy Ruddock and Ian Puckeridge.

spearfishing contestants. This figure would be astronomical if I compared the commercial fishing take-per-hour of effort.

The 1994 U.S. National Spearfishing Championship, held a few miles north of Malibu, California, produced similar figures. Many divers spent weeks, and some months, scouting the contest area. The size and number of eligible fish were strictly controlled. A conservative average of the total hours of individual effort, including the six-hour meet, is 50 hours. The average contestant took 12 fish in those 50 hours of effort, yielding a catch rate of 0.24 fish per hour of effort. This means that the nation's best divers managed a catch rate of one-fourth the average line fisherman's rate.

A biological survey of the meet area, conducted by the San Diego Marine Sciences Group, a division of Ogden Environmental and Energy Services, showed little impact on the fish populations. Trained observers, both scuba and freedivers, surveyed the contest area. Comparison of the precontest fish populations with postcontest populations revealed very few differences.

An important point to consider about the spearfishing contests mentioned above, is their strict limitation on the number of fish per species allowed under the contest rules; unlimited numbers of fish can result in over exploitation. Recognizing this, Australians limit their contestants to just one fish per species.

Seventy-five divers, participating in the sucessful first Australian Bluewater Classic, shot 126 fish in the two-day, 14 hour event. The rate of fish taken on the contest days was 0.12 fish per hour; the number is much lower when one considers the divers' scouting time prior to the meet.

Society also needs to balance the philosophy of individuals who, on the one extreme, would preserve every fish in the oceans, and on the other extreme, would hunt fish to extinction. In the middle is the responsible hunter, who through sound conservation practices, guarantees future fish stocks. Remember, we are a minority, unorganized, with little financial or political power. Our public actions define us. Evaluate the way you act. Be an ambassador. Take time to educate others who are uninformed or misinformed about our sport.

Yellowfin tuna

WORLD-RECORD YELLOWFIN

It is evening at San Benedicto Island, Mexico, October 1989. I am hunting adjacent to a rocky underwater pinnacle, its tip reaching just 10 feet short of the surface, its sides plummeting to the ocean floor 300 feet below. This subsurface rock is a giant fish magnet. Large oceanic predators are attracted by clouds of bait fish seeking both food in the passing currents, and refuge in the pinnacle's crevices and caves. It is evening and a glance toward the horizon reveals just a finger's width of sky under the rapidly sinking sun. Except for a small area of beautiful penetrating golden light from the sun, the deep blue water is now black.

As I make my way, swimming up-current, schooling hammerhead sharks circle just 50 feet below. I have never seen hammerhead sharks in this schooling mode show any aggression toward a diver, nor have I seen them attack a speared fish. Nevertheless, their presence, along with the darkening water, heightens my awareness.

This is a wild time of day! Just a few minutes more and nightfall will force me from the water.

The always nervous bait fish are now frantic. Several times a minute I sense distant bait fish being attacked. Their escaping tails, beating as one, emanate an eerie, deeply pitched thundering sound; it strikes me, reverberating in my chest……

BOOM……BOOM…………BOOM.

I know the tuna are near; I feel them close by. Suddenly I hear, "Tuna!…I'm on!" I look up to see the crew from our mother boat, the

Yellowfin tuna are considered by many to be the premier bluewater gamefish.

PHOTO BY WILLIAM BOYCE

Ambar III, dispatch the chase skiff to aid my fellow diver, heading out to sea, pursuing his disappearing floats.

Once again I dive into the ever darkening water and orient into the current. My heart is pounding. A perfect circle appears at the limit of visibility, now another and another; soon there are four circles, all approaching me on my level. The circles metamorphose into giant yellowfin tuna. Twenty-five feet under the surface, I am very still when the tuna first appear; they are unaware of my presence. At the last minute, the lead fish swerves to avoid me, presenting a perfect shot. Unbidden, my speargun convulses in my hand and the spear strikes the tuna's side. The spear shatters its spine rendering the fish motionless. I swim back to the Ambar III with the fish in tow. Later, my yellowfin's weight is recorded at 255 pounds—a world record.

Yellowfin tuna are found in all of the large oceans of the world, including the Mediterranean Sea. Their vivid yellow color coupled with their hard-fighting spirit earned them their Hawaiian name, "ahi," which means fire. The largest of this species weigh about 400 pounds and measure just over 6 feet long. Resident fish, surrounding the Revillagigedo Archipelago, 200 miles south of Cabo San Lucas, Mexico, are thought to be among the largest yellowfin in the world. Schooling fish, they are seldom encountered as individuals. Schools contain fish with a variety of sizes; frequently the larger, more wary fish trail behind the bolder, smaller fish.

The following are some special techniques for approaching yellowfin. When a school of tuna circles past, just out of range, and when there is no indication that they are going to come closer, try ascending while you still have breath. Very often the tuna will change their path and come directly under you, presenting an excellent shot. (Maybe they think you are a dolphin.)

Sometimes very large tuna appear to be swimming in a straight path, a path that seems unaffected by your presence and one that will not bring them within range. In this case, try to position yourself directly above the fish and dive vertically toward them. Using a full-speed approach, you often can swim very close to the big fish. Jay Riffe's world-record hunt, described later in the chapter, exemplifies this method.

Remember, these fish can be massive. Their size distorts your perception so that a large fish appearing to be 15 feet away might really be 25 feet away. Swim as close to them as you can, withholding your shot until they become nervous and start to veer away.

Bluewater divers have three primary methods for hunting yellowfin. They find them near reefs, in open-ocean schools or in chum lines behind the boat.

Provided the fish are near shore, the easiest method is to patrol bait fish congregations around reefs, and pinnacles and along walls. Evening is the best time, followed by morning—sunrise to 10 a.m. Hunting open-ocean schools was successful in a recent Hawaiian dive described by Brian Yoshikawa later in this chapter.

The last method, which is very productive for pole fishermen but of dubious benefit to spearfishermen, is called chunking or burleying. Have a third diver or crew member toss 1-inch

Terry Maas with his first yellowfin record, 225 pounds, taken at Clarion Island, Mexico.

PHOTO BY JIM MABRY

square pieces of bait meat behind the boat into a light current. Oily fish such as bonito, mackerel or even the red stripe of tuna meat work well. Throw out bait chunks every 30 seconds. The problem is that divers become so uncomfortable dodging feeding sharks that they cannot concentrate on the tuna.

Sharks are also a problem for divers trying to land their catch. California bluewater hunters Doug Ulmer and Tom Mattusch, diving in separate trips to San Benedicto Island, Mexico, each shot yellowfin in excess of 200 pounds. Both lost their fish to sharks. Tom, helpless to the events 40 feet below, watched as his fish disappeared in a savage blur. Galapagos sharks, similar to bronze whalers and ragged tooth sharks, tore apart his catch before he could recover it. Tom retrieved an empty spear. Doug's fish dragged his two buoys down and out of sight for two hours. Searching in the panga (a durable Mexican skiff), he found his floats two miles out to sea. Pulling them in, all he recovered from his fish was a 10-inch square piece of tuna meat attached to his spearshaft. While these particular sharks showed no interest in the divers, it is always a good idea to try for a kill shot and to quickly remove the fish from the water.

Thirty-four-year old Julanne Lum and her husband Matt, both rising stars in California bluewater spearfishing, traveled to Socorro Island, Mexico in early 1994 aboard the *Ambar III,* **hoping to land a big tuna.** The previous year Julanne shot and lost one of the few bluefin tuna speared in California waters that year. The couple's goal was to have Julanne shoot a big tuna before their first child was born. Four months pregnant, Julanne achieved her goal by spearing a 38-pound yellowfin tuna, the North American spearfishing record for women. She remembers:

While I was hanging 25 feet underwater and staring hypnotically into the blue, dozens of bullet-shaped fish started to materialize in the distance. They came toward me fast, and I soon realized they were small yellowfin tuna. Turning to my right, I made two slow kicks away from them to pique their interest. As I had hoped, the school split and circled around me from both directions. Aiming my gun away from the advancing fish and avoiding eye contact, I waited for them to circle in front of me. On cue, the fish edged closer, begging me to pay more attention to them. I chose the closest fish and when I pulled the trigger, the ocean exploded with the sound of 100 tuna tails beating a hasty retreat.

Next came a strange 'whooshing' sound. I looked up to see my buoys zipping past me on the surface, and I knew the fish was still on my spear. As the tuna sounded, my first buoy went under, spilling line out of the line pack. I was amazed at how fast and how strong this fish was. When the buoy resurfaced, I grabbed the float line and began to fight the fish.

My heart dropped when I saw a dozen 6- to 8-foot Galapagos and silky sharks circling my tuna. I pulled faster as Matt dove down to fend them off with his gun tip. When I pulled in enough float line to reach my cable spear line, I took out my knife, preparing to stab the fish in the head. I kept pulling on the cable, but Matt yelled at me to get away from the now dangerous line. I had loops of cable all around me and if a shark had grabbed the tuna, I could have gotten tangled in the wire and been dragged down. I charged the sharks with my empty speargun in an attempt to get them away from my fish because some were getting very close and snipping at my tuna. My actions worked and I quickly handed my catch up into the waiting panga. Matt and I flopped into the boat just as the sharks came back for

The yellowfin's vivid yellow color coupled with their hard-fighting spirit earned them their Hawaiian name, "ahi," which means fire.

<small>Photo by William Boyce</small>

more. I can still hear the voice of my obstetrician, telling me to keep my heart rate down during the trip!

Bluewater hunting for giant tuna is still in its pioneer stages in Hawaii, according to Brian Yoshikawa. One of the most important dangers to the Hawaiian bluewater tuna hunter is the mass of line fishermen intent on the same fish. It is like a national holiday for fishermen when tuna schools appear off the islands. Everyone with a boat overwhelms the docks at first light, and it is not uncommon for more than 50 trolling boats to work a single school of feeding tuna. It would be suicide for a bluewater fisherman to jump into such a melee.

Huge schools of ahi migrate through the islands in May each year and remain through August. Ahi feed predominantly around the 1000-fathom drop-off surrounding the main islands. Some take up residence at fish aggregation devices and buoys anchored in deep water. A few large tuna have been speared off the near-shore drop-offs, pinnacles and buoys, but never before from the offshore schools that roam the 1000-fathom drop-off until the summer of 1994. Here is Brian's story:

Leaving Kihei boat ramp on July 17, 1994, Captain Randy Sasada had on board three spearfishermen. All the line fishermen on Maui think we are insane because of our ventures into what they consider shark-infested waters. Our plan for the day was to work the schools of tuna 6 and 12 miles off the south shore. As we motored offshore, most of the boats took a southeast heading toward the fish they found the day before. Not wanting to contend with the masses, we headed southwest. Using binoculars, we scanned the water for signs of life. There were good indications that the tuna would show because the "tuna-groupie" birds were flying everywhere, and bait fish were scattering off our bow.

We soon encountered a school of feeding tuna. They were moving so fast that it was impossible to get ahead of them and still be able to set up for a shot. We were looking for a school that would hold in one area long enough to allow us to prepare for our approach. Our break finally came when we encountered a feeding frenzy that made my knees weak. A huge flock of birds hovered over a frothing sea containing millions of 1-inch bait getting slammed by three whale sharks, assorted marlin and a school of large tuna. It was a comical scene. Whale sharks were actively feeding on the bait fish, and the bait fish were frantically trying to hide behind the whale sharks. While the bait fish, congregating around the tails of the sharks, were safe from their mouths, they became vulnerable to marlin and tuna boiling around the edges of the fish swarm.

It was the ideal situation we had hoped for—the bait were not running or sounding and there were no other boats in sight. Todd Tyau and Leighton Nakamoto scrambled into their wetsuits as we assembled their rigs. They jumped into the water just as the fish sensed our boat's presence and headed away from the two divers. With a punch of the throttle, the boat's big Chevy 454 came to life and sent us circling the school. Our plan to get on the other side of the fish and scare them back seemed to work as the pile of fish reversed course heading back toward the divers.

We watched as first Todd, and then Leighton, dove into the frothy white cauldron of fish. Both sets of floats bobbed peacefully on the surface as the two divers remained underwater. As the seconds ticked by, I began to wonder if they'd be able to get a shot off. The tuna boiled around them and suddenly Leighton's triple set of floats rocketed off into the distance. The divers surfaced, yelling as their first float duck-dove underwater. Leighton had a fish! We pulled the boat up to him as he began the tedious process of recovering first his floats, and then his fish. It took 15 minutes to recover several hundred feet of line. One float remained submerged while the

Julanne Lum proudly displays her record yellowfin tuna.

Photo by Matt Lum

fish was still yanking a tiring but determined Leighton under water, as the hand-over-hand battle continued. Twenty minutes after pulling his trigger, Leighton's ahi lay in the bottom of the boat, glistening in the morning sun. Its breadth matched the width of Leighton's smile as he viewed his 133-pound ahi, the largest yellowfin speared in Hawaii.

Leighton and Todd later described the underwater scene. Hundreds of tuna swam below them, many twice the size of the fish landed, but Leighton prudently took the closest shot. Even in a feeding frenzy, tuna are extremely wary of divers. Their sensitivity to sound and movement is superb. Seldom does an awkward diver stand a chance at shooting this ultimate adversary. Their speed and strength will test every ounce of muscle in a bluewater hunter, as well as every piece of his equipment. With our trophy in the boat and enough fish for a dozen barbecues, we headed for port.

John Hughes' South African record hunt highlights both the speed of the fish and the dangers of hunting them. Departing the Arniston area in their small boat, National Spearfishing team member ("Springbok") John Hughes, his wife Leslie and buddy Garth Bergis headed offshore to the Blinders bank. On the way, they spotted a school of yellowfin "tunny" feeding on the surface of the blue water, 4 kilometers from shore. Calculating the direction of the fast-moving fish, they maneuvered their boat about 200 meters ahead, where John "crash dove" into the water.

"Within seconds, huge shapes were racing by me about 15 meters deep," John recalls. "I saw a group of three behind me and dove quickly. The fish were moving so fast that I barely had time to train my gun on one. Aiming at the head, my shot hit the last fish in the tail."

Because tail shots do not hit vital organs, and because the spearshaft falls into a streamlined position behind the fish, the fish can develop tremendous mechanical advantage and is free to use its full power and stamina against the diver. During the next hour John was towed up and down the bay, his hands badly cut by the float line. Several times he was dragged underwater, where he eventually ditched his weight belt. The fish pulled him through mats of "blue bottles" (Portuguese man of war jellyfish), stinging his face and hands. John was an exhausted, injured, bluewater diver when he finally landed his country's record—43 kilograms (95 pounds).

In 1995 off Roca Partida, Mexico, National Champion Gerald Lim landed a 265-pound yellowfin. It was late afternoon, the water was 76-degrees Fahrenheit. Gerald remembers:

Visibility is almost 200 feet, rendering the water a startling sapphire blue. The delicate interplay between sun and surface sends fingers of light dancing toward the bottom, like a stained-glass window in a cathedral untouched by human hands. Behind me, a monolithic column of volcanic rock rises vertically from the bottom 250 feet below to greet the air like a gigantic column in a Roman ruin. Schools of nervous baitfish below me dart about as one, reacting with senses far more acute than mine to unseen predators.

Suddenly, this long dormant volcano is once again lit up with living fire as giant yellowfin tuna appear—their backs, a foot-and-a-half wide, are a deep blue-black with metallic flecks. A startling, iridescent-blue-and-gold stripe separates their backs from their silver bellies. Long yellow dorsal and anal fins, the trademark of large fish, trail behind. Their tails sport two rows of bright-yellow finlets, swishing side-to-side with each tail beat. Supreme masters of the moment, these fish exude confidence—almost an arrogance—as they swim by.

My reverie is broken by the realization that I am here to hunt these magnificent creatures. After

National Champion Gerald Lim with a yellowfin tuna from San Benedicto Island, Mexico.

two quick breaths, I angle quietly down toward them. The school responds by angling downward, not panicking, yet keeping their distance. At 60 feet, just as I break off the quest and angle upward, I notice a small group of even larger tuna move into formation with me. Calling on my reserves, I redirect my approach to this new target. I close the distance quickly, aim at the nose of the nearest fish and squeeze the trigger.

The gun recoils as six bands send the 7/16-inch shaft hurtling toward the tuna, striking it at mid-body and sending a plume of greenish blood shooting out. In the blink of an eye, the fish accelerates to warp speed, creates an audible roar and in 2 seconds, carves out three loops of a 50-foot diameter spiral around me, all the while trailing the plume of blood like a crippled fighter plane. As I desperately try to swim up and away from those deadly trail-line spirals, the tuna puts its head down and powers straight for the refuge of deep water, taking those dangerous coils with it.

Just as I reach the surface, my 100-foot elastic trailing line stretches to its full 300-foot capacity and my float is rapidly towed under. As soon as the fish changes direction, however, my float pops back up. Quickly, I catch the float and grab on. The great fish heads for open sea with me in tow. Soon, it slows down, the tension on my trail line lessens and I begin the grueling work of retrieving the stretched line. The fish makes several more short runs until my well-placed shot takes its toll.

Within 20 minutes, I've pulled the fish to within 30 feet of the surface. I hand my trail line to our skiff-tender in exchange for a second-shot gun for the coup-de-grace. I know my shot is true when the fish just quivers after the spearshaft penetrates its central nervous system—the battle is over.

Once in the chase skiff, I admire the great fish beside me. Almost 7-feet long, this fish exemplifies a most perfect design in marine high-performance. Fighting valiantly for its freedom, this noble fish towed me for a mile. Still panting from the exertion and flushed with success and the adrenaline coursing through my veins, I reach out to touch this beautiful creature beside me. I am filled with awe and admiration, and perhaps a twinge of melancholy.

Jay Riffe speared his world-record, 278-pound yellowfin in January 1991 at San Benedicto Island, Mexico. It was late in the afternoon when friend and fellow diver Doug Ulmer suggested that they try the lava flow off the south end of the island. Doug had seen bait there earlier in the day and had shot a 200-pound yellowfin in the same place the year before. The divers found a line of green water close to the flow. Visibility in the green water was 30 feet, while visibility in the outside blue water exceeded 70 feet. Bait fish gathered at the interface of the two currents. Jay dove and saw a school of large tuna swimming cross-current from the green water toward the blue water. Having little experience with big tuna, Jay tried waving his hand to attract them. Unfazed, the huge fish ignored him.

Heart pounding madly, Jay made another dive into the green water. He broke out of the green water into the blue water layered below. Vague shapes below him quickly materialized into tuna as he kept kicking deeper. "The fish were deep and they kept coming," Jay said.

Contrary to what I knew about good bluewater hunting technique, I swam as fast as I could, directly toward the fish, making all kinds of noise. There were four fish, abreast, swimming at a fast clip. I picked out the largest and aimed in front of its nose, knowing that its distance from me and fast speed would affect my aim. Sure enough, my spear hit it in the shoulder immediately in front of its dorsal fin. Just missing the spine, the spearshaft exited midway between the pectoral fins. It did not explode away like other large fish I'd shot, but rather kept going a fast clip. On the

Jay Riffe captured his 278-pound yellowfin tuna at nightfall.

surface, I had just enough time to grab my last float as it raced by. White water spewed behind my head as my two buoys and 300 feet of line held fast to the speeding monster.

The lookout on the mother boat *Sundiver* saw my wake and dispatched a deck hand in the panga who picked up Doug. Shortly, they arrived at my side. I handed my gun up to Doug but was unable to speak because of the water rushing by my face. I held on to the last buoy for 55 minutes while the fish made a great arc, from shore, out to sea and back to shore again. Finally, the fish slowed and I began to retrieve my line. Just as my other buoy surfaced, the mighty fish made another run, ripping the line from my hands. I watched helplessly as all of my gear, including the two buoys, disappeared straight down beneath the waves.

I jumped into the panga hoping to spot the floats in the rapidly fading sunlight. Seconds after turning the boat into the wind, one of my buoys resurfaced. I jumped back into the water and tried to pull the dead weight of the immobile fish straight up from 130 feet. Too heavy to pull up in the water, I got back into the boat and pulled with all my muscles. Like a sack of cement, the big fish came up by inches. I pulled it gingerly, fearing that my monofilament shooting line might part. Many minutes later, we tied the spear line to the side of the boat. Diving down 30 feet with Doug's gun, I tried for a kill shot. The shot was good, as the fish instantly turned color and died. It was dark by the time we got back to the boat, but the flash camera really helped capture its beautiful colors, yellows, blues and silvers—one fish I'll never forget.

WORLD RECORDS FOR YELLOWFIN TUNA

IBSRC WORLD RECORD	Jay Riffe July 1991 San Benedicto Island, Mexico	Official 277.9 pounds 126.04 kilograms
IBSRC WORLD RECORD (W)	Julanne Lum May 1994 Socorro Island, Mexico	Official 38 pounds 17.24 kilograms
Australia	Glynn Dromey October 1972 Ledge Point, West Australia	Official 107.4 pounds 48.76 kilograms
South Africa	John Hughes 1973 WP, South Africa	Official 94.7 pounds 43.0 kilograms

Bluefin tuna

Bluefin tuna, distributed worldwide, are one of the largest gamefish available to the bluewater hunter. In the Atlantic, they reach weights of 1,700 pounds (770 kilograms), while the largest Pacific bluefin, netted in 1989, weighed 1,008 pounds (457 kilograms). My world record of 398 pounds (180.7 kilograms), stood for 15 years. In 1997, Paulo Gaspar's 655-pound (297-kilogram) Atlantic bluefin eclipsed my record. With improved resource management, there will be larger fish taken by spearfishers.

An international tuna commission, the International Commission for the Conservation of Atlantic Tuna, attempts to regulate Atlantic bluefin stocks. Because of their great value (my fish, freshly caught, if jetted to Japan, would have been worth $25,000) and rapidly decreasing stocks, there is always a lively dispute between scientists and fishermen. The scientists, intent on management, caution us against overfishing. Fishermen, intent on feeding their families, insist that things have never been better. The fact is that overfishing by purse seiners in the 1960s severely jeopardized future populations of bluefin tuna by wiping out complete year-classes of these fish.

The situation is even worse in the Pacific, where no functioning plan is in place. In the fall of 1989, night squid netters directed by spotter planes observing mysterious phosphorescent contrails on the surface (giant bluefin tuna disturbing the plankton) started a California bluefin bonanza yielding many fish weighing 600 to 800 pounds. Several netters became millionaires in the space of three months while their deckhands, sharing in the catch, bought new cars.

It is disheartening to think that this marvelous and mysterious migration of huge breeding tuna, perhaps repeated over millennia, was decimated in the span of a few months by man using his highly sophisticated methods. Because of their timidness and great speed, bluefin stocks are at little risk with bluewater hunters who, to date, have taken less than 100 individuals worldwide.

Atlantic bluefin are found off the eastern United States, Canada and the west coast of Europe. Northern Pacific bluefin traverse the ocean from North America to Japan. The Atlantic and North Pacific bluefin are considered to be subspecies of the same species. Southern bluefin, considered a separate species, roam

the South Atlantic, the South Pacific and Indian Oceans.

Prolific breeders, capable of producing 10 million eggs per year, they have been known to reach 30 years of age—my 398-pound bluefin was scientifically calculated to be 11 years old. In the Atlantic, bluefin tuna cannot breed until they are at least six years old (about 100 to 120 pounds). They are not effective breeders until they weigh over 500 pounds, typically at age 15 to 16.

Traveling up to 150 miles per day, these fish regularly make the trip from warm Caribbean waters northward to the cold waters off Nova Scotia and, in some cases, even cross the Atlantic to Europe. One reason these fish are able to travel such long distances and enter cold water is a special physiological adaptation that allows them to retain and accumulate body heat.

The bluefin's heat retention capability is unique among the tuna, and most other fish species as well. Bluefin produce heat in their red muscles (those muscles responsible for slow swimming) and in their stomachs. They conserve this heat with a special capillary system that works as a heat exchanger. The blood-carrying heat, carbon dioxide and metabolic byproducts in most fish are ducted into the gills, where respiration takes place. Bluefin blood first makes a trip through a special set of blood vessels called "retes," which remove some of the heat otherwise lost to the water through the gills.

The significance of all this is that the animal's white muscles (those muscles responsible for sprint swimming) are super-charged with the extra heat and become capable of greater speed. Furthermore, the extra heat allows the larger fish (those over 300 pounds) to extend their range into waters as cold as 45 degrees Fahrenheit. The metabolic price for this adaptation must be expensive because bluefin are voracious feeders, consuming as much as 25 percent of their body weight a day.

Pacific bluefin are fished heavily by line fishermen about 200 miles from the shores of California and Mexico. They find deep fish using depth sounders and attract them to the surface by casting out chum bait. Sometimes a kelp paddy will hold schools of fish. While it is possible for bluewater divers to catch them there, I know of no one who has made a serious effort. Bluewater divers find most of their fish on the edge of steep drop-offs, usually up-current, and usually in association with bait. Spotting yellowtail in the area is a good sign because they frequently associate with bluefin. Hunt the water 50 to 100 feet further out to sea, past the yellowtail concentrations.

Bluefin often swim with such speed (up to 55 miles per hour) that you need to aim at least one-third of a fish-length ahead of them, and on the level of their lateral line. While I suggest using a big gun and three floats, the European divers use a very different system. (The European system is described in the chapter on gear.) Actually, the European blue-water tuna divers are different themselves. Many are tough, nomadic, commercial fishermen who follow the fish around the European continent. Secretive about their catches and their methods, they fish the north coast of France for fish 60 to 90 pounds. The best bluefin fishing is off the Azores in the mid-Atlantic, where divers hunt fast-moving shoals.

To date, many of the largest bluefin

Terry Maas with his 398-pound bluefin tuna.

PHOTO BY HOWARD BENEDICT

Paulo Gaspar with his 655-pound (297.2 kilogram) bluefin tuna taken in the Azores.

UNDERWATER PHOTO BY LARRY TYLER
LAND PHOTO BY DOUG PERRINE

speared have been taken from the waters surrounding Guadalupe Island, Mexico. Noted bluewater diver and researcher Jim Stewart, of the Bottom Scratchers Club based in San Diego, reported seeing the first giant bluefin tuna in 1954. Carrying just a small single-banded gun, and overwhelmed with the size of the hundreds of fish that circled him, he hurried back to his boat. In 1962, Ron Merker went to Guadalupe for bluefin. His 57-pound record held for 20 years. Ron, now a veteran of 5,000 documented dives, says he'll never forget the power of that fish as it dragged him under the water multiple times. Asked why he did not return to Guadalupe, Ron replied that he had seen some very large shark fins in the area as well.

I'll never forget my own Guadalupe Island trip, in 1982, when I speared the largest Pacific bluefin to date.

Bait fish began to gather over the rocks, stepping from 60 to 90 to 120 feet below. I had that special feeling experienced divers get when they know conditions are favorable for big fish. Sure enough, big yellowtail appeared in schools. I yelled to my Hawaiian friend and teammate Dennis Okada, 'Don't shoot the yellows, I think tuna will show!' Two dives later, in the 150-foot visibility water I watched Dennis try to ignore a 40-pound yellowtail swimming toward him. Unable to resist, he shot the fish and headed back to the boat with it.

Alone, I was diving the now famed 'tuna alley' of Guadalupe Island, Mexico. Having trouble with the then-experimental lifeguard float system, which kept deploying its 100 feet of line in the heavy swells, I pinned the line inside the float. I reasoned that if I shot a fish, I could get to the pin and release it as the buoys passed me.

A school of ten, 50-pound bluefin, 100 feet away, mesmerized me. They swam so close to the surface that they occasionally disappeared from my view in the large oceanic swells marching overhead.

Toward the end of a dive, I glanced down, beyond the reef edge into deep water and noticed two small distant tuna swimming in my direction. I froze. Slowly the tuna grew, soon becoming giants. I waited for them to get close enough to make out detail on their bodies before I took my shot. When the closest fish just started to veer away from its course toward me (about 15 feet away), I simultaneously thrust my four-banded gun forward and kicked. I fired. My intent was to give as much forward momentum to the near horizontal spearshaft as possible.

The fish took off so fast that it was impossible to catch my release pin as the two buoys streaked by, almost hitting me. Still joined by the pin, the buoys descended at a steep angle. Seconds later, they started to float back toward the surface, a sure sign my fish was lost. At least I could release that pesky pin.

Suddenly, the floats took off again, towing me in a large circle. I caught sight of the huge tuna, having completed a full circle on the surface, heading straight toward me. I began untangling myself from my float lines and preparing to dodge the monster fish, when it rolled over and started sinking, about 30 feet away. I struggled to stay afloat as the giant tuna's dead weight kept pulling me under. Finally, the chase boat arrived with my second gun. I dove and made a good second shot securing my fish just as the last wing of the first spearhead slipped free. We lassoed the 398-pound world-record by its big tail and brought it back to the mother boat, *Sand Dollar*. We tied it to the boat's swim step while we devised a plan to get it onboard intact.

I'll never forget the unbelieving expressions on the faces of the returning divers, as one by one, they caught sight of that monster fish hanging from the back of the boat.

In the Azores on August 19, 1997, Paulo Gaspar claimed the Atlantic bluefin record—297.2 kilograms (655 pounds). This is a phenomenal catch. Besides its size, what makes this record special is the character and preparation of Paulo himself—a consummate bluewater hunter.

Gaspar was born and raised in the Azores. He enjoyed all water sports, but his passion has always been diving and spearfishing. "Big fish always fascinated me and became an obsession," he recalls. "As the years went by, I began to acquire the utmost respect for the sea,

and all its existence, and I adopted the attitude of a selective hunter. The risk of being attacked by a swordfish, a bluefin tuna or even a shark sparked in me a sense of adventure."

Paulo learned from the local fishermen that the bluefin had come closer to shore and in greater numbers than anytime in 20 to 30 years. However, the fishermen cautioned Paulo that his attempt to land a giant bluefin would end in disaster. They told him of a fellow fisherman who got tangled in his fishing line. The huge tuna towed him 24 meters deep before fellow fishermen arrested his descent and pulled him and the tuna to the surface. Tragically, in the excitement, someone cut the wrong end of the line and the tuna towed the man into oblivion.

Undaunted, Gaspar never stopped thinking about capturing a giant bluefin. He became obsessed whenever he sighted bluefin underwater. He slept fitfully, ate little and spent little time with his family.

Two more tuna encounters brought him to fever pitch. With an inadequate reef gun, Paulo launched his spear at the back of a giant as it disappeared at "supersonic" speeds. Line ripped through Paulo's hands, but in a few minutes, the fish was free, leaving Paulo with a spear bent 90 degrees and a fractured spearhead. "I learned from this experience that I had the wrong equipment," he remembers. "I was trying to shoot an elephant with a BB gun." While waiting for an adequate bluewater speargun, Paulo had another significant tuna encounter.

Still carrying his 130-centimeter speargun, Gaspar fired once more at a large tuna—this time in self defense.

Even today, when I think about this, I get chills. I had been in the water for at least two hours when I spotted a bluefin about 12 meters away and

about 2 meters deep. Its side was toward me and it swam slowly. I stayed completely still admiring this beautiful fish. I was totally impressed with its size and the grace with which it swam.

Suddenly, the fish turned toward me, swimming very fast. Realizing the danger, I aimed my gun. When I pulled the trigger, I knew I wasn't going to capture or kill it. In spite of its speed on a collision course with me, it wasn't at proper range for a kill. However, my intentions were only to divert it. I knew it wanted to bump me.

The fish leaped out of the water and almost came down on top of me. When I think of this, one vivid image stands out: the face of the bluefin so big and so close with a large opened mouth and lots of line (almost like spaghetti) floating all around in the violently disturbed waters.

The day finally came when Gaspar received his Riffe gun equipped with three bands and a shaft with a detachable spearhead. The same day he took his untested gun into the waters 400 meters deep off Silveira Island.

It was 4 p.m. when I arrived in my 18-foot Boston Whaler. I couldn't feel the current and the water was crystal clear. The words of an old fisherman friend spoken that morning echoed in my head. "Paulo, remember you'll only catch one when you fully appreciate its strength. Be careful—that fish is a demon."

Just as I was returning to the surface after a short dive, it appeared in front, just below me at 5 to 6 meters. At the time, I must have been 3 meters deep, moving very slowly and without returning to the surface. Even though I desperately needed to come up for air, I couldn't lose this chance and I went back down a little. I made minor adjustments in my wrist for a good bulls-eye shot. My heart was racing. At the moment it went past me, the tip of my spear must have been 1 meter from its head. I fired. My shot landed 25 centimeters behind its great eye. Instantly, the great tuna stopped, opened its mouth as its tail trembled rapidly in short motions. Finally I can breathe! I was amazed at the

Giannis Margaritis stunned the Greek spearfishing community with his 105-kilo bluefin.

Photo by Giannor Ivanof

amount of blood pouring from its mouth and gills.

I swam toward it quickly, grabbed it by its pectoral fins and with much difficulty swam it to the surface. Its shaking tail helped propel us. I was immensely worried that the fish would emerge from its stunned state. I was afraid it might strike me or tangle me in the spearline.

Still in the water, I grabbed the 2.5-meter line I had previously prepared and tethered the tuna to the boat. Only then did the tuna regain some energy and began thrashing its tail about in the water and spinning the boat around. After what seemed like an eternity, but probably was only a minute, the fish died.

It is difficult for me to decide which was the most thrilling part of this adventure. I don't know if it was when I first sighted this grand fish, when I fired, when I grabbed it, or when I saw it hoisted on the pier. One thing is for sure: it was the most overwhelming experience, and one that I will never forget.

New archeological evidence suggests that bluefin tuna may have played a pivotal role in the southern migration of ancient Greeks from the mainland to the Aegean Sea. Finding large quantities of tuna bones and spears at archeological sites, anthropologists theorize that ancient Greeks followed the migrating tuna, where they corralled them in bays with crude nets, and then speared them.

Bluewater hunter Giannis Margaritis stunned the Greek spearfishing community with the 105-kilogram (231-pound) bluefin tuna he speared in March 1995. Modern Greek divers, hearing tales of giant tuna in their waters, longed for the chance to spear one. Acting on the advice of a fisherman friend, Giannis traveled to a special spot off Corinthian Bay, in 140 meters of water, where he cast bait-fish chum into the water as instructed by the fishermen.

Two large bluefin tuna appeared, swimming up the baited trail. Ten meters deep, Giannis aimed his pneumatic gun and shot the smaller of the pair; his 8-millimeter shaft scoring a perfect hit on its lateral line. His detachable spearhead held fast as the mighty fish pulled out 60 meters of line before it quite suddenly died. Ten minutes after his shot, a proud Giannis hauled the big fish into his boat.

WORLD RECORDS FOR BLUEFIN TUNA

IBSRC WORLD RECORD ATLANTIC BLUEFIN	PAULO GASPAR AUGUST 1995 PICO ISLAND, AZORES, PORTUGAL	OFFICIAL 655.2 POUNDS 297.20 KILOGRAMS
IBSRC WORLD RECORD PACIFIC BLUEFIN	TERRY MAAS SEPTEMBER 1982 GUADALUPE ISLAND, MEXICO	OFFICIAL 398 POUNDS 180.6 KILOGRAMS

Dogtooth tuna

Of all the gamefish profiled in this book, dogtooth tuna, with their average of 20 conical teeth per jaw, most resemble sharks. Frequently found swimming with grey reef sharks, they will turn on a wounded comrade and attack it with the same gusto as the sharks. Native to the tropical Indo-West Pacific, these fish range in an area centered around Australia—from East Africa in the west, north to the Philippines and west to the islands of Oceania. Dogtooth tuna are a resident-pelagic fish, favoring water 20 to 28 degrees Centigrade.

Swimming as individuals or in small groups, they occasionally form large schools. They frequent depths between 50 and 150 feet around coral reefs, preferring the reef's deep sides, leeward sides and channels, and the northern ends of coral atolls. This species is susceptible to overfishing, so expect to find larger fish in more remote locations. Because of their resident nature, some individuals are protected by local divers as pets at tourist locations such as the pass at Rangiroa in Tahiti.

Dogtooth tuna average 15 to 20 kilograms (33 to 44 pounds); the spearfishing record is 55.5 kilograms(121.1 pounds), and the all-tackle record is 131 kilograms (288 pounds). Their flesh is whiter than other tuna and they taste like spanish mackerel. Sharks also like to eat dogtooth tuna. Hooked and speared fish are frequently consumed in feeding frenzies, especially if the escaping tuna are allowed near the bottom, where they may become tethered in a line tangle. Spearing these fish is often a two-way contest—diver versus tuna, diver versus sharks.

Hunting these fish, as with most other bluewater species, is frequently a waiting game. Ferocious feeders, dogtooth tuna can be lured with burley, sound and flashers. Dive to 50 to 70 feet and wait; expect them to circle into range like spanish mackerel. According to Australian Greg Pickering, while the side shot is encountered most frequently, it's better to maneuver yourself above the fish and shoot from there. "This fish is hard to kill from the side," he says. "The most reliable shot is centrally, from above and behind the head at a 45-degree angle. Prangers (multi-barbed spearheads) work very well from the side, but you must be close— 8 to 10 feet—an infrequent event."

Greg tells two good stories, illustrative of dogtooth tuna hunting. Both incidents occurred at Kenn Reef, some 300 miles off the Central Queensland Coast, Australia. In May 1993, Greg and fellow diver Gunther Pfrengle found fish on

the north end of the reef, over several bomies (Australian for coral pinnacles). The pair drifted near another diver's boat, hoping his spearing activity would attract the tuna. In the 100-foot visibility water, Greg spotted a tuna accompanied by several small whaler sharks, cruising midwater around a coral pinnacle. They disappeared, so Greg shot a small trevally and cut it up for bait. A 100-pound dogtooth tuna, with its entourage of sharks, reappeared and brazenly swam quite close, close enough for Greg's shot to knock it momentarily senseless.

Recovering somewhat, the fish took off, taking most of the line from Greg's reel as it headed for the bottom, where it became tangled on a coral pinnacle. "That's when it started thrashing wildly and all hell broke loose," Greg recalls. "About 25 sharks, driven into a frenzy, ripped into the struggling fish. Other large reef fish, including a great trevally (ignoblis) joined the fray. Eventually, the sharks thinned out and I recovered the head and skeletonized remains of the fish, now reduced to 45 pounds."

The next morning Greg and Gunther returned to the same area, working a sand gutter in 80 feet of water, where the tuna were drawn from deeper water. Dogtooth tuna appeared each time they cut up speared unicorn fish for burley. Greg shot an 80-pound fish that eventfully ripped his line on the coral and swam off. On the way up from his dive, he spotted Gunther being towed behind his 25-meter float line. He'd shot a large tuna, which was busily trying to escape both the spear and the 20-odd sharks chasing it. Gunther's pranger spearhead, driven into the tuna's head, held fast. Running out of air, he released his float line, and both divers thought they'd never see his rig again as they chased it into deep water. Luckily, the big

fish circled back as the divers watched it artfully dodge the pursuing sharks. Gunther, still out of breath, asked Greg to try the 70-foot dive for a second shot. Greg's shot was good and the two soon had the big fish rolled into the boat.

Greg reloaded as he swam out to retrieve Gunther's float and several other fish he'd attached to it earlier. Arriving at the float, he found that sharks had eaten the remaining fish, but that three large tuna appeared, circling in mid-water. They were wary, one even sported a scratched head where a pranger spearhead had bounced off the day before. Greg made an extended dive of well over a minute into 60 feet of water, and finally made a long shot. Another 100-pound-plus tuna sped off with all his gear, into water 180 feet deep, so deep that Greg's float burst from the excessive water pressure. Luckily his gun, separated from the buoy, floated up to 100 feet. Greg made the deep dive and released his gun as a pack of sharks devoured his tuna 80 feet below.

Back at the boat, the divers weighed Gunther's tuna. "It weighed 55.5 kilos (122 pounds), slightly heavier than Les Gleaves' 121-pound Australian record, speared eight years earlier," Greg says. "However, we could not claim it as a world record because it was an assisted catch."

South African Jean Napier holds her country's record for dogtooth tuna. Jean had been diving for nine years before her big chance came. She started like many of us—learning to scuba dive. Her instructors and friends were avid spearfishermen and she was soon hooked on the sport as well. Diving in the South African National Championships four consecutive years, she always scored well, placing in the top half of the individuals competing.

A bluewater diver with a dogtooth tuna, named because of the appearance of its mouth.

PHOTO BY ALASTAIR MACNEILL

In 1989, Jean traveled to Inhaca Island off Mozambique, East Africa on a beautiful, hot, windless day. Once in the crystal-clear waters, she headed for a drop-off where she knew large shoals of fish congregated. Kicking strongly in the current, just to stay in place, she saw large reef fish—potato cod and brindle bass—but no big pelagic fish.

Returning to the boat hours later, she was amazed to see a lone dogtooth tunny (South African for tuna) swimming in eight meters of water just below the boat. "I dove down to its level and made a good shot, midbody at very close range," she recalls. "It took off at fair speed, heading straight for the bottom in 12 meters. I managed to hold it off the reef while playing it gently, in order to avoid pulling the spear free. I surfaced, yelled for help, and took off at marathon speed trying to keep up with the fish and thus ease pressure on the float line. By this time I'd realized that this was a big fish and not to be lost at any cost."

Jean's friends arrived in an inflatable boat and followed her for another 10 minutes, spare gun ready. The struggling fish attracted a huge potato bass and another very big tunny. After another 10 minutes, the fish tired enough to pull it to the surface and load it into the inflatable. Amazingly, her spear was not bent, but the clip holding it had to be severed with wire cutters. "We returned to the yacht and hauled it aboard with ropes," she remembers proudly. "I had to cut it into four pieces to weigh it as our scale registered only 20 kilos. It weighed 52 kilos (114 pounds)—a record for me, a South African record and possibly a world record."

WORLD RECORDS FOR DOGTOOTH TUNA

IBSRC WORLD RECORD PENDING	IAN PUCKERIDGE NOVEMBER 1997 WRECK REEF, CORAL SEA, AUSTRALIA	PENDING 182.8 POUNDS 83 KILOGRAMS
IBSRC WORLD RECORD	ANDREW BOOMER NOVEMBER 1996 KATO REEF, GREAT BARRIER REEF, AUSTRALIA	OFFICIAL 168.7 POUNDS 76.50 KILOGRAMS
IBSRC WORLD RECORD (W)	JEAN NAPIER 1989 TRANSVAAL, SOUTH AFRICA	OFFICIAL 114.5 POUNDS 52.00 KILOGRAMS

Greg Pickering holds up what's left of a dogtooth tuna. Frequently found in the company of sharks, this is not an uncommon occurrence. Even fellow dogtooth tuna join the feast.

PHOTO BY GUNTHER PFRENGLE

Jean Napier from South Africa with her 114.5-pound dogtooth tuna.

Top: Photo by East Cape Herald
Bottom: Photo by Allan Ubsdell

Marlin

MAJESTIC MARLIN

Roca Partida, a solitary rock 250 miles off the coast of Baja California, Mexico, is the size of a small gymnasium. Its walls angle sharply downward, 300 feet below the surface. Its tendency to attract and concentrate tuna and wahoo makes it a popular destination for long-range fishermen. Swimming up-current from that rock in 1994, I encountered my first large marlin.

I am 25 feet under the surface, following two 50-pound tuna, another 30 feet below me. Suddenly, they diverge and scatter like frightened minnows. Still focused on where the tuna were, my eyes are unable to clearly distinguish the huge, torpedo-shaped, blue-grey blur, streaking straight up from the depths. WHOMP WHOMP WHOMP WHOMP WHOMP. . . . My body resonates deeply as each beat of the marlin's great tail cavitates the water. It passes the scattering tuna and continues straight toward me, as if to pierce my chest. At the last second it levels off, just inches under me. Still

rocking in its wake, I am unsure of what I have seen because of the animal's great speed.

Now I can distinguish the shape of a huge blue marlin as it eyes me warily, circling me just 20 feet away. It turns directly toward me. We are poised as duelists: the marlin with its mighty sword, aimed directly toward me with the spear tip wavering back and forth, and me with my speargun, aimed and ready.

Should I shoot? It is a trophy and surely a world record! If it were going to hurt me, slashing or stabbing me with its sword, I would already be injured. What if I only wound it and the 500-pound fish drives its sword into me? Just then, it turns, presenting me with a perfect kill shot. It is a mass of muscles, with two distinct longitudinal bands bunching and rippling down its side. I remain in total wonder of one of the ocean's most powerful killers, so perfectly designed with a mighty body and a head shaped like the Concord jet airliner. The moment of indecision passes, and ultimately

the majestic and aloof marlin dismisses me, sinking silently into the indigo depths.

* * * *

Beautiful and ferocious, marlin occupy the crown of the ocean's predatory pyramid. The stomach contents of one 1,500-pound black marlin contained a 150-pound yellowfin tuna—whole! Ample evidence exists to prove that these largest of billfish use their sword to stun and in some cases, spear their prey. World spearfishing champion Terry Lentz, while commercial fishing off Hawaii, cast a skipjack bait into the path of blue marlin. The marlin pierced the middle of the skipjack's body and then swallowed it whole, hook and line attached. In all the excitement, another hook attached to the marlin's line became deeply imbedded in Terry's hand. Only quick action with a sharp knife to cut the line prevented Terry's prompt exit from the back of his boat behind the fighting marlin.

Four species of marlin—blue, black, white and striped—roam the oceans. The largest fish are always female. Like other gamefish, they can be found cruising the deep-water edges of pinnacles and drop offs, and any place where bait fish congregate. Two species, the black marlin and striped marlin, follow bait fish close to shore. Divers find them along rocky headlands off Australia and South Africa. South African blue-water hunters, conducting most of their hunting in the near-shore waters, have some incredible catches chronicled later in this chapter.

Marlin fishermen generally agree that the best fishing in any month occurs during the week with the least moonlight. Fishermen theorize that marlin are forced into daylight hunting because without light on the water at night, they can't feed. Marlin tagging studies show that some fish travel great distances, while others, trapped in specific areas by bands of cold water, stay local, unable to reach the warm open ocean. Some traveling marlin return to the same location yearly.

Whole industries have developed around marlin, including fishing, boating, tackle, publishing, travel and taxidermy. Among the marlin's hunters, the fishermen's trend toward "catch and release" is common today, with anglers limiting their kill to personal records or mortally injured fish. Bluewater hunters, with their worldwide catch of only about 50 marlin to date, follow this creed. As explained earlier in the chapter on ethics, bluewater divers practice "release and catch," preferring to visually "release" unwanted fish and limit their "catch" to special or record fish. Most would be happy with a lifetime catch of one or two marlin.

Having taken 35 fish, South Africans are the undisputed world leaders in marlin spearfishing. "The South African spearfishing community boasts one of the highest records of marlin landed in the world despite a relatively small number of divers," says Darrell Hattingh, a bluewater hunter, marine artist and spearfishing journalist. "Even though we have been hunting marlin for the last four decades, it was not until the last half of this decade that divers have taken marlin in any number. Most spearfishermen feel that advances in gear, diver caliber and the diver's willingness to venture further out into the bluewater have led to this increased success. Our chief target is the black marlin, which come fairly close to shore, especially along the warmer Zululand and Natal coastlines."

We are poised as duelists: the marlin with its mighty sword.

PHOTO BY JAMES D. WATT

No discussion of South African marlin would be complete without introducing the legendary Tony Dicks, who in 1961 at the age of 26, landed a 317-pound black marlin. Before this astounding feat, the pioneering blue-water diver held many fish records, including a 280-pound white shark he took from the infamous shark haunt at Bird Island, Port Elizabeth. When the beast charged, Tony shoved his gun down its mouth and continued to attack the shark's head with his knife while riding its back. Sadly, nine years after his record marlin, Tony suffered a shallow-water blackout and drowned during a spearfishing contest—a contest that bears his name today.

Tony Dicks exemplifies the true bluewater champion's attention to preparation and detail. In long discussions with his mates at the Dolphin Underwater Club of Port Elisabeth, he formulated plans for shooting and managing marlin. "Success in hunting big fish comes, in my opinion, from being able to regulate your mood to that of the fish," he wrote in a December 1961 article in the *Evening Post* with Tony Burke. "Everything depends on being able to keep the curiosity of the fish aroused." Tony made his own speargun—powered by a carbon dioxide fire extinguisher. It fired seven shots between chargings and used hollow 3-foot spears.

Tony's big marlin day began with a ride with fellow divers Clive Tutton and Keith Glynn on their 16-foot ski boat, which looked more like a flattened, elongated surfboard than a boat. (Because of their lack of boat-launching facilities, South Africans are masters at beach launching through heavy surf.) Tony, wearing two thick woolen jerseys, slipped over the side and swam in the crystal-clear water to within 200 feet of the rocky shore.

"I saw a gigantic shape—it became metallic blue and seemed to be giving off color; the ripples from the sandy bottom were dancing along its sides," he recalled in the article. "It was one of the most beautiful sights I'd seen. Swimming just four feet under the surface, with that famous spike sticking straight out and upwards, it moved slowly—not by waving its tail but by flexing its muscles."

Tony shot the fish and after the bubbles cleared, he thought of Hemingway's *The Old Man and the Sea,* as the marlin circled back, looking more like a charging rhinoceros than a fish. Passing Tony, the great fish headed out to sea. Masterfully playing his reel, Tony balanced the strength of the fish's fight against his 210-pound test line. Early into the fight, it towed him 70 feet underwater in less than 10 seconds. Having no floats, he knew releasing his gun would end the day.

Remembering his discussion with his friends, he followed his plan and kept constant tension on the line. He knew if the line went slack, this meant either that the fish was lost, or worse, it was circling back for an attack on him. The fight lasted 45 minutes and covered three quarters of Plettenberg Bay. "I swam in the opposite direction to keep him working," he wrote. "I played him like this until I had swum myself to a standstill."

The big fish swam back into shallow water, slowed and eventually came to the surface, belly up. Tony had played the fish until it drowned. The divers towed the fish to the local pier where the hoist just cleared its 9-foot body from the sand. Tony was an instant hero as word of his catch spread and people gathered to view it.

Marlin occupy the crown of the ocean's predatory pyramid.

Photo by James D. Watt

131

Thirty-three-year-old diver and wetsuit manufacturer Cuan Cronje has 14 years of blue-water experience diving along the Natal coast of South Africa. Here is the story of his marlin:

We launched early and were sounding for reefs off Deep Scottburgh in around 80 feet of water. The sea was very calm, there was no wind and the visibility was a pleasant 50 feet. I had just completed a bounce dive in search of reef structure and was on my way to the surface, when I noticed a marlin approach on my right and begin to circle behind me. Turning to my left, the marlin again came into vision close by, and was clearly intrigued by my appearance in his domain. As I turned my gun toward him, he turned away slightly. Realizing that the placement of my shot was critical, I slowed my movements and swam cautiously toward and yet slightly away from him. This proved decisive; perhaps responding to my faked disinterest, the marlin turned just enough and I fired, aiming for the lateral line just behind the pectoral fin.

It was a long shot, and I was astonished to see the spear flash through his thick, powerful body. Suddenly aware of the reality of my situation, I began to ascend and was surprised at the distance I had to swim to reach the surface. Screaming for the boat, I quickly clipped a second float line onto my buoy, expecting the marlin to scream off into the depths. Instead, the marlin swam steadily and powerfully close to the surface, as I gradually increased the drag on the line. Although I had plenty of opportunity to place a second shot, I resisted the temptation, believing the fish to be a striped marlin and a potential world record.

After an hour and a half, during which time my dive buddies and I fought off the attentions of two zambezi sharks, the marlin simply died and floated upside down. The only visible sign of distress during the chase had been a thin trickle of blood from the left gill plate. Only after boating the fish did I identify it as a black marlin, which later was weighed at exactly 200 kilos (440 pounds.). The whole experience had a very surreal, almost dreamlike quality, which despite my years of experience, I found very strange.

Jimmy Uys has the distinction of holding the official world record for the largest black marlin taken while spearfishing—a 242-kilogram (533-pound) beauty that he nabbed in May 1988. A chemical engineer and competitive diver, Jimmy moved to Durban, South Africa, to "shoot some decent fish."

Jimmy recalls being chastened a year before his record catch by a fellow diver for not spearing a near-dead marlin that had escaped from a long-line boat. Jimmy retorted, "Relax. One day I will shoot my own big marlin." Spoken in jest, Jimmy's words proved prophetic.

Almost a year later to the day, Jimmy and two diving buddies found themselves looking at a wall-mounted 100-pound black marlin while they waited in line to pay for their Zululand campsite. A lively discussion ensued among the three divers about the exact location for a kill shot. One of Jimmy's friends, a marine biologist, identified the lateral line just behind the gill plate as the best spot. Jokingly, Jimmy said, "OK, I'll shoot one today." Everyone laughed.

Signed in, the divers rushed for the beach, launched their boat and headed for the north end of Nine Mile Reef, where they anchored in windy conditions. The water was incredibly clear, the clearest any of them had seen—50 meters visibility. Jimmy recalls:

After relaxing, I made my first dive to 70 feet. Spiraling upwards, I was looking for 'cuda.' About 20 feet from the surface, I spotted a dark looming shape backlit by the sun; its long protruding

Striped marlin herd and attack a bait ball off Cabo San Lucas, Mexico.

PHOTO BY RICK ROSENTHAL

pectoral fins suggested a great white shark. I froze. The fish turned and I recognized it as a marlin. Hundreds of thoughts entered my mind as I acted instinctively, almost in a trance.

I slowly pulled my gun underneath me because of the local belief that fish stay a certain distance from the tip of your gun. The giant fish shone coppery bronze as it passed me at 4 meters. Its large blue eye rolled backwards as it moved, and suddenly I realized I must shoot or lose my chance. In one sleek move, I aimed my gun with two hands, like a rifle, at the exact spot we'd marked on the mounted marlin hours before.

The spear thudded home precisely, stunning the fish. To my despair I saw my spear had penetrated just 8 cm, leaving my barb exposed and unengaged. I grabbed my spearline intending to at least recover my untoggled spear when the fish took off. Nothing happened. Looking closer, I realized that the fish was slack-jawed with blood pouring from its mouth. Slowly the fish toppled over and than sank to the bottom like a stone.

According to Jimmy, the most exhausting part of the battle was hoisting the dead marlin into the inflatable boat.

The McGonagle brothers, Peter and Ian, both American pioneer marlin divers, hunt the waters off Cabo San Lucas, Mexico. One day Peter found bait fish six miles from shore. Drifting through the schools of bait, he saw several marlin swimming deep below, followed later by another pair on the surface. As these two fish sped by, Peter aimed and fired quickly, having just enough time to hit the last fish. "I let it run for 100 feet before locking the drag on my reel," he recalls.

I quickly unlocked the reel again after the fish reached the end of my line, dragging me under and my face mask off. After a minute, I tried relocking the reel, which resulted in a line tangle.

Remembering that I lost my whole rig, gun and all, to a big amberjack three weeks before in a similar tangle, I readied my knife to cut the line should the marlin start to sound. Locking the crook of my elbow on the barrel at the reel, I used the blunt edge of the knife to work out the tangle. While the marlin towed me for about a quarter of a mile, curious wahoo and marlin joined in our train. As the fish slowly tired, I reeled it in to within 15 feet of the surface. I swam down and grabbed its bill, which sent it on one last flight, taking me straight up, waist-high out of the water.

Bluewater diver Don Wert, diving Mexican waters, shot two marlin. Both fish quickly turned to face him, paused, and eyed him, as if to decide whether to charge. Luckily, both fish swam away, spear in tow. "Another gringo was not so fortunate," Don says. "A deckhand friend of mine helped rescue an American freediver who had been speared in the abdomen by a marlin he'd shot."

Recently, Ian McGonagle speared the largest gamefish ever landed by a freediver—a 760-pound blue marlin. Following a tip, Ian and Peter located a current break about 6 miles from shore said to hold 20-pound tuna. A male and a female friend accompanied the brothers in their 16-foot skiff with its sputtering 30-horsepower engine. After diving for a few hours, they returned to the skiff to rest. They'd seen small wahoo and unusually skittish tuna—instead of swimming around boldly, the small tuna darted and streaked about.

At 4 p.m., the team made a final drift in the waning sunlight. Ian remembers:

I could see Peter and Chris in the distance, when suddenly a wall of bait and tuna came rushing toward me. Three tuna broke from the school, one swam between my legs and the other two tried to find shelter in my arm pits. I was busy trying to push one of the tuna far enough away to get a shot with my long gun, when I noticed what provoked such unusual behavior. It was a giant blue marlin, lit up like a neon sign with brilliant blues and golds.

Peter McGonagle with his striped marlin he landed off Cabo San Lucas, Mexico.

Photo by Brenda McGonagle

Jimmy Uys with his 533-pound black marlin.

Above: Cuan Cronje with his 400-pound black marlin.
Left: Ian McGonagle with the largest bluewater gamefish ever speared.

137

One tuna remained as the marlin made several passes in front of me. After what seemed like minutes—but was probably 30 seconds—I fired, hitting the fish in the shoulder area.

My float streaked away like a missile. I yelled for the panga. Peter, who was hunting 100 feet away, heard my big Prodonovich gun fire. The marlin shot by him towing my float behind. "That thing was huge," Peter exclaimed. "It looked like a rocket going by, lit up like Las Vegas." The fish wore neon green and purple-blue bars dancing with pulsating spots of color traveling up and down its body. Its tail made huge 4-foot sweeps.

We jumped in the boat and motored up-current in the direction of the missing float. When we located the float, all we saw was 6 inches of the float's back end as it made its steady way into the current.

I jumped in the water with a second float and quickly tied it to the first. For the next 2 to 3 hours, I was alternately pulling or being pulled. Sometimes I was forced to let go of the line when the fish pulled too fast or went too deep. Peter, unaided by the towing marlin, swam faithfully at my side for my protection. We knew that marlin sometimes turn on fishing boats and spear them.

I tugged so hard that my mask fogged from the exertion. After covering 5 miles with me, Peter took a well-deserved break in the skiff. My line, which constantly pulsed and pulled at my hands, suddenly went slack. I wondered which of the weak points on my gear had failed—the float line, wire cable, speartip or a crimp. When I turned, I realized that the big fish had surfaced and was circling behind me, still glowing like a neon sign—except for a dark spot where the spear lodged. Peter joined me just as the fish took off on its final run. I pulled as hard as I could and the fish finally came up after 10 minutes.

I asked Peter to take a second shot to secure the catch. The fish turned bronze and greenish blue, as it sank, lifeless. I swam up to the great marlin and tried to hug it as if to say, "Thank you for such a wonderful battle." When my hands would not meet on the other side of the fish, I realized that this marlin was indeed huge.

The way three men and a woman got this huge fish into their small boat in the darkening waters is a study in determination. There was no way they were going to tow the big fish in after dark. Three of them pulled ropes attached to its bill and tail while Ian belly-hooked the fish with the gaff. On the count of three they rolled the big fish over the gunnel. It must have been a surreal sight as the four hooted and screamed in the dusk, gliding over the calm sea, the sides of the boat just inches from swamping. That night they measured and cleaned the fish, finding a 25-pound tuna in its belly. After finishing the filleting at 1 a.m. the brothers awoke early for the three trips into town required to distribute the extra meat to the needy.

WORLD RECORDS FOR MARLIN

IBSRC WORLD RECORD BLACK MARLIN	JIMMY UYS 1988 NATAL, SOUTH AFRICA	OFFICIAL 533 POUNDS 242 KILOGRAMS
IBSRC WORLD RECORD STRIPED MARLIN	CHRISTOPHER J. BROWNE APRIL 1997 NORTHLAND, NEW ZEALAND	OFFICIAL 296.3 POUNDS 134.4 KILOGRAMS
IBSRC WORLD RECORD BLUE MARLIN	KEN CHIOCCHETTI APRIL 1985 UMZUMBE, NATAL, SOUTH AFRICA	OFFICIAL 48.1 POUNDS 21.8 KILOGRAMS

Sailfish

Aptly called the "peacock of the sea," sailfish are among the ocean's prettiest inhabitants. Photographer Bill Boyce, flying over eastern tropical Pacific waters in a helicopter, describes a sight that could be called a natural wonder of the world. It was evening as he skimmed 30 feet above the surface, tracking huge balls of bait—expertly herded and driven upward by five groups of sailfish just 100 yards away. Above each group of about 20 subsurface sailfish, eight to ten fish circled languidly on the surface, their sails erect, snaking back and forth as they swam.

"It was a sailing regatta," Bill recalls. "I could see 70 sailfish subgrouped into eight ferris wheels. The golden glow of the sun was stunning, setting on a mercury sea behind the fishs' black-spotted blue sails!"

Their majestic multipurpose sail serves these ferocious hunters well. Fully raised, it increases their visual impact fivefold—instantly turning this slender fish into a monster. Groups of sailfish use their size-enhancing sail to corral schools of bait fish. Swimming at multiple depths, they scare and force bait into tight columns.

Videotaping a Costa Rican sailfish, I had a good opportunity to document another use for the sail. The hungry fish, with its sail tucked down into its back, chased a hookless fishing lure. Approaching the bait, the fish unfurled its sail as it made an incredible 90-degree turn, using its sail as a high-speed brake. Another scene in the video documents the fish striking a lure, slashing its bill sideways. Yet another shows its chameleon-like ability to change color in seconds, from black to iridescent pale blue.

Sailfish are found in both large oceans of the world. Pacific sailfish are larger and more colorful than their Atlantic relatives. Tagging studies show that Caribbean fish range widely, from Florida to Venezuela. In contrast, Australian release studies prove that their fish remain local. Needle-nosed and muscular, this fish has been clocked at speeds of up to 68 miles per hour.

Rarely targeted specifically by bluewater hunters, only a few fish are taken each year. Because of their soft flesh, it's easy to lose a fish not speared with care.

"These fish are strong fighters, but they do not dive to the bottom, like dogtooth tuna," Australian champion Greg Pickering says. "They pull along just under the surface, where they gradually tire. Provided your gear is set up properly, they can be handled without too much

drama. I remember, however, hanging onto my rig for 15 minutes while sharks rose to have a go at a 'sail' I'd shot. This feisty fish used its pointed bill to fend off the sharks at the same time it was fighting my spear."

"Kill shot" Robert Torelli of Australia displayed his marksmanship on the sailfish pictured on the next page, taken at Imperious Shoal. Steve Crabtree, whose diving buddies call him "Eagle-eye Action-man Crabtree," spotted a group of sailfish cruising behind their boat. Everyone raced overboard and Robert, finding the school of five fish first, took several pictures before making a serious attempt to spear one. Sprinting on the surface, he swam 50 meters to catch the moderately slow swimming fish. He dove to the fish's level. "Eyeball to eyeball with one 10-foot fish, I looked for the best penetrating shot. From my angle, I calculated a shot near the spine would traverse the fish, letting my flopper toggle on the other side. My shot was perfect. While not fully penetrating the fish, the spear did hit its spine, and within 10 to 20 seconds I could confidently drop my spearfishing rig and start taking pictures."

South African René Neethling is one of the few divers in her country to have taken a sailfish. Starting her relationship with the ocean early, 5-year-old René hung onto her dad's belt as he cruised around shore rocks hunting for lobster. At age 9, she shot her first fish.

"Unfortunately my father died when I was 10, and I think my love for the sea is a way of seeking contact with him," she says. "It is a world that we both loved and shared. To this day no experience can be better than that of a deep dive in crystal-clear water, with myriads of fish coming to investigate me—this strange creature invading their territory." Graduating from shore diving, she longed to dive from an offshore boat and spear a big gamefish. She credits members of the Wahoo dive club of Durban for making her dream become reality.

Two days before Christmas 1991, René woke up from a dream where she'd shot a 37-kilogram (81.5-pound) sailfish. Later the same day, she realized her dream by landing a sailfish off Aliwal Shoal. A strong current forced her and fellow divers to drift-dive the reef. She floated through shoals of many kinds and sizes of sharks, all intent on eating bait fish—small red-eyes. She spotted a metallic blue shape in the distance. "My eyes popped out of their sockets," she recalls.

> The sailfish approached me on the surface, and I simply exhaled slowly and sunk about one meter. For a second or so, I couldn't decide if I should shoot. Then the bad part of me took over and just as the sailie turned, I leveled my gun and pulled the trigger. I made a good shot, but this was a strong fish. I was towed through the water with such force that my snorkel was ripped from my mouth and all my boatman heard from my screaming mouth was a gurgling noise, sounding more like obscenities than anything else. The fish made one terrific run and stopped. Thinking it was finished, we hoisted it aboard our boat. Suddenly, it came to life and several unprotected shins were shaved and badly grazed until a sharp thinker covered its head. Luckly for me, I was still in the water and escaped injury.

Back on the beach, the fish weighed 37 kilograms, precisely the weight in her dream! René has great respect for this fish. "Nothing can compare to its colors when it lights up to feed, and when it unfolds its sail like a velvet mantle," she says. "I think most divers will shoot only one sailfish. When they see that blue eye, I'm sure they will vow never to shoot another; little else other than a world record might cause them to break this rule."

The sailfish—peacock of the sea.

PHOTO BY WILLIAM BOYCE

Rob Torelli's sailfish taken at Imperious Shoal, Australia.

PHOTO BY ROB TORELLI

Diver with a South Pacific sailfish.

PHOTO BY GREG PICKERING

WORLD RECORDS FOR SAILFISH

SOUTH AFRICA	A. HEYDORN 1992 ZULULAND, SOUTH AFRICA	OFFICIAL 139.6 POUNDS 63.4 KILOGRAMS
AUSTRALIA	GLYNN DROMEY APRIL 1976 NINGALOO, WEST AUSTRALIA	OFFICIAL 112 POUNDS 51 KILOGRAMS
NORTH AMERICA	JACK KEARNS MARCH 1988 FLORIDA	OFFICIAL 54.0 POUNDS 24.5 KILOGRAMS

Large mackerel (spanish and king)

A fish with many names, large mackerel species from the genus scomberomorus, are hunted in tropical and subtropical waters worldwide. Australian bluewater hunters pursue the narrow-banded spanish mackerel from their country north through Malaysia, where they're called "tengirri." South Africans hunt the "couta," and for the U.S. Virgin Islanders, it's the "king mackerel."

"Large mackerel have a reputation for being a tricky fish to spear, capable of tremendous speed and power. They are also blessed with excellent eating qualities," Australian spearfishing champion Greg Pickering says. Writing in the *Australian Free Diving and Spearfishing News, Issue number 1*, 1993, Greg offers the following information on the Australian spanish mackerel:

> We eagerly await their southern migration during the summer, when water temperatures reach 20 degrees Centigrade (68 F) or more. Prolific feeders, equipped with razor-sharp teeth, these fish have a high growth rate and a high edible flesh content (70-80 percent). Spanish mackerel prefer deeper edges adjacent to headlands and reefs, channels between exterior coral reefs, offshore islands and current lines. The best conditions for these fish occur during the morning with a rising to full tide, in water visibility 20 to 40 feet. Clear water makes them spooky and they simply don't show in dirty water. Often the first sign of this fish is the appearance of its black stabilizing fins on the tail; sometimes it's the only thing we see of the fish, hiding just at the edge of our visibility.

> Usually found grouped in midwater or near the surface, we rely on their curiosity to bring these fish within range. Shooting a small fish, or swimming away from the school, sometimes attracts them. Diving down to midwater, hunters often wait for a minute or more for an approach. When spanish mackerel swim in their typical S-fashion, good divers anticipate a turn toward them for their final approach to the fish. Australians prefer to hunt this fish with a relatively long gun (stock length 1.2 to 1.5 meters), and a

René Neethling with a nice couta (king mackerel or spanish mackerel).

PHOTO BY RENÉ NEETHLING

thin-fast shaft, equipped with a single barb—mounted 8 centimeters from the tip.

We avoid head shots because of the soft flesh and because, with its long body, it can gain enough leverage on the spear to free itself. Instead, hunters aim for the spine, or the area several inches under the dorsal fin in the mid-body (see page 150). Anticipating several strong bursts of speed, divers need to confirm the open position of their single barb, on the far side of the fish, before they apply too much braking pressure. Once subdued, we grab the fish through the gills, around the throat, and try to avoid its teeth. We improve the quality of its flesh by promptly killing and bleeding it, cutting its gills at the throat.

California bluewater hunter and dentist Gerald Lim grew up in Singapore, where he hunted the large mackerel called tengirri. He divides his methods for hunting mackerel according to where they're found:

Over reefs, we hunt them on the surface, in midwater and on the bottom. I prefer either midwater or the bottom, where I position myself on the up-current side of a reef or a high spot, on the flats past the reef drop off and anywhere I find bait concentrations. Depths range from 40 to 70 feet. Dropping quietly to the bottom, with minimal head and fin movements, I lie absolutely still and face into the current. About one in four curious mackerel, sensing my presence by pressure changes caused by the current flowing over my body, will come within range.

For the other three in four fish that stay out of range, my method is to simply run them down. Abandoning all finesse, I swim behind them as fast as I am able. Mackerel, so confident of their amazing speed, will frequently slow down. Because this swim covers 30 to 50 yards underwater, I'm usually purple by the time I shoot! These fish never seem to turn completely and offer a broadside shot. Instead, the best angle they offer is a 10- to 20-degree divergence from their straight path. Even with this poorly positioned going-away shot, bluewater hunters, equipped with a powerful speargun and a detachable tip, land a surprising number of these fish.

Off larger islands, we sometimes hunt in sand patches. Lying on sand flats in 40 to 60 feet of water, we again remain very still and patient. Often, a mackerel cruising inches off the bottom will pass on its patrol of the reef edge. There needn't be any bait fish in these areas for mackerel to be present.

Midwater hunting is my favorite. I dive 10 to 25 feet, and becoming neutrally buoyant, just float there and slowly scan to intercept curious fish. A variation of this technique is the slow-spiral descent, where sinking slowly with my head still, I scan in all directions.

Hunting from the surface is our least favored technique. Because these fish generally travel in a straight line, and when we see one it's too late to make an intercepting approach, we must chase them down.

According to Gerald, Malaysian divers hunt large mackerel around primitive fish aggregation devices (FADs.) Anchored on featureless sand or mud-bottomed high spots, in 150 feet of water, FADs offer a collection point for bait fish in an otherwise barren area. Native fishermen construct them from a rock anchor, a rope with coconut palm fronds attached every 10 feet and at the surface, large bamboo-pole floats.

"I hunt mackerel near the FADs on the surface or in midwater," Gerald says. "The FADs themselves offer a special hunting option by providing hanging points for the diver, who maintains his position by holding on to a rope or palm frond. The tricky part is keeping a speared fish from tangling on the FAD, too deep to retrieve."

An Australian diver with a spanish mackerel.

PHOTO BY GREG PICKERING

Vee King Shaw, from Hong Kong, shot what is probably the largest mackerel taken by any bluewater freediver. Diving from Pedro Blanco, a point 60 miles east of Hong Kong, Vee King spotted an immense school of a thousand tengirri. It was March 1979, in water 16 to 18 degrees Centigrade, when Shaw dove to 40 feet and intercepted the last fish in the school. Shooting what he considered to be one of the smaller fish, Vee King was eventually dragged 5 kilometers during the resulting fight. Luckily, a passing speed boat observed him being towed through the water and stayed with him until he landed the fish.

Examining the fish later, they found his shot was well placed. The detachable head entered just behind the gills and toggled on the fish's spine. The fish was so large that it had to be cut up into pieces for weighing. It weighed an incredible 135 kilograms (280 pounds).

Vee King Shaw with the largest of the large mackerel species!

PHOTO BY VEE FONG SHAW

South African René Neethling considers her country's large mackerel, the couta, one its fastest gamefish. "What it lacks in strength, compared to the ignoblis (giant trevally), it makes up in speed," she says. "I've seen feeding couta move so fast through the water, that all I'm left with is a blurred vision of a few black dots on their caudal peduncle as they disappear into the blue." She continues:

At times these fish form massive shoals, made up mostly of small individuals ranging from eight to 16 kilograms. Larger fish travel alone or in groups of up to three fish. Favoring the deeper water near offshore pinnacles, they venture close to shore during our annual sardine run. We hunt them at the head of the current, above bait fish concentrations, about 15 meters deep. Very well camouflaged, they are especially difficult to spot swimming over sand.

My best hunting tactic is to dive to their level, swim with them and abruptly stop; invariably they will turn to investigate. You've got to be ready with your gun extended because they only give you one chance for a shot. I have shot nearly all of my couta on their first investigation— if they return for a second look, it's generally out of range.

Once shot, these fish make two runs. The first is very fast, the second is much slower and more circular. At this stage it's important to keep constant pressure on the line to prevent slack and a resulting closed-barb from which they can easily slip free. A short rubber bungee helps maintain the desired line pressure. When there are lots of fish around, we use two guns. It's tricky at first, but easily mastered in one season. The first gun's line is 40 meters long, the second gun's line, equipped with a marlin clip, is only 20 centimeters long.

Shooting the first fish usually keeps the school occupied long enough for me to go to the float for my second gun. After shooting the second fish, I loop and snap the short-gun line around the longer line and retrieve both fish in at once. The South African record is 34 kilos, but further north, outside our boundaries, Eddie Dunn has taken a 56-kilogram fish.

My own 26-kilogram couta gave me a workout. Spying it from above, I dove and followed a small couta school until my lungs practically burst. When I stopped, one fish made a leisurely turn, giving me my shot. It took off at record speed, pulling my line through my hands, burning them. Making two long runs, it continued to fight as two dusky sharks arrived, attracted by the commotion. The harder I fought, the more the fish struggled until I finally managed to pull it in and kill it under the watchful eyes of the duskies. Keeping my other loaded gun aimed at the sharks, I swam to shore with my fish. Fortunately, their interest waned and I managed to beach my fish intact.

U.S. Virgin Islander Mark Marin hunts the king mackerel. "Because these fish are both stealthy and rare, spearing that first 'kingfish' has long represented a major rite of passage among underwater hunters of the Caribbean," Mark says. A North American record holder, skindiving journalist and independent-school headmaster, Mark covets this fish more than any other because of its speed and beauty:

We typically find them near the bottom, swimming as individuals or in groups of two to three fish. Only occasionally do they come into shallow water for a rare feeding foray. Weighing 15 to 30 pounds, they tend to come into our waters more often around the new moon and exhibit seasonal migratory patterns which vary throughout their southern Atlantic range.

Since they swim near the bottom, and tend to stay below 50 feet, hunting them requires much luck or clear water or preferably, both. Remember, in clear water if you see them, they have already seen you. If your dive brings you down behind the fish, it will almost certainly disappear with a casual flick of its tail. Similarly, if it senses you ahead of it on the same level, it will turn away with an uncanny knack for keeping a foot or two out of range.

I find a 90-degree approach works best. Since a kingfish will seldom deviate from its line of travel, I try to plot an intercepting course that puts me right on its back. This requires that I spot them early enough to lead them during the descent. In an attempt to 'stone' the fish, I aim for the lateral line or the spine, and if I miss vital areas I'm surely in for a ride.

The North American spearfishing record is in the 50-pound range. "But," says Mark, "all of us have our own stories of the 'seven-footer, thicker than a telephone pole, that ran 150 feet off my reel before it pulled the spear free.' That's the one we all dream of boating. With a bit of luck, one of us will!"

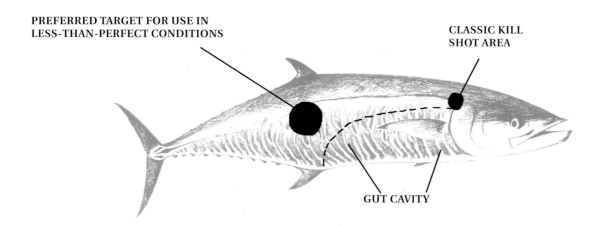

PREFERRED TARGET FOR USE IN
LESS-THAN-PERFECT CONDITIONS

CLASSIC KILL
SHOT AREA

GUT CAVITY

Because of their soft flesh and large gut cavity, mackerel can be lost if the shot is not well placed. When close, aim for the classic kill shot area; otherwise aim for the firm muscle midway between the dorsal and ventral fins, at the base of the tail.

WORLD RECORDS FOR LARGE MACKEREL

AUSTRALIA	ARNOLD PICOLLI SEPTEMBER 1982 CORAL BAY, WESTERN AUSTRALIA	OFFICIAL 80.4 POUNDS 36.5 KILOGRAMS
SOUTH AFRICA	J. ANDREWS 1990 ZULULAND, SOUTH AFRICA	OFFICIAL 74.8 POUNDS 34 KILOGRAMS
NORTH AMERICA	MICHAEL VOGEL SEPTEMBER 1987 ST. THOMAS, U.S. VIRGIN ISLANDS	OFFICIAL 53 POUNDS 24 KILOGRAMS

Wahoo (ono)

Wahoo, among the fastest and best-tasting of all fish, are found in most of the world's temperate and tropical oceans. Their name originates from the Hawaiian Islands, where appreciative settlers, intending to name the fish after the island Oahu, misspelled the word writing "Wahoo" instead. Native Hawaiians call this fish "ono," their name for "good."

Wahoo have a well-earned reputation as aggressive hunters. One fish, while chasing a pole-fisherman's lure cast from a large fishing vessel in Mexican waters, leapt over the deck and smashed through a glass cabin window, coming to rest on the galley floor—just in time for dinner!

I'll never forget the sight of a large wahoo attacking a school of two-pound bait fish. Drifting over a school of about 100 fish near a Mexican pinnacle, I saw a silver streak hit the center of the grouped fish. The wahoo's charge was accompanied by the sounds of water cavitation noise, much like the sound a motorboat makes, and ended in a loud WHACK, as bait fish scattered in all directions. One unlucky bait fish remained, cut in half by the wahoo's incredibly sharp teeth. The great fish made a leisurely return, taking its meal in two gulps, and as so often happens in the ocean, the bait fish reschooled, feverishly consuming the remaining bits of their brother.

In Mexico, wahoo prefer shallow water, about 100 feet deep, near pinnacles and drop-offs. Although they swim at depths anywhere from 3 to 60 feet, they seem to prefer 20 feet. Found in schools and pairs, they regularly make 15-minute circuits, passing the edge of the bait fish boundary on their return from open water.

Wahoo are attracted to any kind of vertical line, anchor line or buoy chain. This includes your own anchor line, around which they tend to collect as the day passes. In the morning, they concentrate into schools and are easier to approach. Later in the day, they become progressively more solitary and shy. South Africans and Australians successfully attract them with flashers.

A brightly barred, 'lit-up' wahoo is a beautiful sight, especially close to the surface, where unfiltered sunlight enhances their intense colors. Like many fish, they have a chameleon-like ability to change color; their dark vertical bars and their electric blue body fade into steel grey, seeming to disappear into the ocean's background. Their languid swimming style is curious. They appear to rock, left and right like a log, while at the same time opening their mouths

Wahoo are among the fastest and best-tasting of all fish.
PHOTO BY RICK ROSENTHAL

wide, revealing razor-sharp teeth.

The best way to approach wahoo is straight-on, as they swim toward you, either from above or from below. Because of the wahoo's lateral sensitivity, it's difficult to make on-level approaches, especially from the side. Watch their dorsal fins closely; if that fin rises and you are within range, take your shot because the fish will not allow you to move any closer.

Aim for their lateral line just behind the gillplate, or anywhere centered in the forward third of the fish. The wahoo's initial run is so strong that most shots in the rear two-thirds of

the fish will allow the shaft to rip free. This burst of speed is spectacular. Surface observers have confused the sound of the escaping fish with that of a water skiier as the fish's tail chopping the water, and then the diver's float, race by at 20 miles per hour. But wahoo tire rapidly—a steady, weaker, pull follows the first run. Allow several minutes to pass before pulling them in. Play them carefully because too much back pressure on the line will rip the spearhead free.

An uncommonly speared fish in Australia, they are found more often north of latitude 30. Generally a solitary fish, wahoo sometimes form

"Dead-eye" Bob Caruso with a Mexican wahoo.
PHOTO BY HOWARD BENEDICT

schools as Greg Pickering found in 1993 at Nine Mile Reef off Tweed Heads. "We found a school of 30 wahoo, their tails sticking out of the water as they basked in the oily calm water," he recalls. "We hunted them by jumping in up-current, and kept track of them by raising our heads out of the water and looking for their tails in the air. Once close, we threw a handful of burley in the direction they swam. This allowed us to approach them, as they stayed swimming just below the surface. That day we bagged three fish—30, 48 and 60 pounds—all exceptional by Australian standards."

Brian Yoshikawa holds the official North Ameri- can record for wahoo at 68.5 pounds. Brian describes himself as a new breed of Hawaiian spearfisherman, a true bluewater hunter. "Unlike the typical Hawaiian spearfisherman, content scrounging the reefs for a stringer full of small fish, I chose to explore the deep-blue waters, hunting fish that swim fast, fight hard and live where some divers dare not tip their fins," Brian says. "I like hunting the lava flows that richly surround the Hawaiian Islands. These lava flows pour into the ocean, forming dramatic cliffs, pinnacles and radical drop-offs, some rising several hundred feet while others fall thousands of fathoms into the

153

Pacific. Currents, washing the lava flows, pull nutrient-rich waters from the azure depths. This begins a wondrous food chain, starting with the tiniest creatures and ending with the largest gamefish known—wahoo and tuna.

"The most easily accessed flows and pinnacles are heavily fished in Hawaii—consequently trophy fish are seldom found there. The best grounds for spearing wahoo are the remote, hard-to-find, hard-to-get-to waters where conditions are the roughest, windiest and nastiest. Sharks guard these waters. Wahoo will spook when they sense you are near because they have either been chased, baited, hooked and shot at, or they have witnessed their schoolmates succumb to hooks and spears."

With that introduction to Hawaii ono hunting, Brian chronicles the hunt for his record:

> As I pulled a shimmering tuna to the surface, the monster ono reappeared, a second time, from deep water. Observing my tuna with one eye, and keeping its other eye on me, the big fish slipped back into the depths. Feeling depressed at blowing my second chance in three minutes, I swam my 30-pound ahi back to the boat where I convinced our boat captain, Randy Sasada, to pick up my fellow divers, Todd Tyau and Mike Kimura, for another try at that big ono. After hearing my story of the big fish, Todd and Mike smiled, nodded their heads, and wondered aloud if I had hit my head or held my breath too long.

> Conditions were great. Bait fish were everywhere and schools of mahi-mahi, tuna and smaller wahoo came through, grabbing a bite before swimming on. My big fish was nowhere to be seen. Ready to call it a day, I was surprised to see Todd and Mike intently tracking a large shape about 50 feet ahead of them. I took a quick breath, dropped down 20 feet and swam an intersecting course. If it maintains its course, it should be in view by now, I thought, as I fought off my first urges to breathe. Slowly, a spherical

shape materialized, first a grey cylinder, next a silver torpedo and finally a metallic, phosphorescent-blue gamefish. As it came within range of my outstretched gun, I realized that this crafty ono, intent on eluding my friends, was not aware of me. Patiently, I waited for its arrival, my lungs now screaming for air. It was too late for the fish when it noticed me; my spear rocketed into its collarbone, snapping its spine—the stalk was over. After two blown chances against that mythical ono, I made good on the third.

Divers must be careful to avoid the wahoo's sharp teeth. Even dead fish pose a risk to the unwary. The slightest bump with the fish's open mouth will leave a large gash, as veteran San Diego diver Howard Benedict knows.

Howard tells an incredible story of his three consecutive world-record wahoo taken in less than 20 hours. Howard, a dentist, and his brother Mike, a dental technician, planned a three-month circumnavigation of the Baja Peninsula, Mexico, in Howard's 26-foot boat. The brothers intended to spear fish along the way, from San Diego, past the cape and up into the Gulf of California. They looked forward to diving on the legendary Thetis Bank with two large pinnacles, the sides rising 200 feet from the bottom, 300 feet below. The 100 feet of water above these pinnacles contains some of the best gamefish in the world. It is a popular destination for the San Diego-based long-range fishing fleet.

Very few divers have ventured to Thetis because of its remote location, 23 miles from shore and two-thirds of the way down the Pacific Coast of Baja California. The ones who make it there are treated to the silhouettes of hundreds of mating hammerhead sharks circling in the indigo-clear water at 80 feet. A strata of yellowtail and amberjack circle above the sharks in 60 feet of water, while wahoo cruise the surface 20 feet above them all.

Howard Benedict with two of his three wahoo taken at Thetis Bank, Mexico. The largest weighs 102 pounds—an unofficial world record.

Photo by Mike Benedict

It was the fall of 1984 when Howard and Mike reached Thetis Bank, just two weeks into the trip. In spite of extremely rough conditions, with high swells and winds over 20 knots, they entered the water the evening of their arrival. Just before dark, Howard shot his first wahoo—an 80-pound record.

The next day, half-an-hour after first light, Howard shot another wahoo, weighing 90 pounds. Motionless at first, the fish bolted toward the bottom, taking a kicking Howard with him. Watching the scene from above, Mike swam a safety line to Howard, who for a few seconds before the fish died, remained spread-eagled between the fish below and the line above. "I was so excited after landing my second fish that I could hardly talk," Howard said.

Mike and I continued to dive through midday. Mike shot two fish while I waited for bigger prey. My patience paid off as I spied three wahoo, looking like marlin without bills, coming directly toward me. I dove and leveled off, remaining suspended and motionless as they nearly swam into the end of my outstretched gun. When they finally turned broadside, I shot the biggest, which never moved as I swam it back to the boat.

The seas were really rough by this time, and when I finally got the big fish over the swimstep and onto the engine hatch, a big swell sent the open-mouthed fish sliding into my leg. I looked down to my shin, now spurting blood from a 3-inch gash, exposing my leg bone. My first thought was of infection so I jumped back into the ocean and washed fish slime from the wound. The horizontal nature of the cut caused it to gape wide, making it too large to tape; it would have to be sutured. Mike took one look at the wound and admitted he could not handle suturing it.

No medical help was available, even on shore, hours away. Reluctantly, I gathered my medical kit and wedged myself against the sea in the cabin below. Shaving the area first, I used five large sutures to close the wound. I taped it liberally and was back in the water within half-an-hour. Soon, however, our lack of sleep took its toll, and too tired to spend another night on the bank, we headed for shore.

We anchored in a calm bay where we weighed my last and largest fish on two identical scales. The scales read the same, 102 pounds, an unofficial world record. We finished our trip two months later. My leg healed without problems. Back in San Diego, I confirmed the accuracy of the scales.

WORLD RECORDS FOR WAHOO

SOUTH AFRICA	C. GRAVE 1990 NATAL, SOUTH AFRICA	OFFICIAL 94.7 POUNDS 43 KILOGRAMS
NORTH AMERICA	BRIAN YOSHIKAWA APRIL 1992 HAWAII	OFFICIAL 68.5 POUNDS 31.1 KILOGRAMS
AUSTRALIA	GREG SMITH SEPTEMBER 1988 NEW SOUTH WALES, AUSTRALIA	OFFICIAL 52.8 POUNDS 24 KILOGRAMS
NORTH AMERICA	HOWARD BENEDICT OCTOBER 1984 THETIS BANK, MEXICO	UNOFFICIAL 102 POUNDS 46.3 KILOGRAMS

Giant trevally (ulua)

Like the dogtooth tuna, the giant trevally is a resident-pelagic species, sometimes taking a local residence, other times moving or migrating away from their "house." It's one of the strongest fish to fight when speared, so anything less than a good head- or spine-shot often leads to loss of the fish as it invariably heads straight for the bottom.

In South Africa, where giant trevally inhabit the east coast, they are regarded as a premier gamefish. Found near offshore pinnacles, 20 to 40 meters deep, they also appear near the shore, where they hunt at night. During the annual sardine run, they come very close to shore, just before dawn and just after sunset, where their large eyes facilitate nocturnal hunting.

As with most gamefish, smaller fish tend to be curious and congregate in schools, ranging from three to hundreds of fish. Larger fish become solitary and wary, spending their days hiding in caves and caverns. While the average giant trevally weighs 10 to 16 kilograms (22 to 35 pounds), much larger fish have been taken—up to 60 kilograms (132 pounds) in northern South Africa.

René Neethling, a South African bluewater diver, shot a 35-kilogram fish off Protea Reef. The big fish took off with her gear, float and all. "Fortunately, the fish could either not find its cave or the spear prevented its entry, and it surfaced 15 minutes later, still struggling madly," she recalls.

Across the world in the Hawaiian Islands, Todd Tyau holds the official North American spearfishing record for the giant trevally, which Hawaiians call "ulua." According to Todd, lava structures make perfect homes for ulua, especially when the lava forms tubes and caves with multiple entrances. Because this fish is frequently fought on the rocky bottom, Hawaiians use cable line and detachable spearheads.

In May 1992, Todd and diving buddy Halii Iaea anchored on the shore-end of a 150-yard lava finger. The divers worked each side of the finger out to sea, where it ended in sand 75 feet deep. Having no luck, they retraced their path. "I looked to the left and all I saw was bait fish scattering," Todd recalls.

Instantly, I knew something bigger was feeding on them. Seeing nothing, I watched and waited. Sure enough, a large ulua charged the bait from the sand channel below. It attacked again and swam in a haphazard course. Taking a chance, I descended, hoping my path would meet one of its charges. My timing was perfect. Having noticed me, the big fish swam straight toward my outstretched speargun.

It turned and I fired, making a perfect spine shot,

Top: A beautiful, free-swimming Australian giant trevally.

PHOTO BY GREG PICKERING

Left: Todd Tyau proudly displays his pending record, a 120-pound, Hawaiian ulua.

PHOTO BY RANDY SASADA

paralyzing the fish. Swimming to the surface, I noticed my spear had not fully penetrated the fish so I subdued it on the surface. Halii, attracted by the noise of my gun discharging, yelled, 'You got it. You got the hundred-pounder!' With those words in mind I held the fish tightly to me as I swam back to the boat.

World kickboxing champion Dennis Alexio broke Todd's record two years later. Early in the morning on July 2, 1994, Dennis and two buddies, Henry "Henele" Keawe Ayau Jr. and Danny "Kaneala" Robertson, swam a quarter-mile offshore of the Big Island—Hawaii.

There they encountered a large school of star jacks (blue-spotted trevally). Henele, using his secret teaser, successfully attracted a 60-pound ulua that was scouting the edge of the schooled jacks. After taking the teaser into its mouth twice, it spooked when Henry made an approach.

A few minutes later, Kaneala yelled to alert Dennis that a large ulua was below, near a ledge, 80 feet deep. Dennis dove outside the ledge, parallel to the fish, and then turned abruptly angling toward the ledge. Kicking with all his strength, he gradually got closer to it, even though it had increased its pace. Expecting the fish to disappear any second, Dennis lunged forward and made a desperation shot.

The spear hit the ulua about two feet in front of its tail, high in its back. Like a freight train, it roared off into a cave, where it holed up. Dennis resisted its run for 15 seconds, but since he'd already been down for some time, he was forced to surface. After Kaneala handed Dennis his gun, Dennis dove for a second shot. His head-shot, exiting through the gills, was good and all the divers could hear the big fish banging and thrashing about in the cave below. The second spear, protruding two feet out of each side of the ulua's head, restricted its movements. "As I watched the fish struggle, I realized how big it was when it turned its head sideways," Dennis said.

Fearing it would escape over the ledge and into the 600 feet of water below, Dennis grabbed his knife and dove. "Entering the cave, I found the ulua with its back to me," Dennis recalls. "Cautiously, I pulled the fish to the side and observed it for a few seconds before surfacing."

By now, Dennis was really excited; he attempted a third shot to secure his catch. "As I rolled into the cave, I realized it was now dead. My heart was thumping madly as I swam the big fish to the surface. On shore, we recorded its weight at 131 pounds, a Hawaiian record."

WORLD RECORDS FOR GIANT TREVALLY

AUSTRALIA	LARRY SPRINGALL OCTOBER 1971 LIZARD ISLAND, QUEENSLAND, AUSTRALIA	OFFICIAL 120.88 POUNDS 54.88 KILOGRAMS
SOUTH AFRICA	P. DEXTER 1975 NATAL, SOUTH AFRICA	OFFICIAL 100 POUNDS 45.4 KILOGRAMS
NORTH AMERICA	TODD TYAU MAY 1992 HAWAII	PENDING 120 POUNDS 54.5 KILOGRAMS
NORTH AMERICA	DENNIS ALEXIO JULY 1994 HAWAII	PENDING 131 POUNDS 59 KILOGRAMS

Dolphin fish (dorado, mahi mahi)

Dolphin fish are distributed worldwide. They are extremely tasty, which probably explains why every fishing culture gives them a special name. Bluewater hunters generally do not target these fish, but consider them a welcome bonus.

Dolphin fish grow at an incredible rate—some gain 30 pounds in one year. Even their eggs develop rapidly, hatching in just 60 hours. These fish age quickly, too; grandfather fish are only four years old. Strictly an open-water species, they are particularly drawn to flotsam of all kinds. They begin life as schooling fish but frequently form pairs as they age. It is not uncommon to find a mixed school—small females accompanied by several large males.

Males develop a distinctive forehead crest which further distorts the shape of this unusual fish. Fish that appear huge from the side are almost laughable when viewed from the front; they seem to be squeezed as thin as a pancake. These are among the sea's most beautiful fish, capable of kaleidoscopic, almost instantaneous, color changes, from gold to electric blue to silver.

Bluewater diver Peter McGonagle tells the story of his world-record catch: "I was employed as a deckhand for a fishing boat working out of Cabo San Lucas, Mexico. We headed for a huge school of dorado about 20 miles out. Most of the fish were female weighing up to about 45 pounds. The fishermen onboard caught 12 fish until they ran out of bait. Now was my chance to slip into the water.

I was immediately engulfed by female fish, but I could also see several large 60- to 70-pound males stealthfully cruising the outer edges of the school. I found that the largest fish stayed way out on the periphery as long as I swam with the school but became curious when I left it. It would follow me a short distance until we made eye contact and then dart away. Keeping its distance, it would then follow me back to the females. The fish and I kept repeating this dance until I changed my tactic.

I laid perfectly still on the water for 30 minutes, gun at my side, floating like a drifting log. The big fish would approach, circle me and then dart away again. Finally it came close, almost within range, then darted straight down. I continued to remain still as it reversed course and came within 10 feet, close enough for a good shot.

Right: Dolphin fish like this female are capable of kaleidoscopic, almost instantaneous color changes, from gold to electric blue to silver.

<small>PHOTO BY JAMES D. WATT</small>

My shot was true, hitting it behind the gill plate. It jumped out of the water and then headed straight down, instantly stripping 150 feet of line from my reel. Pressure on the reel's drag finally stopped it. The fish stayed deep, continually swimming on its side. Half an hour of gentle pulling passed before I was able to move it toward me. On the surface, it darted around in circles as I reeled in my loose line. I finally pulled it close enough to shove my hands into its gills. That's when I realized how really big it was. I held it, bear-hug fashion, until I could swim back to the boat, where everyone onboard was impressed with its beauty and size.

WORLD RECORDS FOR DOLPHIN FISH

NORTH AMERICA	RON CUTLER MAY 1979 ST. CROIX, U.S. VIRGIN ISLANDS	OFFICIAL 44.0 POUNDS 20.0 KILOGRAMS
SOUTH AFRICA	C. HEINZ 1994 NATAL, SOUTH AFRICA	OFFICIAL 25.1 POUNDS 11.4 KILOGRAMS
NORTH AMERICA	PETER MCGONAGLE 1990 CABO SAN LUCAS, MEXICO	UNOFFICIAL 70.0 POUNDS 31.8 KILOGRAMS

Peter McGonagle with his beautiful, 70-pound record dorado.

<small>PHOTO BY STEVE HOWARD</small>

Yellowtail (kingfish)

Yellowtail, distributed worldwide in various sub-populations, are one of the most popular gamefish hunted. Bluewater hunters take more of these fish than any other species. Prolific members of the jack family, they grow rapidly, reaching maturity in two years. The oldest fish recorded lived just 12 years. Yellowtail migrate in open water according to water temperature, preferring 63 degrees Fahrenheit (17 C) in nearshore North American waters, and 64 to 75 degrees Fahrenheit (18 to 24 C) in the waters off Australia. As with other bluewater species, little is known about their natural history.

Usually swimming in pairs or schools of same-size fish, yellowtail get their name from the distinctive yellow stripe running the length of their bodies, ending in their yellow tail. As with other bluewater species, larger fish tend to be more solitary. Strong and fast-moving, they are capable of drowning a diver, as Adam Smith and Ian Puckeridge warn in the *Australian Free*

Diving and Spearfishing News, issue number 3, 1994. "In Australia, biologists have found that yellowtail live nearshore and along the continental shelf," they write. "Juvenile fish (up to 60 centimeters) tend to remain in a limited area, but as they grow older their territory spreads." Ian speared a fish off Sidney that had been tagged and released in New Zealand waters.

Yellowtail taste good. They can be barbecued, smoked, canned or eaten raw as sashimi. Unknown in North America, several cases of fish poisoning (ciguatera) from yellowtail have been reported in Australia.

Bluewater divers hunt yellowtail near the up-current end of pinnacles and kelp beds, offshore under kelp patties, under flotsam and in balls of bait herded toward the surface. Curious fish, it is not uncommon for them to circle a wounded fish fighting the spear, or approach a captured fish strung to the float. I used this curiosity as a basis for an effective yellowtail lure. Made from

Gerald Lim with a nice yellowtail taken at Guadalupe Island, Mexico.

PHOTO BY TERRY MAAS

flat, white plastic, articulated in two places, and shaped and colored to match the fish, this lure is attached to my float line and trails behind me, 20 feet deep.

Yellowtail frequently school about 20 feet down and have a habit of swimming circles around a diver, getting closer with each successive pass. When they school deeper, a successful method for bringing them up is to make a rapid descent and ascent through 50 to 60 feet of water. Yellows are attracted to speared smaller species, such as bonito, still fighting the spear.

It seems each yellowtail diver develops his own method for attracting fish. Some strum their speargun power bands or tap their gun. Others wear white-tipped gloves and wiggle their fingers or wave their hands, or unsheathe their knives and glint them in the sunlight. Team divers often delay the retrieval of a speared yellowtail knowing it might attract others in the school, making it possible for a team member to make a shot. Occasionally yellowtail attract sharks and other predators. (See Jeremy Williams' story in the chapter on marlin.)

Yellowtail are ferocious feeders and work together in their hunting. Bluewater photographer Bill Boyce found himself caught up in a feeding frenzy in the Sea of Cortez, Mexico. Bill was diving against a steep shore drop-off when he heard what he thought was a motorboat engine headed his way—a very scary sound for the freediver who cannot delay his ascent to the surface for air. Ascending close to the rocks to avoid the boat, he became engulfed in a mass of fleeing bait fish, so densely grouped that they intermittently blocked all light.

Small yellowtail expertly herded the bait against the rock wall, trapping them there. Still ascending, Bill heard the motor getting louder. Too loud for a boat, the noise became terrifying! Almost at the surface, hundreds of cormorant bodies pierced the water around him, like a scene from the movie *The Birds*. Surfacing in this mayhem, Bill shrieked, partly in panic and partly to scare the birds, plunging all around him

inches away. They soon departed. Following the yellowtail-driven bait, the birds formed a continuous aerial hemisphere—much like a Chinese fan, as they emerged, flew up and dove again, chasing the bait into the distance.

"Because of its cold waters, my country has few bluewater species," veteran bluewater hunter Steve Crabtree of New Zealand says. "What it lacks in variety, it makes up with its mighty yellowtail—the largest in the world." In the pioneering 1960s and, 70s, kingfish (as they call them) formed huge schools close to shore. The magic weight of 100 pounds was often reached. "With so many skilled hunters chasing the kingfish so avidly, the fish population has suffered," Steve says.

Although the species is still common, the larger fish are becoming rare. Kingfish have been saved in New Zealand because they have little commercial value, but for this same reason, they have not been seriously studied. Little is known about the age or habits of larger fish, except that they soon disappear from an area that is regularly hunted. Sometimes fatally curious, kingfish quickly learn that divers can be trouble. When I hunt untouched reefs for a week, I can count on getting the biggest fish the first day. By the end of the week, they become progressively more wary, and all I get are fleeting glimpses of smaller fish.

There are few sights in this world of underwater hunting that can match the beauty of a large school of big kings. Hundreds of them, swimming straight up from the depths, can surround you in seconds. Fascinated by divers, they circle for minutes, bigger fish at the edges, smaller fish within arms reach. It is difficult to make a shot at an individual fish in a whirling mass of thick green bodies. Divers commonly get 'schooled' by these fish and have to end the dive without a fish.

The power of a large fish, when not properly hit, is frightening; brushing aside heavy spears, they head straight down and don't come back. This power makes spearing them a tricky business, often leaving divers empty handed and spearless. More a street fighter than a bluewater thoroughbred, the yellowtail is as tough as they come!

On the other side of the Pacific there is another subpopulation of large yellowtail far off the coast of Chile. That's where René Rojas, a U.S. world spearfishing team member and Los Angeles champion, took his American record. "While the waters near the coast of Chile are mostly cold and green, the water surrounding Robinson Crusoe Island, several hundred miles from shore, are incredibly blue and clear," explains René. "You get excited just sailing over these transparent waters covering a craggy, rocky bottom." The water temperature is in the 70s, but there are no corals, tropical fish or kelp—just huge yellowtail. Chilean divers tell stories of spearing yellows over 100 pounds, and 50-pound fish are common.

René's big day did not start well. Having a cold, he had trouble clearing his ears. His gun tip had broken off a few days before, and he knew the only way he could land a fish was to shoot his headless shaft completely through the fish and toggle the shaft on the other side. René decided to make a close dive trip in a sandy bay near his boat. After several hours without seeing any fish, he swam back toward his boat anchored near some moorings and a pier.

"Looking behind me in the shallow water, I was amazed to see a midsized yellowtail following me in five feet of water," he said. "Making a shallow dive, I moved my gun under my belly and made a hip shot. The shot was good; the spear went completely through the gills and toggled on the other side. The fish made several strong runs to the bottom that I am grateful was sand-covered—it would have surely tangled in a rocky bottom. I unsheathed my knife and grabbed its gills. When my forearm was swallowed up in its huge gill plate, I realized I had a big fish." René's official American record weighed 80.5 pounds.

Marine biologist Mark Steele took his 68.3-pound North American record from the La Jolla kelp beds of California in May 1990. Shore diving, Mark entered the water by timing the mild sea swells and letting them sweep him off the rocks. Twenty minutes later, he was patrolling the outer edge of the kelp forest growing from 70 feet of water. The water was 67 degrees Fahrenheit, warm for that time of year, but the visibility was only 15 feet. He leveled off at 20 feet and watched schools of jack mackerel, streaming by and milling about aimlessly, obviously not threatened by gamefish. Finding a school of barred sand bass, the biologist in Mark took over as he observed the breeding fish at 40 feet.

"As I neared the level of the bass, I sensed motion to my right," Mark recalls.

Hugging the kelp, a big yellowtail swam directly toward me. Knowing the fish would get spooked if it sensed my gun movement, I turned my gun carefully. True to form, this fish, which appeared to weigh 40 pounds, veered sharply away. I swung the gun as fast as I could. Aiming at the disappearing fish, I calculated where it should be, compensated for the distance by aiming high and shot into the gloom. I headed for the surface as line spun from my reel. Its initial run toward open water was short lived because it returned to tangle in the kelp 60 feet below.

Adrenaline coursing through my body robbed me of valuable oxygen as I attempted to dive and assess the quality of my shot. The good news was that, even though the fish was hopelessly tangled in the kelp, my fixed spearhead (not a detachable) was wrapped up tightly so that it could not slide back through the fish. After catching my breath, I returned to dispatch the fish with a quick stab to the brain. Next, I became a human lawn mower cutting the kelp free from the bottom. I pulled the whole floating mess to the surface, where I untangled the fish. I strung the fish on my back where its five-foot body rode for the swim to the beach. Tourists asked the usual questions:

'Do you always get fish like that?'

'No, I wish I did.'

'Must've been a good day?'

'Yep!'

The best part of the day was yet to come. Mark drove to the nearby homes of California legends Jack Prodonovich and Wally Potts, whom he credits with doing more for the sport

of bluewater hunting in the United States than any other divers. "These guys helped me out when I was getting started," Mark says. "Their incredible excitement and enthusiasm for my catch was a special reward, one I'll long remember."

Right: Four-time New Zealand national spearing champion Darren Shields took this 45-kilogram (100-pound) yellowtail off East Cape, New Zealand, in January, 1993.

PHOTO BY STEVE CRABTREE

WORLD RECORDS FOR YELLOWTAIL

NEW ZEALAND	ALLAN LANGTON FEBRUARY 1974 THREE KINGS ISLAND, NEW ZEALAND	OFFICIAL 105 POUNDS 47.7 KILOGRAMS
AUSTRALIA	STEVE BRABANT AUGUST 1985 LITTLE SEAL ROCK, N S W, AUSTRALIA	OFFICIAL 94.7 POUNDS 43.00 KILOGRAMS
SOUTH AFRICA	T. SCHOEMAN 1974 SOUTH WEST AFRICA	OFFICIAL 84.6 POUNDS 38.4 KILOGRAMS
NORTH AMERICA	MARK STEELE MAY 1990 LA JOLLA, CALIFORNIA	OFFICIAL 68.3 POUNDS 31.0 KILOGRAMS

Left: René Rojas with his American record of 80.5 pounds taken from Robinson Crusoe Island off the coast of Chile.

PHOTO BY JACKIE ROJAS

*At first light, a 40-pound white seabass cruises a Channel Islands kelp bed,
60 miles off the California coast.*

Photo by Terry Maas

White seabass

California bluewater hunters prize the elusive and tasty white seabass more than any other local gamefish. Seeming to appear from nowhere, these fish require a skillful approach. The key to hunting them is learning just how close you can get before they bolt, disappearing in a blur.

The California Fish and Game Department limit is three fish daily except for the period March 15 through June 15, when the limit is one. White seabass populations have been on the decline, but there is now good news for white seabass fishermen. State and sportsmen-supported propagation and grow-out facilities, coupled with the ban on commercial nearshore gill nets, should help ensure increasing numbers of fish.

Baby white seabass live behind the surf-line in drift algae. Older fish (over 4 inches) occupy bays and shallow coastal waters. From there they mature in deeper coastal waters, usually not more than 350 feet deep. Some fish reach five feet in length and live for 20 years. A 28-inch fish (the legal length for possession) is about 5 years old. Spending the winter months hunting squid in deeper water, spawning fish move into the kelp beds between March and October. The peak months are May, June and July.

Divers usually find white seabass in and around kelp beds and in bays free of kelp and over deep-water pinnacles. Whites have even been reported many miles offshore under floating kelp paddies. They frequent kelp beds in the early morning and early evening, generally descending deeper during midday. Periods of slack current are good also because the fish tend to school higher in the water at that time. A lucky diver will sometimes find one "sleeping," its nose nestled behind a kelp stalk 10- to 45-feet deep.

One of the best locations for whites is the up-current end of a kelp bed or reef, where they can be found swimming into the current or patrolling the bluewater edge of the underlying reef. When the current changes and the kelp rises to the surface, they'll be swimming along the kelp bed toward the new up-current end. With mild current changes, they may stay at the down-current end of the kelp. Another favorite location is a bluewater opening into the kelp forest overlying a sand channel. Some specific kelp beds will have no fish in clear water with a current, but will hold fish as the current slackens and the water visibility drops below 25 feet. They are often near bait schools of mackerel, sardines and blacksmith. Catalina Island pole fishermen report that their most effective bait is blacksmith fish.

Spawning whites return to the same areas yearly, and they tend to stay there for three to four weeks. I captured their mating behavior on video; seven 20-pound silver males followed a 25-pound zebra-striped female through the kelp, taking turns rubbing against her body. Another time, 20 feet below the surface, I watched as three males swirled around a female in a shallow sand bowl. The female was probably laying her eggs.

Sometimes white seabass, members of the croaker family, make their presence known with their distinctive, deep-throated *KRAAK-------ah---ah, KRAAK-------ah---ah.* The sound tells you whites are near—the croaking will actually resonate in your chest—unfortunately it offers no directional information. Some divers attract whites by mimicking the croaking. Try two quick, deep-throated croaks—*bump-bump*—and observe the effect on the fish. If they are hunting, they may scatter; otherwise they may swim close and join you as a member of their school.

Mark Barville, who is particularly knowledgeable about white seabass hunting off Palos Verdes, California, used his finely tuned musician's ear to call in hundreds of whites weighing from 10 to 60 pounds. They circled him for minutes, the larger fish staying as close to him as the smaller fish. In the evening, when shadows block sunlight from the kelp edge, you can find them swimming slowly and croaking to attract others. If the sound becomes louder, wait motionless and they may pass in view.

Their croaking, useful in keeping the school together in dirty water and at night, conveys danger as well. Just one distressed croak from a wounded fish alerts the rest of the school, and fish within a large radius will disappear. This is an excellent reason for making a kill shot—to prevent the fish from making distress croaks. Bill Kroll, 1994 Catalina Bluewater Meet champion, once shot a white seabass that he discovered would croak when he put pressure on the fish's side. He "croaked" his fish while swimming it back to his waiting boat. The friendly sound he induced attracted a school of white seabass that followed him for minutes.

White seabass are very sensitive to sound and motion. Croaking aside, this is one fish you must hunt silently. I have seen them flee after being alerted by noisy divers clearing their ears or squeaking their fins. One very successful hunter literally creeps over the kelp forest, using only his fingers for locomotion. When you approach a kelp bed with your boat, shut off the engine and drift quietly into the bed. Let out the anchor noiselessly and avoid stomping around in the boat. Slip over the boat's side silently and avoid splashing.

How and where you hunt white seabass depends on the timing of their breeding cycle. After their winter absence, whites reappear in March and April, taking up residence in a specific kelp bed that serves as their home base. For three to four weeks this kelp bed becomes the center of their breeding activity. They might separate and stray during the day to feed, but they often regroup, especially in the early evening. Late evening and early morning are the best times to hunt white seabass because they are more curious and easier to approach. In the morning, look for "sleepers."

Later in the day, look for them cruising slowly under and around the edges of their kelp forest. White seabass hunters are often treated to breathtaking images of cathedral-like shafts of light dancing through the kelp canopy and filtering into the blue water below. For many bluewater hunters, images like this account for a successful dive even though they speared no game.

Long guns, with barrels 56 to 60 inches long, work well for white seabass because these fish move slowly and the extra length of the gun does not pose tracking problems. It does, however, offer a long shot. Hunters prefer three types of terminal gear. Many use a reel that contains at least 150 feet of line. I like a 75- to 100-foot trail line. Attach a flagged buoy for hunting at the outside edge of the kelp. Substitute a very small

streamlined buoy for use in the kelp forest. It should be small enough (egg sized) to pull easily through the kelp yet large enough to float your line.

The trick to hunting white seabass in the spring is finding the *specific* kelp bed they have settled into. Look for signs within the bed to decide where to start your diving. Birds working one end of the bed are a good sign. Look for concentrations of bait fish up-current or in kelp clearings.

There are two types of successful white-seabass fishermen: the chargers and the creepers. Al Schneppershoff was a charger, often covering a mile of coastline in less than an hour. Chargers swim quickly but silently, working the outermost 20 feet of the kelp and the bluewater edge beyond. They look for solitary sleepers under the kelp and groups of fish cruising the bluewater edge of the kelp forest. They slow when they hear croaking or when they approach a bait school. Charging is an excellent way to locate a breeding kelp bed. Once the bed is located, try creeping.

Successful creepers have the advantage of knowing that white seabass are near. Good divers are totally silent. They restrict their motion by relaxing their bodies into something like a deep-sleep state. Some become so loose that their bodies undulate like the seaweed in a passing swell. Breathing is slowed to four or six breaths per minute and is imperceptible. When they start underwater, they break the seal around their snorkel, flooding it at the surface to prevent noisy bubbles.

You should dive to the depth of the fish (15 to 40 feet) and level off, neutrally weighted. Remain suspended and motionless for about 10 seconds. Then, using the smallest fin motions, slowly swim 10 feet and stop again. Focus your eyes in the distance, and look for the first clue—usually a gill plate, a yellowish fin or a slight change in the water color. Using kelp stringers as camouflaged stopping points, repeat this slow progress through the kelp until you need to ascend. Back at the surface, advance 20 to 30 feet then start the next dive.

Mark Barville is one of the best creepers I know, and he has some interesting stories. He once found a school of sardines packed tightly into a kelp room by corralling white seabass. When he entered the kelp clearing, moving almost imperceptibly, he was immediately engulfed by the frightened sardines. Seconds later, a marauding 40-pound white seabass slammed into Mark's shoulder and then swam around facing him, as if to challenge. Another day, a white swam up and hit the end of his speargun, taking the bright spearhead into his mouth. These are exceptional encounters because many hunters consider themselves lucky just to see one or two distant fish in an entire season.

There is some controversy among successful white seabass hunters about what type of head movement is best. The purists rarely move their heads, instead using only their eyes for a lateral scan of the 180 degrees in front of them. A 360-degree scan provides the advantage of detecting fish from behind.

"I think they try to school-up with you," says veteran white seabass hunter Harry Davis. He knows that a white seabass following his fin-tips is almost impossible to shoot by turning in the water and aiming. One day, he spotted a 50-pound fish trailing about five feet from his fin-tips. Not wanting to risk turning, he aimed the gun backward, over his shoulder and, activating the trigger with his thumb, made a perfect shot.

"When you follow a white seabass, keep in mind their lateral line is very sensitive," world-record holder Skip Hellen says. "Try to track parallel to them, or fall in behind them, but do not approach them at a right angle." Successful tracking requires stealth, keen observation and a few tricks. There are two opportunities to close the gap. One occurs when the fish passes behind a large kelp stalk. Just as its eyes disappear, increase your pace or cross behind the other side of the kelp stringer and cut the fish off. The other trick again relies on the fish's head and eye position as it swims. Time a gentle increase in speed just as it rolls its head and eyes away. If the fish gives no opportunity to close the gap, try stopping dead still in the water or croaking. Many times the white seabass, sensing your speed change or hearing the croak, will turn 90 degrees and present a perfect shot.

When the visibility is poor (less than 20 feet) and if the fish spooks, stop and hang on the kelp or lie on a rock and continue aiming where it disappeared. A shining gill plate or a white tail may be the only sign that the fish has returned. Some individual fish will habitually return to the exact location from which they vanished. Return to that location in five to 10 minutes and repeat the same approach. There is a good chance it will reappear.

It takes experience to judge when a fish will bolt. Watch its tail; one gentle flick is not a problem, but a second one is generally followed by the fish's disappearance. Other indicators of a pending bolt are a flair of its dorsal fin or a double twitch of the muscles along its lateral line—as if it were "setting its spring." Long-time white seabass expert Ron Merker says he can tell a white's intent by watching its head. "When it rolls its eyes forward and its head shakes, take your shot."

Harry Davis' story of his 70-pound fish illustrates just how sensitive white seabass are. "One morning while swimming at a depth of 15 feet along a narrow dark Catalina Island kelp channel, I swam up behind the tail of a giant sleeper. There was no possibility for a successful shot without first turning the fish. After stopping 10 feet behind and at the same level as the fish, I slowly pointed the gun at its tail. I used three separate but very slight and slow gun jabs to get its attention. The fish turned sideways and presented me with an excellent profile shot."

Sometimes, when you are on the surface, white seabass will swim directly under you. Immediately dive so that you are facing along the direction that the fish is swimming, and go for a shot behind the head. If the fish is off in the distance, follow quietly on the surface. They frequently stop under bait or on the far side of a kelp stalk. Try a vertical dive behind a kelp stalk and level off in their direction. Another good approach is to angle 45 degrees away from the fish, level off out of sight, and then angle back toward it. You can dive directly down to deeper fish if you are weighted heavily enough not to have to kick the last part of the approach. Use only the slightest changes in your fin angulation to keep your path converging with the fish.

Bill Kroll uses a special approach for shallow white seabass visible from the surface. He weights himself so heavily (using an extra four to five pounds) that he is neutrally buoyant on the surface. When he exhales, he becomes negatively buoyant and starts descending. He sinks like a falling leaf with his gun outstretched and still. Bill limits these dives to 20 feet.

"Expect to feel 'lung-squeeze' and anticipate a little difficulty in overpowering your weights returning to the surface," Bill says. Obviously, the overweighted diver is at risk for shallow-water blackout because he would sink at depths of less than 15 feet. Bill says that he uses this technique only for very shallow dives of short duration and when all other approaches fail. These conditions are very unlikely to result in shallow-water blackout.

Small whites, especially fish weighing up to 15 pounds, are so quick they will roll and dodge your fired spearshaft. Spearshafts take a quarter of a second to travel 15 feet, long enough for the fish to react. When Harry Davis fired at a white seabass straight-on, the fish moved so quickly that the shaft hit it broadside. The shaft went completely through the fish and threaded it again on the other side as the fish turned yet again.

Once shot, these fish are swift and depart in a straight line. Apply enough pressure on the shooting line to pull the spear free, leaving the speartip to fight the fish. Apply suitable line pressure. Too much restraint on the line will pull the spearhead free and will turn the fish causing tangling in the kelp. Too little pressure may allow the fish to run free without tiring. A hot fish, tangled in the kelp, is easily lost because its soft flesh will not hold the spearhead.

Later in the season, August through November, white seabass become more pelagic and true bluewater fish. They are found further offshore. The kelp beds now become their hunting grounds as they patrol the outer edges or corral bait fish in tight balls inside kelp clearings. In the winter, be alert for fishermen reporting squid runs because the whites will be near. Because a winter storm changes the salinity of the water, shutting off the squid spawning in deeper water (100 feet or more), whites will move closer to shore for a few days.

Whites follow the cooler water north, preferring temperatures no warmer than 64 or 65 degrees. As the water warms in Southern California, they migrate to the northern part of their range, which includes the northern Channel Islands and the coastline from Santa Barbara to Santa Cruz. Whites in summer also tend to group more often and swim over deep-water pinnacles 60 to 80 feet deep, where the water is cooler.

Biologist Mark Steele both studies and hunts white seabass. "When the fish move outside the kelp, a very effective technique is to kneel on the bottom and move only your head to scan for fish," Mark says. "This often seems to attract fish. Other times, when they are not attracted, it will often be the only effective angle of attack. Whites don't seem to expect predators to come from beneath them, and they will frequently swim by, oblivious to you."

Yas Ikeda found his world-record 79.3-pound white seabass asleep in the kelp at Catalina Island in June 1971. Skip Hellen, current holder of the world record for white seabass at 80.5 pounds, tells how persistence paid off in the three-day hunt for his record fish.

Early in March 1994, Skip's friend Steve Leigh reported seeing some large white seabass at Palos Verdes, California. The Palos Verdes peninsula is not far from Los Angeles and is a popular destination for local bluewater divers. Its kelp beds, although approachable by boat, are most often accessed from the shore, where divers must negotiate "Cardiac Hill." The almost vertical 150-foot dirt path to the water's edge filters out all but the most serious hunters. Divers find white seabass in and around the kelp beds extending parallel to shore about 1/4 mile outside the beach.

Skip and Steve got to the water early the first day, and at 6 a.m. they swam out to the seaward edge of the outside kelp bed. Skip used a four power-band gun with 100 feet of polypropylene line attached to the end of the gun. Working his way up-current, Skip located bait at the head of the current. Three times he spotted several white seabass, but could not get close enough for a shot. The school must have drifted down-current because Steve shot a nice 38-pound fish as the school rose under him.

Skip stayed where he was for an hour, but the fish were gone. He decided to drift down-current on the outside edge of the bed. By now the current had picked up, gracefully bending the kelp stringers over, forming a waving variegated carpet 8 to 10 feet below the surface. He spotted a 5-foot white gliding just above the carpet, swimming slowly into the current. Diving toward the big fish, he watched as it veered from its course and disappeared.

"This huge fish really got my juices flowing," says Skip, who stayed in the bone-chilling water another two hours. The surface temperature of the water was 57 degrees Fahrenheit, and below the thermocline, where he was diving, it was probably five degrees colder. After six hours of steady diving, his teeth rattling from cold, Skip finished the day by spearing a 51-pound white.

Skip started day two at first light. The 40- to 50-foot visibility barely allowed him to see the bottom through the haze. He worked both the inner and outer kelp beds for three hours without seeing a fish. Swimming the inner edge of the outer kelp bed on his way back to shore, he dove, spotted another giant and watched it disappear

into the haze. This was his second big-fish sighting in as many days. Only twice before, in his 30 years of spearfishing, could Skip remember seeing white seabass so big. Skip remembers day three as the record day:

> The surf was down, but the visibility had decreased to 20 feet. I worked both the inner and outer kelp beds for about four hours, and I was getting cold and tired as I decided on one more pass through the outer kelp bed, where I'd seen the big fish the day before. Since the water was less clear, I spent less time on the surface and more time at midwater, 20 to 30 feet down.
>
> Spitting my snorkel out to prevent bubbles, I dove in the middle of the kelp bed and leveled off at 25 feet, just hazing out the bottom below. The current, strong enough to keep the bait up-current at the point of the kelp bed, laid the kelp fronds down about four feet below the surface. Swimming level, I entered a kelp room (a clear opening in the kelp). Noticing motion to my right, I watched as a huge white seabass swam a semicircular path in front of me. I made two slight kicks, just enough to propel me within range (12 to 14 feet), and I fired.
>
> The fish bolted, taking my polypropylene line in tow. My spearshaft shot completely through the big fish, and I feared the spear line might saw through its soft flesh. As the end of my gunline came into my hand, I swam in the direction of pull, applying a slight braking pressure. The white soon entangled itself in the kelp, giving me time to inflate my float and tie it to the gunline. I used my knife to dispatch the fish with a stab to its head and to cut it free from the entangling kelp. Twenty minutes later, I headed back to the beach. I knew this fish was big, but it wasn't until I tried to pull him over the rocks that I realized I might have a record.

White seabass numbers are not threatened by freedivers. We have seen gill-netters wipe out whole schools of fish. It is not uncommon for line fishermen, in one day, to take many individuals from a single school when the whites are feeding on squid. Bluewater divers are happy to take one or two fish from a school.

WORLD RECORD FOR WHITE SEABASS

NORTH AMERICA	SKIP HELLEN MARCH 1994 PALOS VERDES, CALIFORNIA	OFFICIAL 80.5 POUNDS 36.3 KILOGRAMS

Skip Hellen proudly displays the world-record white seabass he took at Palos Verdes, California, in March 1994.

PHOTO BY TOM MURRAY

Striped bass

Striped bass, commonly called "stripers," are the premier gamefish of New England. Stripers have been recorded as heavy as 125 pounds and measuring as long as five feet; any fish weighing over 50 pounds is considered a trophy. Stripers can live longer than thirty years and range from North Carolina through New England to Nova Scotia. Rhode Island, with its rugged rocky coast, deep coastal water and convergence of strong oceanic currents, is one of the most productive states for stripers.

The seasonal migration from their spawning grounds in the Chesapeake, Delaware, and Hudson bays, begins late May to early June as the water warms.

U.S. national spearfishing team champion Dave Sipperly says, "When the water temperature rises to 50 degrees Fahrenheit, the bass are in. Small 'schoolies' weighing 3 to 10 pounds, arrive first, followed by larger solitary 'cows.'"

Striped bass populations were rapidly declining in the early 1980s due to heavy commercial and recreational fishing pressure. Strict conservation measures such as a three-year fishing moratorium, increased size limits, and imposed bag limits have helped restore this species. Divers report seeing more and larger fish. Spearing stripers is legal in all New England states except Massachusetts, Connecticut and Maine. Limits are typically one fish per day, with a minimum length of 36 inches (40 inches commercial). Be sure to check the current fish and game laws.

Spearfishermen find these fish in shallow water, feeding early in the season (June, July) and swimming around offshore reefs later in the summer (August, September). Mike Laptew, a former competition diver, still spears stripers but he uses most of his energies now to capture them on video.

U. S. national spearfishing champion John Plikus with a nice catch of striped bass.

PHOTO BY DAVE SIPPERLY

Mike says, "Striped bass follow their favorite food—herring and menhaden. Look for locations that hold these important prey. They can be found at tidal flows into estuaries or breakwaters adjacent to tidal salt ponds. Such places include the mouth of the Charlestown breachway or the Pettaquamscutt River. You will find striped bass behind large boulders on each side of the river mouth. They lie in the eddies behind the boulders to rest and ambush unsuspecting bait fish passing in the current."

Later in the season, striped bass become more nocturnal in their feeding habits and congregate near deep-water reefs. Examples of good Rhode Island locations are Brenton Reef and Lands End in Newport, Beavertail Point in Jamestown, Sugar Reef and Watch Hill Reef off Westerly and the Lighthouse and the rock islands off Sakonnet Point. In New York, Montauk Point is a famous and often very productive striper hangout. These spots have in common a rough rocky bottom and pinnacles where strong currents bring up an ample supply of bait fish and dissolved oxygen. Stripers like to cruise by these rocky ledges and pinnacles. Other times, they will hug a sandy bottom, resting from the current behind small sand knolls.

The time of day and current conditions are both important. According to Dave Sipperly, the best time to hunt stripers is at dawn and dusk and preferably at high tide, when the water is slack. "I try to fish forty-five minutes before slack, the slack, and forty-five minutes after slack or until the current becomes too strong." Ideal conditions occur with the converging of slack tide either at dawn or at dusk.

Stripers can be found in depths of 5 to 60 feet, with most in the 25-foot range. For shallow-water hunting, Mike Laptew advocates learning one area well. He says, "Because of the limited visibility (10 to 15 feet), it is important to learn bottom contours and the best ambush points. This is more productive than trying several unfamiliar sites."

As they move offshore, stripers become true bluewater fish and are attracted to underwater buttes and rock pinnacles—the more prominent, the better. A good example is an area Mike has dubbed "*Striper Alley.*" With its 30-foot crown and shear edge drop-off to 80 feet, it acts like a bass magnet. Bait fish swirl above and behind the reef. Like all reefs, position is important. Find a spot on the edge of the drop-off where the bait fish congregate and orient yourself aiming out into open water. To locate these highly productive buttes, consult a local underwater survey chart and target the many deep-water pinnacles that rise to a diveable depth.

Ted Warnock, 1990 individual U.S. national spearfishing champion, holds the world record for striped bass. His 31 spearfishing seasons make him a New England expert. Ted shot his record 58-pound, 12-ounce fish in 1971. He remembers:

It was an unusual day with a rough tide. It was 3 p.m. on a bright sunny day. I swam out from Hull's Cove, Jamestown, Rhode Island, expecting to hunt a 15-foot wall. Before I reached my spot, I made a 20-foot dive. I saw a huge fish disappear into the gloom. Thinking that this probably was my only shot for the day, I continued out towards the wall. Finding my ledge, I dove and settled into the seaweed-covered bottom. I wore black, my gun was black. Motionless, I waited as suddenly a big fish came from behind me. He nearly swam in front of my gun. I shot after a slight adjustment to my aim. It was a good shot. The fish made six good runs before I could get my hands on him.

National champion Ted Warnock with the 58.75-pound striped bass he speared in 1971.

PHOTO BY RICHARD DELUCA

Mike, Dave and Ted agree on their hunting style and are constantly learning from each other. They recommend relaxing and settling to the bottom with minimal movement. Don't waste time with a dive that results in less than perfect positioning, for example, settling out away from the edge of a ledge. There are no man-made noises that will attract these fish; you must be absolutely quiet as any noise will spook them. Freeze your position and look carefully if you hear the *ba-boom* of a frightened fish as others may also be near. Water cavitation by the fish's tail is responsible for this sound which Mike says resembles a kettle drum; its sound resonates through your body.

These divers advise us to become one with the water and invisible. Make long dives on a good ambush spot; dives of one minute are adequate. Stripers are easiest to approach from below. Expect them to swim very close, but never swing your gun in their direction. Ted broke this rule twice, surprisingly landing nice fish. He discovered later that both fish suffered from cataracts, blind to his side.

Ideal gun lengths are 42 to 48 inches with two 5/8-inch rubbers and a 5/16-inch stainless steel shaft. A detachable head is also recommended. Dave Sipperly is developing a new gun combination. "In the past two years my teammates and I have successfully used a heat-treated 9/32-inch pinned shaft with a 3 inch barb, and a single 5/8-inch band. This gives us more speed, accuracy and penetration without excessive drag or reloading time."

Some divers use reels, while others prefer floats. Mike Laptew has invented an ingenious system that arrests his descent in midwater. The thick wetsuits required in the cold water compress at depth, causing an increasing negative buoyancy. Mike says, "It's easy to blast right through a school of stripers with no way of stopping without spooking the fish. I use two floats. One is a surface float for my flag. The other float is a lobster buoy tied to my weight belt with an adjustable length line. I adjust its length to the fishes' depth, for example, 30 feet. As I swim down and approach 30 feet, the smaller buoy arrests my descent nicely, allowing me to level off without excessive leg or hand movements. I can sink quietly right into the fish without scaring them."

WORLD RECORD FOR STRIPED BASS

NORTH AMERICA	TED WARNOCK	OFFICIAL
	JUNE 1971	58.75 POUNDS
	JAMESTOWN, RHODE ISLAND	26.6 KILOGRAMS

Bluewater photography

WHALE SHARK AND MANTA RAYS

The manta rays of San Benedicto love freedivers. Wild and magnificent, they become tame once you touch them. One lucky day, when the tuna were scarce, these giants came to play. Temporarily dropping my buoyed gun to the bottom, I yell to my friend and fellow bluewater hunter Bob Caruso to get his camera.

A manta ray rises under me, its jet-black body and white wingtips contrasting sharply with the brilliant blue water below. Taking a deep breath, I swim toward it. Two large remora fish, their ugly heads firmly suctioned to the ray's back on either side of its flat mouth, make perfect reins. Sensing the increased drag as I grasp the remoras' tails, this winged stallion of the seas surges forward and down, starting a giant outside loop. We're flying! Now upside down, 40 feet under, its massive body shields me from the sun. Water rushes by my ears as its great beating wings return me to the surface, where I dismount for air.

Suddenly a shark-like form appears in the indigo distance, light rays playing off its speckled back. Recognizing it as a whale shark, I wonder, 'They don't bite, or do they?' As it turns toward me, I'm relieved to see that its bearded mouth has no teeth. The 'beard' is really dozens of foot-long hitchhiking remora fish lined up under its jaw. It passes close enough for me to gently grasp its dorsal fin. Expecting either an acceleration in speed or a quick slap from its tail, I'm surprised to find that it just accepts my weight—and off we go. I hold on as long as my breath lasts. Soon it returns me to the pinnacle, where my fellow divers join the fun. Entranced, we ride these wonderful animals for hours, accumulating stories for a lifetime.

In the evening, exhausted and out of film, we move our boat the Ambar III to shelter, miles away from this magical spot. Returning the next day, we are astonished to find the whale shark and manta rays still circling the same pinnacle, welcoming us back for another day of wild rides.

Bob Caruso's image above is a beautiful composition of Terry Maas riding a manta ray, sun rays and a small fish for perspective.

PHOTO BY BOB CARUSO

Keen observers, bluewater hunters witness an amazing range of sights, from the beauty of our ocean environment to complex fish behavior, including feeding, aggression and courtship. Using either a still camera or a video recorder, we can document these scenes and our catches. The resulting images effectively bridge the comprehension gap between us and our landlubber friends, and lend credibility to the story of the "one that got away."

This chapter starts with advice from some of the best bluewater image hunters; the balance covers a simplified approach to creating top-quality still and video images.

BLUEWATER IMAGE HUNTERS

Some of the greatest bluewater hunters I know don't carry a gun. Rick Rosenthal, from Washington state, has filmed production sequences in the midst of feeding frenzies, with marlin, sailfish, tuna and sharks all trying to steal a bite. James D. Watt, from Hawaii, sometimes dives with whales, close enough to be knocked senseless by their powerful tails; other times he dives with sharks capable of chomping him in two.

James says it's important to do research before attempting bluewater photography. "Study your subject, learn where it can be found and under what conditions. Once in the water, try to descend before your subject sees you and avoid eye contact. Good freediving skills contribute more to the production of outstanding bluewater images than do photographic skills."

Californian Bill Boyce learned how to stalk bluewater species in close quarters. A biologist working aboard tuna fishing vessels for an international marine fisheries commission, his job was to report the bycatch of dolphin. Although it wasn't in his job description, he used his freediving skills to rescue dolphin from the nets. These experiences later led to a career transition, from biologist to professional photographer, and enhanced his ability to capture beautiful images on film.

Bill had the opportunity to make some interesting observations about dolphin. He literally dove in the tuna purse-seine nets as they surrounded and concentrated acres of marine life in their ever-tightening circle. Once, Bill found himself swimming with tons of tuna as the net, one-mile wide and 500-feet deep, contracted. The frantic, tightly-packed 100-pound fish buoyed him to the surface, and forced him to swim on his back to protect himself from their stiff dorsal fins, as they thrashed through the water. "When someone tells you dolphin pair and mate for life, don't believe them," he says. "More than once, in the space of minutes, I've seen a female accept the advances of up to four males."

His favorite experience was playing with dolphin babies. Arching his back and holding himself still on the surface, he mimicked the posture of several females making a "raft" as they lie packed, parallel, side to side. Creeping sideways, he eased himself next to the raft, gradually gaining the confidence of the dolphin mothers. Baby dolphin, at first braver than their mothers, would swim a circuit around the raft and through Bill's outstretched arms. Over and over, the babies repeated their swim through his hands. Sometimes mothers themselves would join in the fun, letting Bill pet them, and scratch their bellies like a friendly dog.

Australian Rob Torelli and Americans George Kuznecovs, Bob Caruso, Howard Benedict and I are just a few of the bluewater spearfishermen who augment our experiences with film. The following is a simplified approach to underwater photography suitable for the bluewater hunter, who juggling a camera in one hand and a gun in the other, needs to use the least-complicated methods available that yield acceptable images. Readers interested in learning more about this subject should read *Howard Hall's Guide to Successful Underwater Photography* (Macor Publishing, 1990) or the *Pisces Guide to Shooting Underwater Video* by Steve Rosenberg and John Ratterree (Gulf Publishing Co., 1991).

PRINCIPLES COMMON TO VIDEO AND STILL PHOTOGRAPHY

The distance between you and your subject is important for two reasons: focus and color filtration. Bluewater fish are generally far enough from the lens (more than 5 to 7 feet) that problems with focusing, common with macro (close) shots, are minimal. With the appropriate film selection, *f*-stop and shutter speed, it should be easy to preset the lens focus for a range of 5 to 12 feet. Since water distorts the focus of subjects further than 12 feet from the camera, it is not necessary to have the in-focus range set to include distances beyond 12 feet.

Color filtration increases with the length of the water column through which light travels. Include in your calculations both the distance between you and your subject *and* the distance from the subject to the surface. Warm colors, first the reds and next the yellows, are absorbed so quickly that most of our images, shot through a color-absorbing water column of more than 15 feet, are condemned to shades of blue. The light-absorbing quality of water is the same for a subject one foot away and 14 feet below the

Rick Rosenthal, freediving, films Terry Maas for the video Blue Water Hunters. *Rick's scuba gear is for emergencies or extended filming in deep water.*

PHOTO BY TOM ROSENTHAL

water as it is for a subject 14 feet away and one foot under the water.

The most colorful images are made on sunny days in shallow water with the subject next to the lens. Wide-angle lenses allow you to get close enough for quality color, yet do not cut off parts of your subject like narrower angled lenses. Be sure to rub your lens with your hand to remove small air bubbles that collect, especially just after entering the water, or encountering foamy surface water. Amber color-correction filters, by selectively blocking the blues, help restore balance to pictures shot through a long-water column. Professional photographers shun the use of these filters, preferring instead to correct their images in the lab. One disadvantage to these filters is that they block light, thus requiring the lens to open larger. This results in less depth-of-field (the range of distance that subjects will be in sharp focus). However, filters are useful in newer video housings, equipped with flip-down filters and large color monitors, making it possible for on-the-spot color correction (white balance adjustment).

External light sources, such as strobe lights for cameras and movie lights for video, are of little value to us because their maximum effective range is just 6 to 7 feet (3 meters). A water column 12 to 14 feet long (6 to 7 feet out and back) absorbs all of the external light source's colors. Because of their excessive bulk and because most gamefish do not come within effective range, bluewater divers find lights unacceptable as companion equipment to their spearfishing gear.

One way I have found to make cameras and video recorders more useful is to build a pistol grip handle with a trigger mechanism. Design your trigger to engage the shutter, or on-off switch, for instant shooting. Fabricate it from ultra-high-molecular-weight (UHMW) plastic, a material easy to form and machine. It is relatively inexpensive and has the same density as water, making weight adjustments unnecessary. Smooth rough edges with a gas torch, and blacken its white color with indelible markers. With a good handle, you become a regular "two-gun Pete," capable of carrying your speargun in one hand and your image-maker in the other.

Bluewater hunters are naturals when it comes to a steady hand and an accurate aim. It takes a little practice, however, to focus using two eyes, one over the camera on the subject, and the other through the lens. Use the same target you made for speargun practice to develop your focus and aim.

STILL PHOTOGRAPHY

The Nikonos V is the best choice for bluewater hunters because of its small size and simplicity. You can make it more versatile by fabricating a neck carrier with a rubber bungee cord and Velcro, or a weight belt holster from UHMW plastic. Remember to make anything attached to your body easy to release and remove in an emergency, such as a line tangle. Rick Rosenthal suggests darkening any shiny or bright object on your camera; this helps the camera blend in with the ocean and allows you to move closer to your subjects.

While the 35-millimeter lens that comes with the camera is good for images shot at distances

This camera is equipped with a left hand-hold and trigger fabricated from UHMW plastic. Divers can hold it in their left hand and shoot their gun with the right.

greater than 10 feet, the length of the water column washes out most color. Using a wider angle lens lets you get much closer to your subject, decreasing the water column and increasing color. Both the 28-millimeter and 15-millimeter lenses work well. The 15-millimeter lens allows you to shoot within the closest range, but it is a very expensive lens ($800 to $1,500). The more reasonable 28-millimeter lens is the best choice for beginners because of its versatility and price (about $300). Prefocus, set the depth-of-field and leave it alone.

More than 90 percent of the best images, dependent on natural light, are made aiming up, toward the surface, at a slight angle. This offers a beautifully variegated background and the chance for enhancing rays of light to stream through the image. Look for composition; a small fish in the frame enhances the quality of the image by adding perspective, both in size and distance. (See Bob Caruso's manta ray picture on the previous page.) Don't forget the trick of making a speared fish appear bigger by positioning it closer to the lens than its captor.

To beginning bluewater photographers, experts suggest this approach: for level, or upward shots, shoot at a speed of 1/60-second. Shoot at 1/30-second when pointing down. Use 100 ASA film or faster. Film selection is based on experience. James Watt suggests using Kodachrome 64 for water that is more blue than green, and Fujichrome Provia for water more green than blue. In low-light conditions, without a flash, try Kodak's Ektachrome Lumiere 100, setting the ASA to 200 on the camera. Be sure to tell the developer to "push" the film one stop. All of the films mentioned produce slide transparencies preferred by professionals who project their work or expect to sell it to magazines. Beginners who want snapshots for their friends, might consider using print film, which offers greater latitude in colors and exposure settings.

Make most of your adjustments using the *f*-stop feature on the camera. With lots of available light, use settings of *f*/8 or *f*/11. As the light decreases, use *f*/5.6 or *f*/4. Remember, as you lower the *f*-stop the depth-of-field is decreased, making your focus and distance estimating critical. The *f*-stop setting also effects the "sun ball" visible in the background when you shoot upward; the lower the *f*-stop, the larger the ball (the *f*/4 ball is huge). If you have some doubt about your settings, err on the side of underexposure (*f*/8 or higher). A photo lab can do a lot more with an underexposed image than it can with a burned-out, overexposed one.

Bill Boyce suggests setting your *f*-stop, shutter speed and focus in advance; then leave them alone and be patient. Wait for your subject to become centered and within the focus range. Make a few well-composed shots rather than many sloppy ones. Panning shots, for moving fish, should be taken as if you are skeet shooting. Pan at the same speed your subject is moving. Keep panning as you squeeze the shutter, and

continue following your subject for a few seconds after you shoot. The best way to get good sun-ray pictures is to use speeds 1/125 or faster.

VIDEO RECORDING

According to Rick Rosenthal, one major advantage video recorders have over movie cameras—besides expense—is that they're quiet. Their virtually silent recording mechanisms allow you to get closer to shy bluewater subjects than do more noisy film cameras. Another advantage video recorders have is their ability to capture images in very low-light situations. This ability, termed "low-lux," provides for images impossible to capture with conventional film cameras. As the light decreases, expect the images to become more grainy and monochromatic.

The best video images are taken in water no deeper that 35 feet. Under ideal conditions, when there is full sunlight shining straight down into very clear water, this depth can extend to 50 feet. Try to aim horizontally or down, and keep the sun at your back. For crisp images use shutter speeds of 1/125 to 1/250 in shallow, clear water. When the water is dirty or deep, or the sun is behind clouds or at a low angle, place the shutter-speed setting on "auto."

Let's examine the equipment first. The most popular video recorders for underwater image making use the small, yet clear, Hi-8 format. Manufacturers are constantly improving video cameras and their housings. Using less power and equipped with long-life batteries, the Sony TR series of video recorders operate for an average of two hours. An improved auto-focus feature decreases "hunting," which is the transient in-and-out lens motion of the electronic circuitry focusing on an image. The Sony's modest size permits a small housing, which leads to increased maneuverability.

One of the finest video housings is the Stingray, manufactured by Light and Motion Industries. Its small size, superior optics, electronic controls,

Left: The compact and versatile Stingray housing is ideal for bluewater video recording.
Right: A video recorder mounts to the docking plate that makes all electronic connections.

expertly crafted seals and locking mechanisms make this a versatile and reliable housing for the bluewater hunter. With just three housing penetrations, one for the back plate, one for the lens and one for the flip-down color filter, the number of possible water leakage points is minimal. Compared to other housings, camera installation is simple. All cable connections are made from the camera to a docking plate outside the housing, where big fingers are no problem. The whole assembly is inserted into the housing, which receives the electronic connections from the docking plate, much like plugging in an electrical outlet. For purposes of illustration, I'll highlight each aspect of video recording and relate it to a specific feature available on the Stingray.

Focusing is easy for the bluewater hunter unconcerned with close-up images. The 90-degree, optically correct lens is unique among other housings because of its ability to maintain focus throughout the full zoom range. For fixed-distance subjects, set the focus once and zoom away.

Should you use the auto-focus feature of the video recorder? The answer depends on light conditions, the subject and your experience with the camera. I prefer to use the auto-focus mode to "snap to focus" on my subject and once focused, disable the auto-focus, leaving the camera fix-focused in the manual mode. Leaving the recorder set in the auto-focus mode risks the possibility of the electronic circuitry temporarily losing focus and "hunting" as it adjusts in and out in an attempt to recapture the correct focus. The resulting image is blurry and ruins the sequence. Auto-focus circuitry becomes more dependable in highly illuminated, clean water and less reliable in poorly illuminated, dirty water. The auto-focus feature provides a definite advantage for filming subjects that continually and rapidly change their distance from your lens, such as a fish swimming toward you.

Use the Stingray's 3-inch color monitor to accurately compose your shot, monitor color reproduction (white balance) and check the displayed camera functions. View the monitor with the recorder held relaxed ahead of your chest, instead of close up against your eye. The advantage of arms-length viewing is that you can see your target easily, over the camera, thus simplifying adjustments to your aim. Do not use it for focus as your eye cannot accurately judge fine-focus through the monitor.

Left: An image of a sailfish taken from one frame of a video sequence.

VIDEO BY TERRY MAAS

White balance is the setting responsible for the correct representation of color. It's usually set at "sunlight" or "auto," but you can experiment with the proper setting while shooting. Professionals set white balance with a white slate they carry; viewing the slate for five seconds through the lens sets the electronics.

Another way to adjust color is to use the Stingray's nifty flip-down color-correction filter hinged *inside* the camera housing. Use it to restore red and yellow colors when shooting through a water column more than 15 feet long. The filter is most effective when light is plentiful for example, clear tropical waters between the hours of 10 a.m. and 3 p.m. The filter will help to restore warm colors in both a turbid water column of up to 20 feet and a clean water column of up to 50 feet. Check the filter's effect in the monitor; setting the white balance to "sunlight" may introduce a red hue to the image, especially near the surface.

One problem common to all currently available housings is their limited space for batteries. The extended two-hour operating time is still short. Bluewater hunters, spending so much time in the water, will find it inconvenient to return to their boat or to shore to change video recorder batteries.

IMAGE PROCESSING—NOW AND IN THE FUTURE

The illustrations on the left demonstrate some imaging and editing capabilities currently available. The top picture is a "video grab" derived from the analog signal of a video recording I made off Costa Rica. Because the videorecorder shoots 30 frames per second, the number of potential images are astounding. The lower illustrations show how Howard Benedict's excellent photograph of my bluefin tuna was enhanced and retouched by Vance Carriere for the cover of this book. Using his computer and a popular photo-enhancing program, Vance separated the background from the diver and from the fish, providing them both with more contrast. The gun slung over the diver's shoulder was removed and a fintip was added.

The future of underwater imaging is exciting. The promise of electronic storage cubes, capable of holding thousands of images in a small three-dimensional format, may make videotape obsolete. There will be no more lost time in the warm-up period (several seconds) as the tape starts moving. Each of the 30 frames-per-second will approach 35-millimeter quality, making an unlimited number of high quality plates possible.

The advent of digital storage of images and digital editing will make enhancing your images easy. Marginal pictures will be converted to masterpieces. The art of original photography will be the primary casualty of this digital revolution. Virtually any image can be enhanced or changed—you will not be able to distinguish the differences. Enjoy the images you see today—they are the last of the originals.

Whether by film or video, capturing images of your bluewater experiences helps them last a lifetime. Share them with your friends and educate them about your sport. The creativity and challenge of underwater photography are addicting. No doubt some of you will find yourself shooting more pictures than fish.

The photograph on the left is the original. The image on the right was digitally enhanced for the cover of this book. The speargun over the diver's shoulder was removed, a fin-tip and bluewater were added and the contrast between the diver and the water was increased.

PHOTO BY HOWARD BENEDICT

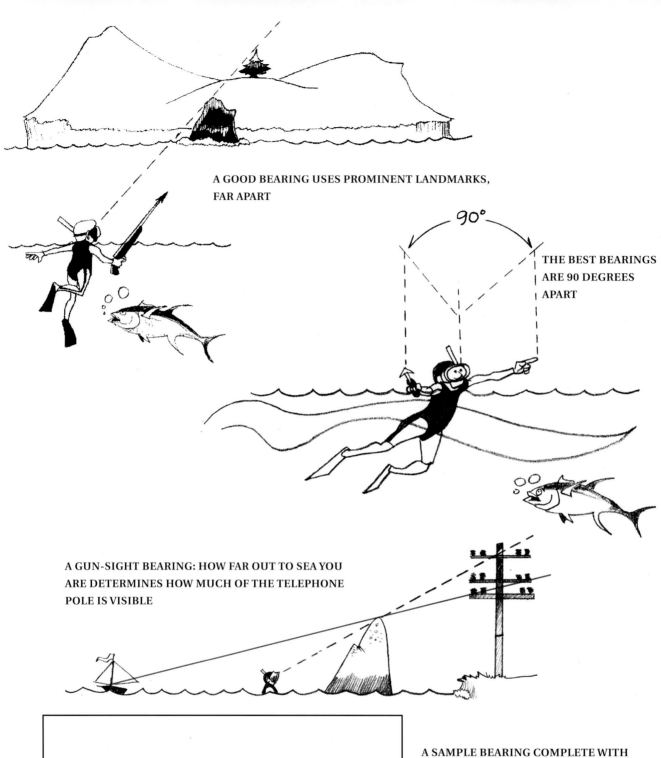

A GOOD BEARING USES PROMINENT LANDMARKS, FAR APART

THE BEST BEARINGS ARE 90 DEGREES APART

A GUN-SIGHT BEARING: HOW FAR OUT TO SEA YOU ARE DETERMINES HOW MUCH OF THE TELEPHONE POLE IS VISIBLE

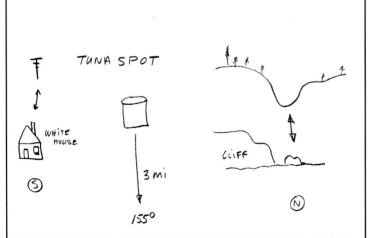

TUNA SPOT

WHITE HOUSE

3 mi

155°

CLIFF

A SAMPLE BEARING COMPLETE WITH A GENERAL LOCATION BEARING— THREE MILES STRAIGHT OUT FROM A WATER TOWER AT 155 DEGREES

SOUTH, THE CHIMNEY OF A WHITE HOUSE LINES UP WITH A TELEPHONE POLE. NORTH, A WASH ROCK LINES UP WITH A PROMINENT DIP IN THE HILL BEHIND

APPENDIX I

Reference bearings

Since many good bluewater fishing spots are located over a specific pinnacle or reef, relocating them is a good reason to learn and use bearings. Simply defined, a bearing is a straight line connecting two points. While the GPS (global positioning system) coupled with a depth sounder will return you to your favorite location, good reference bearings are more accurate and repeatable and will help you identify and maintain your position over the bottom when you cannot see the bottom.

Many good bluewater hunting locations are subject to strong currents that ebb and flow throughout the day. Without a reliable location reference, it is easy to drift far off your hot spot in just a few minutes. Good bearings can even help you estimate the direction and strength of the current. The bearing line is used as a location reference. Some bearings are so accurate that you can relocate a single rock a mile offshore, while others, many miles from land, are good if they get you within a quarter-mile of your spot.

Shore bearings provide excellent position orientation when adequate land references are available. The best bearing is made between two easily recognizable structures located far apart. A good example would be the sharp edge of a surf-side rock that lines up with a tree on a distant hill top.

Choose your bearing landmarks carefully. Avoid motor homes that may drive away and bushes that grow or die back. Cliffs, mountain tops and the edges of rocks or pinnacles all work well. Be sure to look at these landmarks during different times of the day. A cliff edge, very distinct in the morning, might disappear in the midday sun.

Check the bearing for accuracy by swimming to the right and left of your position and observe changes in the position of the landmarks. Select another landmark if there is no relative movement between them because they will be inaccurate.

Two good bearings, 90 degrees apart, will pinpoint any underwater location. A good method for establishing a second 90-degree bearing is to position your arms away from your body at 90 degrees. Alternating right and left sides, line one arm up with the established bearing and sight down the other arm for the location of the second bearing. Many times a second bearing, 90 degrees from the first, is not available. A second bearing at another angle (45 degrees to 135 degrees) is still useful if it provides good relative movement between landmarks while moving in on the first bearing.

Sometimes only one bearing is available; in that case look for a "gun-sight bearing." A "gun-sight bearing" is a single bearing capable of providing both your location along a straight line and the distance from shore. Distance is estimated by using vertical references on the two landmarks. The farthest point becomes more or less exposed depending on the distance out to sea. These bearings suffer some inaccuracy, but they are much better than a single line.

Some bearings do not come into view until you are very close to them, making them difficult to re-find. In this case, make a general bearing to help you get into the area where the specific bearings can be seen. A compass bearing to a prominent landmark works well for a general bearing, or use a GPS fix. When it seems impossible to find good movement between landmarks, try using binoculars (seven power maximum.)

"There is nothing more maddening than to be unable to locate your dive spot because you forgot the bearings," Harry Davis says. "Be methodical about recording all information. Take notes, photographs or videotapes and transcribe the information later into a permanent book." Video recordings and photographs provide good bearing data and, unlike scribbled notes, are not subject to misinterpretation.

Your anchored boat or buoy makes a good temporary reference when the shore is neither visible nor useful for bearings. With experience you can maintain your position accurately by judging your angle and distance from the boat. If land is visible, sometimes you can use the boat as kind of a floating landmark and line it up with objects on the shore. Be sure to anticipate shifts in the wind and/or current that will change your position relative to the boat. Adding a second, separately anchored buoy about 200 feet away from the first makes an excellent reference for temporary bearings. Line them up like shore bearings or maintain their relative relationship for good position awareness.

Sometimes you will come across another boat anchored on a spot that looks like it might be good. There is a way to get precise bearings of their location without disturbing them. Simply position your boat outside the other and find a suitable bearing that lines up with their boat. Move your boat and find another bearing as close as possible to 90 degrees to the first one.

APPENDIX II

Currents

Two types of currents, oceanic and local, are important to bluewater hunters because of their profound effect on the day's diving conditions. Large oceanic currents, meandering offshore, sometimes bring exotic fish within reach. Local currents, whether driven by the tides or winds, or both, may become strong enough to vanquish the strongest swimmer among us, literally blowing us off our spot.

Good examples of oceanic currents are the Gulf Stream off the east coast of the United States, the California Current off the west coast, the Mozambique Current off the east coast of South Africa, the East Australian Oceanic Current off the east coast of Australia and the Leuwin Current off west Australia. With the exception of the cold California Current, they are welcome occurrences for bluewater divers, generally bringing in clear, warm water, loaded with exotic fish.

These currents frequently arrive with the seasons. The Gulf Stream for instance, brings warm-water fish close to shore in the summer. It influences much of the east coast as it advances from Florida northward. Sometimes, with careful observation of the weather, it is possible to predict the meandering of currents like these. Typically a strong, steady onshore wind of several days duration will bring these currents close enough for bluewater hunters to enjoy the riches they bear.

Most of our best bluewater locations are also subject to local currents, which bring in nutrients and bait. Fishing conditions are generally best when local currents are mild to moderately strong. Some locations become lifeless in slack current, while others become impossible to dive when the current is running at full strength. Tide changes during the night do not directly influence our ability to swim, but they do affect water visibility. Very high tides can wash dirt and silt from the shore, increasing suspended matter and reducing visibility. The prediction of these currents, both night and day, allows us to plan our diving trips for the best days.

Harry Davis and I independently studied the effects of the tides on the currents surrounding Santa Barbara Island, one of the Channel Islands of Southern California. After correlating hundreds of current observations with graphic tide tables, we are now able to predict the direction and the magnitude of the currents about three-quarters of the time. Listed below, in descending order of importance, are the major factors influencing local currents at the island.

1. Direction of tidal change—high to low, or low to high.
2. Magnitude of tidal change, measured in feet of water moved per hour.
3. Location of dive site on the island.
4. Tide reversal—a small tide change between larger changes.
5. Prevailing oceanic currents, in this case the California current.
6. The wind.

In most cases, the currents are weakest when the net tidal change is from high to low (Figure A, Examples 1 and 2). When the net change is from low to high, expect strong currents (Figure A, Examples 4and 5). We feel that the prevailing oceanic current opposes and cancels an outgoing tide resulting in less local current, and augments an incoming tide resulting in more local current.

In general, expect more current on days when the magnitude of the tide change is large. This is especially true for incoming tides. Estimate the magnitude by dividing the number of feet of tide change by the number of hours during which the change takes place.

While the net trend of tidal change is important, a significant reversal in the tide's direction, can offset the trend (Figure A, Example 4). To get an idea of how these local currents work, imagine a jar of molasses superimposed over the graphical representation of currents available on tide calendars (Figure A). When you tip the jar of molasses, the fluid takes some time to start moving; once started however, it gains momentum. Tipping the jar in the opposite direction does not immediately change the direction of flow; it takes a while to overcome the initial momentum. The steeper the graph, the faster the molasses moves. The flatter the graph, the slower the molasses moves. This seems obvious for simple tide changes with a strong trend (Figure A, Example 2). However, the molasses analogy helps most when we consider the effects of tide reversals on tide trends.

A trend is a tidal flow, over several periods, which peaks to high or low. It might contain a small intervening opposite tide—a tide reversal (Figure A, Examples 1, 3, 4 and 5). A trend allows the molasses to build momentum, and a small reversal will do little to overcome its initial momentum. It works the same with the currents; with a large tide trend and a small reversal, expect a strong current (Figure A, Example 5). A strong reversal, on the other hand, will tip the jar of molasses in the opposite direction enough to slow the trend; in this case, expect a weaker current (Figure A, Example 4). At the end of a trend, expect a change in both the direction and force of the local current.

Your position on the island is very important. Some locations close to the island are shielded from the current, whereas others are affected by eddy currents (described later). Other locations, far from shore, are less affected by local geography and more affected by open-ocean trends. It's not uncommon to dive one area in relative calm when at the same time, currents a mile away make diving from an anchored boat impossible.

Two factors that are unrelated to the tides are wind-generated currents and large oceanic currents. Several days of strong, steady winds can create a significant but transient surface current. Such currents promote up-wellings of cold, sub-surface, nutrient-laden water that encourages

195

SANTA BARBARA ISLAND TIDAL CURRENTS

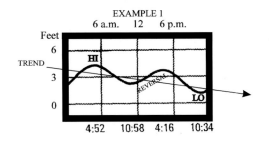

This is as good as it gets. The small outgoing trend (high to low), broken by a small reversal, makes the most favorable conditions. Expect minimal currents.

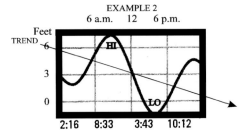

This will be a good day. Even though a large amount of water moves and there is no reversal, the net outgoing trend is good.

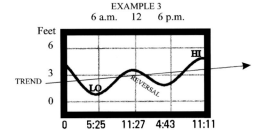

Expect light to moderate currents all day, slowing slightly at 11:27a.m. The trend is slightly incoming.

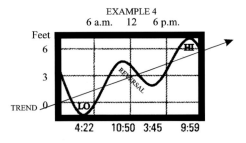

Expect moderate to heavy currents. The midday reversal will slow the current slightly. The incoming trend is large.

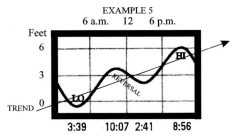

This will be a strong current day—stay home or plan to use a "live boat." The small reversal will do nothing to counter the large incoming trend.

Figure A

visibility-destroying plankton blooms. The California Current, flowing down the coast, changes in direction and force. It is unpredictable and is probably the wild card responsible for our missed predictions.

Figure A summarizes our observations for Santa Barbara Island. While these observations are specific to this island, I have found them to be accurate for other Mexican Pacific Islands, far to the south. You probably will not be able to predict your local currents by using the specifics we use for Santa Barbara Island, but using the same factors we identify, and your own careful observations, you should be able to develop an adequate current-prediction model. Currents from one direction might bring in the fish, while currents from another might kill your spot. Predicting your local currents accurately is a great time saver and allows you to plan vacations with confidence.

Local geographic structures have an important impact on currents, sometimes allowing the clever bluewater diver to remain in conditions that cause others to throw in the towel. Look at the bait fish in strong currents. They know where the least current is. The water above and down-current from a subsurface pinnacle will flow faster than the bait fish prefer. Instead, you will find them bunched at the up-current side of the rock.

Water driven by the currents acts exactly like water flowing over a rock in a stream; it gets forced upward before it flows over a pinnacle or high reef. This temporary upward deflection slows the current considerably. I have seen divers kicking for half-an-hour with maximal effort to swim just 50 feet over the top of a pinnacle. Their reward was reaching the slower water in front, where they could rest and maintain their position using much less effort.

Diving along a current-swept wall offers another opportunity to find favorable eddy currents (light currents flowing in the opposite direction of the strong prevailing current). Many times the area just ahead of, or behind, a small prominence projecting from a wall will offer a rest from the current and a place to ambush unsuspecting bluewater species. Larger points or prominences will create strong eddy currents. Try making a circuit by following the eddy currents against the main current, and then joining the main current for a ride back.

Eddy currents are curious; while the strength of most simply varies directly with the intensity of the current spawning them, others develop only in the strongest of currents.

In 1974, Bill Ernst, John Ernst and I won the U.S. national spearfishing team championships in large part because of our understanding of these eddy currents. Brenton's Reef off Rhode Island is almost impossible to dive in a moderate current. During a strong current, however, special eddy currents develop. We identified these unique eddies exactly one month before the meet. (The tides at any given location are very similar to the tides at the same location 28 days later.) We used these relatively calm eddy currents to spear fish from the 6-knot current, just 6 feet away, when everyone else found it almost impossible to dive.

Record and study your local conditions and you will soon develop enough knowledge about the effect of the tides and local weather on the currents to confidently choose the best days for a diving trip or vacation.

APPENDIX III

Deep diving

This discussion on deep diving appears in the appendix because the ability to do so is not a prerequisite for successful bluewater hunting and because the risk of shallow-water blackout increases with each deep dive. Experts consider dives in excess of 60 to 80 feet to be deep. In most cases, dives are from 1½ to 2 minutes. Many successful bluewater hunters rarely dive deeper than 30 feet. Everyone agrees that a deep-diving freediver must be attended by a safety diver. Recall Tommy Botha's rescue of Gyula Plagiani in the chapter on survival.

If it is so dangerous, why dive deep? Because sometimes the only available fish are found in deep water. Additionally, many deep-diving techniques apply to freediving regardless of the depth; consequently, deep-diving training will broaden your freediving skills. For this discussion, I draw heavily on the knowledge of three well-known bluewater hunters. Carl Butler from the U.S. Virgin Islands holds many North American records for gamefish. Dave Sipperly, a member of the 1993 U.S. national spearfishing champion team, teaches advanced scuba and freediving. Australian 1989 National Spearfishing Champion, Greg Pickering, introduced earlier, learned deep-diving techniques by trial and error. Despite the geographic gulf between these divers, their approaches to the subject are very similar.

Deep divers never hyperventilate rapidly. Instead, they take long, slow, deep breaths without forced inhalation. Their breathing rate averages about six to eight breaths per minute, which is about half of their normal resting rate. All agree that in order to dive deep you must be relaxed.

"I relax my mind as well as my body," Carl Butler says. "I developed my own style of 'soaring' down to the depths. I kick down to my negative depth, relax every muscle in my body and begin to soar. Dropping a shoulder or feathering a fin is all that's required to manage changes in direction. Looking forward, by extending my neck, causes the muscles in my back to tense and contributes to a feeling of air hunger. Returning my head to its neutral position always made this feeling disappear.

"Practicing total relaxation helps me enjoy the ocean more. Learning to manipulate buoyancy and pressure makes me feel as if the ocean is holding me with her support—something I can rely on. When you realize that you are not fighting her anymore, you become a better diver."

Self-taught deep-diver Greg Pickering has made documented dives to 135 feet. "The key to deep diving is relaxing, staying warm and practicing," he says. On poor visibility days, unsuitable for spearfishing, Greg makes 60- to 80-foot practice dives, lies on the sand for 1 minute, then returns to the surface, resting for 3 minutes. He repeats this sequence for hours. Other days, he practices in the pool, swimming laps underwater. His goal is a rapid return of his resting heart rate, which he monitors with a hand on his chest; when his rate slows, he's ready to dive. The time required to recover varies with the depth of the dive—3 minutes for 70 feet and 5 to 7 minutes for dives in excess of 100 feet. A common limitation to prolonged periods of deep diving is cold intolerance. Striving to relax, deep divers slow their heat-generating metabolic processes and eventually get cold. This diminishes their bottom time.

Dave Sipperly, who studies deep divers, emphasizes efficiency in the water column. "Deep divers do everything possible to conserve oxygen while keeping their drag profile down," he says. He recommends a slow, one-legged pike-dive to start the descent. "Kick smoothly, reduce your drag area by keeping your legs as close together as possible. Use your calf and ankle muscles, and then fall into a negative descent, kicking only when necessary to keep up your momentum." While some divers find that closing their eyes relaxes them and slows their heart, Dave keeps his eyes open, alert for game. To conserve valuable oxygen, he does not swim after deep fish, but relies instead on their natural curiosity to bring them within range.

Conserve energy by making smooth ascents, using a slow kick; a fast, panicked swim only increases the chances of blackout. Dropping your shoulders and folding your hands at your groin cuts down the excessive drag that squared shoulders present.

Deep divers modify both the physical aspects of their gear and the way they use it. Masks are designed to decrease internal air volume. As divers descend, water pressure squeezes the mask to their face. It takes valuable air, forced into the mask, to equalize outside pressure and decrease this squeeze. By using rubber or silicone inserts to fill any area of your mask not required for vision, you can greatly decrease air lost to equalization.

Removing weight from your belt is important for three reasons. At depth, compression of your wetsuit and lungs requires less weight to offset your decreased buoyancy. Less weight makes both swimming at depth and ascent easier. However, the greatest benefit of a light weight belt is that you will reach your neutral point earlier and become buoyant deeper—an important consideration for the survival of shallow-water blackout. Divers sometimes use 8 to 10 pounds of ballast, intended for release on the bottom and for recovery later, to help them reach a fish or an anchor. In any case, don't forget to release your weight belt at the first sign of trouble.

Rubber-powered spearguns are preferred to pneumatic guns, which lose their punch as the depth increases. A trail line makes recovery of your gun easy, and hopefully, you will be less hesitant about leaving it in midwater if an air problem arises. Use a trail line that develops less drag than a reel, and don't be afraid to release your gun along with your weight belt if there is doubt about reaching the surface conscious.

"Spearguns are a major source of drag," says Dave. "Keep your gun close to your body, and hold it at the handle, or at the muzzle, with a loose comfortable grip. It is common for uncomfortable divers to hold their gun tightly—another cause of oxygen loss. This method feels a little awkward at first, but it is quickly mastered."

An unexpected hazard for very deep divers with long endurance is decompression sickness, commonly referred to as the bends. Polynesian commercial breath-hold pearl divers sometimes become afflicted with a variant of this disease known as the "staggers," characterized by difficulty in walking. Some physicians think that "micro-hits" of nitrogen bubbles to the nervous system build in a cumulative fashion, leading to this progressive disability.

South African Edward Hayman, a 23-year-old bluewater diver, survived a white shark attack to his foot, and later became a truly deep diver. After diving a five-hour international spearfishing contest in 1994 off False Bay, South Africa, he developed a documented case of the bends. During the contest, he spent the first-half hour diving to 20 meters in the 4-meter-visibility water. Lured into the clearer water below, he dove the remaining four-and-a-half hours into depths of 20 to 30 meters. "I felt no pain, nor did I feel the need to stop diving," he recalls.

Six hours after the meet, Edward's speech started to slur and his handwriting deteriorated. Very tired, he went to bed early, only to awake the next day still tired with increasing problems in speech, writing and now walking. He was unsteady on his feet and his leg muscles twitched uncontrollably. Reporting to the hospital, a provisional diagnosis of the bends was made and immediate hyperbaric and drug therapy was started. After seven hours in the hyperbaric oxygen pressure chamber, most of his symptoms disappeared. An MRI brain scan confirmed a central nervous system hit (an area of the brain suffering a decrease in oxygen supply caused by nitrogen-bubble pressure on the blood vessels). After two weeks of hyperbaric oxygen therapy and after weaning from his medications, Edward recovered.

Edward's physician, Major G. Van Niekerk, did a marvelous job of treatment and follow-up documentation. "Mr. Hayman spent 50 minutes at depths exceeding 20 meters," Dr. Van Niekerk writes in Hayman's medical records. "This is at least 10 minutes longer than the U.S. Navy no-decompression limits for diving with compressed air." In further discussion, Dr. Van Niekerk pointed out that the first documented case of the bends resulting from freediving was published by Professor Paulev (*Journal of Applied Physiology*, 1965, 20; 1028–1031), who developed the bends from doing "bottom drops" to 20 meters. As a medical officer in a submarine escape training tank, he had made 60 freedives over a five-hour period, each dive lasting 2 1/2 minutes.

In Edward's records, Dr. Van Niekerk suggests a three-point strategy to help freedivers prevent the bends. "An objective guideline would be to ensure that the total dive time does not exceed the no-decompression limits for compressed-air diving, even though it is known that repeated ascents while diving with compressed air increases the risk of developing the bends. Adequate hydration—the intake of 250 to 300 milliliters of fluid every hour—should be mandatory. Overall better record-keeping of dive profiles by surface support personnel will lead to a better understanding of the problem and its scope."

APPENDIX IV

World-record rules

Up from the depths comes a huge steel-grey tube scattering bait fish in its wake. It's almost within range when you recognize it as the largest fish you've ever seen—possibly a world record. You shoot. As the fish rockets into the depths you wonder what you must do to preserve this catch as a world record.

Your first thought must be safety. The blue water is deep, dangerous and filled with powerful fish capable of drowning you in a line tangle, or maiming you in an attack. Your potential record might tow you into an offshore current or out to sea at night. Only when you satisfy this safety requirement should you consider your actions to preserve your record.

With the astounding increase in awareness of bluewater hunting as a separate and bona fide sport worldwide came the realization that while many countries have functioning organizations for their national records, there is no international organization dedicated to bluewater records.

An international group agreed to formulate an organization for the certification of world records—the IBSRC. Two main goals emerged. The first goal was to establish a committee to evaluate each country's historical records and combine them into a worldwide registry. Eligible fish are bluewater species such as tuna, marlin, wahoo and sailfish. To keep the committee international, these species must be available to divers on more than one continent, thus yellowtail (kingfish) made the list but white seabass (mulloway) did not.

The other goal was to establish and publicize a set of rules by which future records would be judged. These rules stress safety and provide specific criteria for performance. Basically, the rules call for the catch to be made independently and unassisted. Because bluewater hunting is inherently dangerous and safety problems such as shark attack, nightfall, fatigue, etc. might prevent one from meeting the record criteria, the late Bill Kroll recommended a special award for those meeting all the criteria for a record but for one safety-related infraction. Such near-record catches are recognized by a separate and prestigious class of Meritorious Awards. Meritorious Awards are also available for outstanding catches that while not world records are still noteworthy.

Since the Underwater Society of America (USOA) has a functioning non-profit organization in place with goals similar to the International Bluewater Spearfishing Records Committee (IBSRC), it was approached to sponsor the committee. With the enthusiastic support of the USOA, the committee soon grew to 33 governing members. In keeping with its goal as a truly international organization, members include recognized bluewater divers from such countries as Australia (6), New Zealand (2), Greece (2), South Africa (2) Brazil (1) England (1) Mexico (1) and France (2).

International Bluewater Spearfishing Records Committee (IBSRC)

The mission of The International Bluewater Spearfishing Records Committee (IBSRC) is to promote ethical, safe and sporting spearfishing practices, to establish uniform regulations for the compilation of world-bluewater gamefish records, and to provide basic spearfishing guidelines for use in bluewater contests and any other bluewater spearfishing activities worldwide.

RULES

The words "Bluewater spearfishing" are defined as capturing, or attempting to capture, with a muscle-powered speargun, while breath-holding and submerged, wild edible bluewater gamefish species. There are some aspects of this activity that cannot be controlled through rule making, however. Bluewater spearfishing regulations cannot insure an outstanding performance from each fish, and world records cannot indicate the amount of difficulty in capturing fish. Captures in which the fish is not truly wild do not reflect credit on the bluewater freediver. Only the individual spearfisher can properly evaluate the degree of achievement in establishing the record.

Only fish caught in accordance with IBSRC rules, and within the context of these rules, will be considered for world records. The general concept is: Breath-holding divers, using muscle-powered spearguns, must spear and subdue their wild bluewater catch unassisted. They will make every effort to land their catch once speared. Each application will be reviewed by the certification subcommittee. Committee members cannot vote on a record they possess, or in which they have a commercial interest .

CLASSES OF AWARDS

1. WORLD RECORDS:

a. For a period of one year after certification of the committee by the Underwater Society of America, the IBSRC will publish in several worldwide spearfishing publications, its rules and an invitation to submit past records for certification.

b. Current records from such organizations as the Australian Underwater Federation, South African Spearfishing Federation, IUSA and Underwater Society of America, or any organization with similar record rules or standards, will be considered valid.

c. Future records will be awarded in conformance with the rules of the IBSRC.

d. Records will be maintained for men and women.

2. MERITORIOUS AWARDS:

From time to time the IBSRC will award a meritorious award to an individual who makes an unusual catch of a listed or an unlisted species. Examples: (1) An unusual fish; (2) or a fish very close to an existing record considered, due to its extreme size, unlikely to match the current record; or (3) a record-weight fish which but for one rule infraction would otherwise become an official world record.

GENERAL REGULATIONS

Divers must be completely submerged when they fire their gun.

Divers must remain in the water and unassisted until their fish is subdued.

Divers must retain contact with their float and/or line at all times. If they lose contact with their gear, they must find it and reestablish contact with it unassisted and while remaining in the water.

While potentially dangerous, the use of chum or burley or flashers is allowed provided, however, that with the use of chum, divers make and distribute it themselves in the water unassisted (fish used for this purpose must be shot by the diver using it), or in the case of flashers, they carry it themselves unassisted.

Fish must be free-swimming, not restricted by nets, traps, fishing lines or other devices.

Recently tagged gamefish, still exhausted from their recent capture, are ineligible.

Fish must not be in an artificial environment such as penned-in bays, or in close proximity to fish nets, fish rearing pens or sanctuaries.

The catch must not be at variance with any laws or regulations governing the species or the waters in which the fish was caught.

A buddy diver may provide a second or additional unloaded gun to the spearfisher, provided he/she does not assist the diver in any way to subdue their catch.

In most cases mutilated fish, depending on the circumstances, are not allowed.

The use of artificial light sources for night spearfishing is not allowed.

DEFINITIONS

Subdued fish: Any fish taken ashore, or tethered to a boat with a line no more than 3 meters long.

Mutilated fish: Any unhealthy fish. Examples: a fish which is weakened by being previously speared, or attacked by sharks, or injured by commercial or recreational fishing processes (a recently caught and tagged marlin).

Sanctuary: An area in the ocean, protected by governmental decree, where the hunting of certain bluewater species is prohibited.

Muscle-powered speargun: Any speargun that stores potential energy provided from the spearfisher's muscles only. The gun may only release that amount of energy that the diver has provided to it from his/her own muscles. Common temporary energy-storing sources for spearguns are: rubber, spring and compressed air.

GEAR

1. Spearguns:
The gun must be charged with muscle power only; no explosive or compressed power is allowed.
2. Terminal gear:
Trail line or reels are allowed.
Any float, or temporary aggregation of floats, shall not exceed 150 pounds (68.1 kg) of floatation. Divers must propel themselves unassisted and without motors.
3. Use of safety boat:
Divers must pull their fish up unassisted.
A buddy diver or crew member may pass unloaded guns to the diver.
4. Powerheads: Powerheads are prohibited. They may be carried by the diver for defense, but they may not be used to spear their catch.
5. Artificial breathing apparatus: No artificial breathing apparatus is allowed.

ELIGIBLE FISH

Albacore (genus, sp: Thunnus alalunga)
Amberjack
    Atlantic amberjack (genus, sp: Seriola dumerili)
    Pacific amberjack (genus, sp: Seriola rivoliana)
Bonito (genus: Sarda)
Broadbill swordfish (genus, sp: Xiphias gladius)
Cobia (genus, sp: Rachycentron canadum)
Dolphin fish, Dorado, Mahi Mahi (genus: Coryphaena)
Mackerel
    Atlantic mackerel (genus, sp: Scomberomorus cavalla)
    Pacific (genus, sp: Scomberomorus commerson)
Marlin
    Striped (genus, sp: Tetrapturus audax)
    Blue (genus, sp: Makaria nigricans)
    Black (genus, sp: Makaria indica)
    White (genus, sp: Tetrapturus albidus)
Sailfish (genus: Istiophorus)
Spearfish (genus: Tetrapturus)
Trevally, giant (genus, sp: Caranx ignobilis)
Tuna
    Bigeye (genus, sp: Thunnus obesus)
    Dogtooth tuna (genus, sp: Gymnosarda unicolor)
    Yellowfin (genus, sp: Thunnus albacares)
    Pacific bluefin (genus, sp: Thunnus orientalis)
    Atlantic bluefin (genus, sp: Thunnus thynnus)
    Southern bluefin (genus, sp: Thunnus maccoyii)
Wahoo (genus, sp: Acanthocybium solandri)
Yellowtail
    North American (genus, sp: Seriola dorsalis)
    South American (genus, sp: Seriola lalandi)
    Australian (genus, sp: Seriola grandis)

DOCUMENTATION

1. Weighing requirements:
a. The fish must be weighed by an official weighmaster (if one is available) or by an IBSRC official or by a recognized local person familiar with the scale. Disinterested witnesses to the weight should be used whenever possible.
b. The weight of the sling or rope (if used to secure the fish) must be subtracted from the total weight.
c. At the time of the weighing, the actual gear used by the spearfisher to catch the fish must be exhibited to the weighmaster and weight witness.
d. Only weights indicated by the gradations on the scale will be accepted. Visual fractionalizing of the gradations is not allowed. Any weights that fall between two gradations must be rounded to the lower weight.
e. All record fish should be weighed on scales that have been checked for accuracy by government agencies or other qualified and accredited organizations. All scales must be regularly checked for accuracy and must be current within 12 months, or quickly recertified after the weighing.
f. If there is no certified scale available, then the scales must be checked by weighing objects of recognized and proven weight similar to the weight of the fish.
g. In extremely remote areas where no weighing scales are available, it will be permissible for the spearfisher to use his/her own scales provided that they are high-quality scales and have been properly certified both before and after returning from the spearfishing trip. Fish measurements should accompany this application.
h. The IBSRC reserves the right to have the scales recertified if there are any indications that the scale might not have weighed properly.
i. Weighing fish on a boat at sea: Weighing at sea shall be allowed, provided that the scale is certified and that the weight registered is video taped for a minimum of two (2) minutes. The lowest weight recorded is the official weight.
2. When it is impossible or impractical to weigh the fish on a certified scale, a formula based on width, girth or other measurements may be used, provided the formula is approved by the IBSRC and a penalty reduction is applied. The penalty will ensure that measurement will produce a weight reduction so that 99% of the fish so measured will be larger than the formula results, when weighed.
3. Catch weighing or measurement must be witnessed and as much documentation as possible should accompany the application for the record, include any catch-and-release tag information.
4. Tissue sample: In order to better help the scientific community, and to positively identify the fish, the committee requests a small frozen tissue sample be provided. One gram of frozen muscle is sufficient.

APPLICATION:

For application for Associate Membership or for a world record, write: IBSRC
    552 North Victoria Ave
    Ventura, Ca., 93003, USA (fax 805-650-3014)

Glossary

Antihistamine: A drug that decreases the release of histamine in body tissues. Histamine released in nasal and throat tissues causes swelling, often leading to difficulty in ear clearing. Some newer antihistamines do not cause as much drowsiness as the older ones. Antihistamines are frequently used to prevent sea sickness.

Apex predator: A carnivorous fish at or near the top of the food chain with few natural enemies. Examples are adult tuna and marlin.

Apnea: Absence of breathing. Freedivers are apneic throughout the duration of their dive.

Atoll: A ring-shaped coral island that nearly or completely encloses a lagoon.

Bag limits: The maximum legal number of fish allowed to be captured and possessed, usually in one day.

Bait ball: A tightly packed mass of schooling bait fish. **Bait fish** herded or under attack merge into compact groups which seem to move as a single unit. A natural defense phenomenon, its formation signifies that predators are near.

Bait boundary: The farthest distance that reef-based **bait fish** will venture away from the security of their shelter in search of food. A distinct line or boundary generally forms in light to moderate currents as the fish orient up-current into the bluewater.

Bait fish: Any fish eaten by **bluewater gamefish**. Their behavior is useful in predicting the presence and direction of approaching bluewater game.

Bank: A large elevation in the ocean floor, that can range in size from a few acres to many miles. Some banks collect bait and subsequently attract **bluewater gamefish** species.

Bearing: A straight line defined by two reference objects that pinpoint a location. Two bearings, taken roughly 90 degrees apart, can be relied on to precisely locate a reef or **pinnacle**.

Bends: Decompression sickness. In a normal ascent, dissolved nitrogen gas escapes slowly from the body. When divers ascend too quickly, the nitrogen gas forms destructive bubbles in body tissues which, when occuring in the brain or spinal cord, can cause palsy or paralysis. While rare among freedivers, this condition can occur if the cumulative depth and time spent underwater exceeds standard decompression tables. It can be prevented by observing depth-duration schedules and is treated in a recompression chamber.

Blowing off: The rapid elimination of carbon dioxide by rapid or deep breathing.

Blue bottle: The South African name for the Portuguese man of war, a stinging jellyfish. These blue jelly fish sail in large mats on the surface of the ocean and present a hazard to the ascending freediver.

Bluewater gamefish species: Traditional angling gamefish such as marlin, tuna and yellowtail. Frequently found in or near deep water (more than 100 feet deep). The fish profiled in this book are all considered bluewater gamefish species.

Bluewater Meet: A freediving spearfishing contest in which, with few exceptions, only pelagic bluewater species are eligible. Generally, rules allow for only one fish per species. Examples are the California Catalina Bluewater Meet and the Australian Bluewater Classic.

Bluewater: Anywhere spearfishermen hunt open-ocean gamefish species. It's generally deep, blue and clear but sometimes may be shallow, green and even turbid.

Break point: A deep-ocean floor edge abruptly dropping into very deep water. For example, a gradually sloping bottom might extend offshore from an island to 50 fathoms, where it abruptly changes to a steep angle sloping into much deeper water. Bluewater species frequently congregate at these drop-offs.

Breathing up: Freediver's jargon for the process of drawing deep breaths in preparation for a dive.

Burley: An Australian term for chum, or chunk bait. Drifting chunks of fish strung to a diver's float, or pieces of fish cut up on a boat and cast into the water used to attract fish. Australian experts shoot a small fish and make deep vertical cross-hatching incisions along its entire side.

Shallow filleting cuts send hundreds of tiny bits of flesh into the currents. The commotion of frantic bait fish snapping up the chum attracts predatory species.

Bycatch: The incidental, non-targeted catch made by commercial fishermen. Sometimes the quantity of unwanted species is much greater than those sought after.

Capture guides: Machined spearshaft tubes mounted on the speargun barrel. They retain the spearshaft in both the vertical and horizontal planes and prevent a spearshaft from whipping and deforming under high-release loads.

Cavitation: The separation of water molecules that occurs when the water is cut by a large force such as a boat propeller or the quick tail movement of a powerful bluewater species. With fish, this is accompanied by a loud booming sound.

Ciguatera: A serious type of fish poisoning that affects as many as 50,000 people worldwide per year. A nerve toxin, it can cause death or chronic nervous disorders characterized by sensation reversals—for example a cold can of juice might feel hot. It's found in such fish as grouper, snapper, spanish mackerel and amberjack. Cooking does not destroy this toxin, which is impossible to detect. Some people test for the poison by feeding suspect fish to a cat or pig; if the animal remains well, they consider the fish safe.

Color correction filter: A lens, usually amber, used by underwater photographers to return warm colors (reds and yellows) to their images when these colors are removed by the selective light-absorbing qualities of water.

Continental shelf: The submerged, gradually sloping border of a continent extending from shore to a point hundreds of feet deep, ending in a steeper descent to the ocean floor, sometimes miles deep.

Core temperature: The central temperature of the body. A variety of mechanisms hold this temperature remarkably steady. Changes to the core temperature, as seen in fever or hypothermia, cause drastic changes in bodily functions and in oxygen consumption.

Cows: Large striped bass.

CPR: Cardiopulmonary resuscitation. A body of first-aid techniques aimed at reviving a victim whose breathing and/or heart has stopped.

Crimp: A device for binding line or cable. A tube made from aluminum, copper or stainless steel, it is swaged tightly around the line with a special crimping tool.

Croaking: Making a fish-attracting sound while submerged. Divers recycle air through their vocal cords and mouth to create a variety of sounds. Under certain conditions the correct sound will attract bluewater species.

Crustaceans: Aquatic arthropods, including shrimp, crabs, lobster and barnacles. All have a segmented body and a thick exoskeleton (shell).

D-ring: An openable chain loop, excellent for making attachments in the **terminal gear** chain. A positive closing device not subject to accidental opening.

Decompression: A scuba diving technique of slow ascent, usually with rests for five to 10 minutes at several points to help prevent nitrogen bubble formation in the body. Obviously, it's unavailable to the freediver.

Dehydration: The loss of body water, which may lead to thickening of the blood and make divers more susceptible to the **bends.** Seen in freedivers who don't drink enough water to balance the increased loss of body water resulting from breathing through a snorkel and increased urination.

Depth-of-field: The range of distance from the camera lens in which all subjects are in focus. For example, objects in focus anywhere from two feet to 12 feet would represent a large depth of field, while objects in focus from only one to two feet would represent a small depth of field.

Depth sounder: An electronic device capable of detecting the depth of fish and the ocean floor. Simple depth sounders report on the area immediately below the boat, while more sophisticated ones range below and far to the sides. Experienced boat captains, using a good depth sounder, can recognize individual fish and species by the distinctive marking they leave behind on the meter screen.

Detachable spearhead: A two-piece spearhead held to the spearshaft with an adaptor. Once the spearshaft is shot, the spearhead is free to separate from the shaft and toggle, either on the other side of the fish, or in its body. An average of 18 inches of cable or line connects the spearhead to the spearshaft.

Diving reflex: A rapid slowing of the heart seen in all humans just after the head is immersed in cold water.

Docking plate: A video-camera-housing part holding the video camera. It slides into the underwater housing, securely holding the video recorder in place. Sometimes these plates make electrical connections within the housing.

Ecologically sustainable development: Development that does not outrun the environment's ability to replenish resources, and therefore can be sustained indefinitely. The way we use, conserve, and enhance the community's resources so that our total quality of life, both now and in the future, is secured.

Ecosystem: A biological unit defined by both the physical environment and the species of organisms living within it.

Eddy current: A counter-current running in the opposite direction, and at the edges of, a large current. It's a much smaller current proportional in size and speed to its parent current.

Emergency locator: An electronic signal generator that when activated, sends out an emergency signal which may be received by passing boats, airplanes and satellites. This discrete frequency is monitored by governmental agencies, who use the signal to find victims who have turned on their locators.

Equalization: The maneuver a diver uses to increase pressure behind his eardrum, through the eustachian tube, to equalize the water pressure outside his eardrum.

Estuary: A body of brackish water where salt and fresh water mix, usually at the mouth of a river.

Exsanguination: The medical term for bleeding to death.

F-stop: A calibrated setting of the diameter of opening of a camera's lens aperture. The greater the f-stop, the less light enters the lens and the greater the **depth-of-field**.

FAD: A fish aggregation device. A man-made fish-attracting device fashioned to mimic natural fish congregation points, such as seaweed or **flotsam**. Typical devices are made from anchor buoys festooned with ropes or plastic streamers, or floating mats of buoys with submarine projections made of rope, plastic and sometimes natural elements such as palm fronds. FADS are

most useful in congregating fish in a specific area where there are no natural fish-attracting points (reefs, **pinnacle**s).

Feeding frenzy: A state of excitement in feeding fish, characterized by rapid swimming, biting and an abandonment of their usual wariness and timidity. Sharks, in their excitement, have been known to attack their own kind. Feeding **bluewater gamefish** species frequently abandon their usual caution and become easier to approach.

Fish street: A path along the edge of the **bait boundary** traveled by **bluewater gamefish** species.

Flasher: An artificial fish-attracting device trailing behind the diver or jerked like a fishing lure. Made from a combination of shining objects and multicolored plastic streamers.

Float line: See **trail line**.

Floppers: Moveable metal barbs attached to the spearhead. They hug the head in a low profile when the shaft is fired forward. When the shaft is pulled backward, the barb opens to about a 45-degree angle. A small turned-up tip at the end of the barb helps it deploy by catching water or flesh as the shaft is pulled backward.

Flotsam: Anything floating on the sea. Logs, boxes and cargo nets can gather barnacles, **bait fish** and **bluewater gamefish** species.

Flying gaff: A large gaff useful in bringing large **bluewater gamefish** into the boat. The hooked end of the gaff is detachable; it is attached to the boat with a rope. Temporarily attached to a floating gaffing pole, it releases after it engages the fish. Divers pull the rope in to recover their fish.

Fouling organisms: Plants and animals that attach themselves to fixed or floating objects. **Flotsam**, with these life forms attached, become more attractive to bait and subsequently **bluewater gamefish** species.

Freediver: A breath-holding diver whose only source of oxygen are his lungs filled with surface air, taken between dives.

Gill net: A curtain of netting suspended from the surface by floats. Single nets may be linked into a "wall of death." Fish swim into them in darkness and are caught by their gill covers.

GPS: The global positioning system developed and maintained by the United States military. This system of electronic triangulation

Fish parts:

DORSAL FINS

CAUDAL PEDUNCLE

PECTORAL FIN

ANAL FIN

PELVIC FIN

FINLETS

LATERAL LINE

KILL SHOT AREA

DORSAL FINS

PECTORAL FIN

ANAL FIN

CAUDAL PEDUNCLE

uses satellite-generated signals that allow the user to identify his exact position anywhere on earth with an accuracy of 75 feet or less.

Grow-out facility: A holding pen, usually located in a harbor or protected bay, where small fish are received from the hatchery and fed until they acclimate and grow large enough that they can be released into the wild.

Gun-sight bearing: A bearing along a straight line incorporating vertical references for triangulation. It's useful when there are no bearings 90 degrees to the original bearing.

Headlands: A point of land, with a sheer drop at the shore, adjacent to deep water. A cliff at the shore where bluewater hunters sometimes find **bluewater gamefish.**

Hip shot: A shot made from below the diver,

with the gun held near his waist, usually at close range when there is no time or opportunity to extend the gun for normal aiming. Correct your aim low to compensate for parallax.

Hyperbaric oxygen treatments: Treatments whereby oxygen is supplied under pressure in a recompression chamber to patients suffering from the **bends** and other medical conditions. May be of some use in recovering patients with brain injury after **shallow-water blackout.**

Hyperbaric therapy: A treatment for patients afflicted with decompression sickness (the **bends**). Divers are placed in a sealed pressure chamber that develops air pressure similar to the water pressure experienced in diving. The treatments are designed to redissolve nitrogen gas into the blood, reducing destructive bubble size and thus hopefully limiting or reversing symptoms. The divers breathe oxygen, which corrects tissue starvation for oxygen caused by nitrogen gas blocking the bloodstream.

Hyperventilation: An increased rate and/or depth of breathing. Carbon dioxide blood levels decrease with little corresponding increase in oxygen blood levels. If the diver engages in hyperventilation to excess, he may diminish his desire to breathe, long enough to become unconscious.

Hypothermia, acute: The rapid cooling of a diver's core temperature. A serious condition, it starts with mild confusion and muscle weakness, then progresses through a full range of deteriorating body processes frequently ending in unconsciousness or death from heart irregularities.

Hypothermia, progressive: A gradual cooling of a diver's core temperature, that takes consecutive days of diving to develop. Because the cooling is so gradual, many of the signs and symptoms of acute hypothermia do not appear. It can lead to a gradual, unnoticed but serious decrease in a diver's performance and safety.

Immersion diuresis: An unexplained condition characterized by the increased rate of urine production. It's one cause of diver dehydration.

Incidental catch: See **bycatch**.

Inflatable: A small skiff relying on inflatable rubber pontoons for flotation.

Kelp paddy: A floating mat of seaweed, usually created by strong waves and surges breaking the seaweed's anchorage to the bottom. Detached, it floats to the surface and drifts in the currents. It can attract sea life of all kinds.

Laryngospasm reflex: A protective reflex that causes closing of the vocal cords to prevent passage of air or water into the lungs. This reflex occurs in unconscious persons or those slightly anesthetized when an irritant such as water comes into contact with sensitive tissue near the vocal cords.

Lateral line: A line running down the side of a fish from just behind its gills to its tail. Composed of pits of exposed nerve endings that can detect subtle changes in pressure and thus helps the fish detect movement.

Light box: A long box emitting a very thin straight edge of light used to assess the straightness of a spearshaft during the straightening process.

Line pack: A receptacle-holding **trail line** that can be attached to a speargun or a float or anywhere between the two. Equipped with a mechanism that releases the line when a powerful fish fights, it does not release in the weaker forces of ocean waves pulling at the float.

Line tangle: Entrapment in a line. A freediver caught in a line tangle may be prevented from reaching the surface or pulled underwater.

Live boat: An unanchored boat manned by a spotter. It transports and watches over divers hunting in currents too strong to swim against.

Local currents: Small currents usually generated by tides and/or surface winds. They may become quite swift.

Lung squeeze: The crushing effect of water pressure on the chest cavity. The deeper a diver descends, the smaller his chest cavity becomes. This can cause discomfort in many divers when they descend below 90 feet with lungs fully inflated at the surface, and as shallow as 20 feet when the lungs are only partially inflated at the surface.

Mask squeeze: Pressure exerted to a diver's face resulting from increased water pressure outside his dive mask. Divers must inject air inside the mask to balance this external pressure.

Mating wound: A wound inflicted by a male shark on the "shoulder" of a female shark during copulation.

Maximum sustainable yield: A fisheries-management term meaning the greatest take that can be taken harvested from a fish stock year after year without depleting the species. It's used as a reference point for management purposes to describe the maximum potential productivity of a stock in terms of catch. Can vary yearly.

Metabolism: The totality of the chemical processes in the organs and cells of the body responsible for life. These processes slow in cool bodies, such as those with mild hypothermia (not shivering, which increases metabolism), and increase in bodies warmed above normal temperatures, such as those with fevers. Oxygen consumption is proportional to the rate of metabolism. Expert freedivers probably exert some control over their metabolism by slowing their heart and decreasing muscular activity.

Micro-hits: Small bubbles of nitrogen that form in decompression sickness (the **bends**), causing localized tissue lesions. They may be cumulative, causing clinical symptoms such as itching, pain, weakness and other nervous system problems.

Modulus of elasticity The measurement of the elastic force retained and delivered by the **propulsion bands**. Bands with a high modulus of elasticity retain and deliver greater force than bands with a low modulus of elasticity.

Negative depth: The depth at which a diver's weight becomes negative and he sinks.

Neutral point: The depth at which a diver neither floats nor sinks. Neutral buoyancy typically occurs anywhere from 10 to 40 feet, depending on how much weight he carries on his belt.

Oceanic current: Large bodies of flowing water, generally with different fish, visibility and temperature than the surrounding water through which they flow. An example is the Gulf Stream off Florida.

Olfactory apparatus: A fish's organ of smell, which is very sensitive in many bluewater species. Diver-generated scents can either repel or attract fish.

Panga: A Mexican name for a durable streamlined skiff powered by an outboard engine and carrying up to six people. A good craft from which to attend spearfishermen, it can also be used as a rescue or pickup boat working from a yacht.

Pelagic fish: A fish that spends most of its adult life in open ocean environments. Not associated with the bottom but traveling midwater in the currents of the sea, pelagics are generally narrow in shape and capable of traveling great distances.

Pinnacle: Steep-sided, underwater, rocky prominence. When they are located in an area frequented by bluewater fish, pinnacles often offer good ambush points for bluewater hunters.

Pinned shaft: A spearshaft equipped with pins or tabs located near the release-mechanism end used to anchor loaded power-band wishbones. It may be welded or attached mechanically with holes drilled into the spearshaft.

Pinniped: A suborder of carnivorous marine animals including seals, sea lions and walrus.

Pneumatic speargun: A gun powering the spearshaft with a piston, driven by compressed air. It's limited to one muscle-loading sequence when the diver forces the shaft into the barrel, causing the air piston to compress. These guns

lose power in deeper water.

Positive buoyancy: The tendency to float. Any time a diver's weight is insufficient to sink him or keep him level in the water, he will be "positively buoyant" and float.

Powerhead (banger, popper, smokey)**:** An explosive device mounted on a pole or spear, used to defend against shark attacks. It explodes on contact with the shark's body and may or may not contain a slug. The shell is actuated either by a built-in firing pin or the point of the spearhead itself.

Propulsion bands (power bands, rubbers)**:** Tubular rubber bands are attached or looped through the muzzle of a speargun on one end, and connected to the wishbone on the other. One or more bands propel the spearshaft. The average force required to load a band is 80 pounds.

Push film: A film-developing term that means the shooting and processing of film at a higher ASA (film speed) setting than the film's actual ASA rating. Shooting and developing ASA 200 film at 400 ASA is pushing the film. This technique allows image making in low-light situations

Push-rod: A lightweight but strong metal rod connecting the remote trigger of a center-handled gun to the **release mechanism**.

Recoil: The backward and upward force delivered by the **propulsion bands** to the barrel when the spear is released.

Reef: An elevation on the ocean floor composed of rocks and/or coral. Many reefs, especially steep-sided or offshore, are good gathering points for **bluewater gamefish** species.

Reel: A device like a fishing reel, used by spearfishermen to play and recover speared fish. While angling reels can be used, most reels used for spearfishing are fabricated from heavier stock. They are frequently equipped with a variable drag and a **release mechanism**. Reels are subject to **line tangles**.

Release mechanism: Usually a two-piece assembly of levers responsible for releasing the spear. One part is activated by the trigger and releases the lever retaining the spearshaft; when the second lever pivots out of the way the spearshaft releases.

Retes: Blood vessel loops that act like radiators, allowing, most notably, bluefin tuna to maintain their internal heat at a higher temperature than the surrounding water. (Retes are found in some other tuna and wahoo as well.) Retes collect heat and return it to the body before blood reaches the gills, where other bluewater fish lose most of their heat to the water.

Rigging: The composite of a spearfisherman's gear from the speargun to his floats.

Rookery: A place on the shore where seals and sea lions "haul out" to rest and breed.

Schooled: A diver's confusion and inability to make a shot when surrounded by a large school of fish moving so fast and erratically that it's difficult to single out one fish.

Schoolie: A small striped bass found in a large school of similarly sized fish.

Seamount: An undersea mountain, rising from the ocean floor, with a peaked or flat-topped summit.

Shaft twist: The rotation of the fired spearshaft generally caused by an asymmetrical spearhead.

Shallow-water blackout (SWB): An unconscious state divers experience when the brain becomes deprived of oxygen. Frequently instantaneous and without warning, this condition causes death in a significant number of freedivers.

Shark billy: A sharp-pointed pole carried by divers to fend off sharks. Divers hope that poking a shark's sensitive snout with this device will drive it away.

Shoal of fish: A school of fish.

Slack current: The slowing of a local current to negligible levels.

Spear guide: A device designed to keep a highly powered spearshaft tracking in a straight line during its travel down the barrel. Some barrels are grooved, while others support individual machined guides. See **capture guides.**

Spear line: The section of line connecting the spearshaft to the **trail line** or the speargun barrel. Also called shooting line.

Spearhead: The sharp pointed device at the spear-tip end of a spearshaft that pierces the fish, and is equipped with **floppers** or "wings" that toggle inside the fish or on its far side. It may be as simple as a sharpened spearshaft with a single flopper or as complicated as a **detachable spearhead** designed to separate from the spearshaft and toggle on the far side of fish.

Spearhead adapter: A device that screws onto the end of a spearshaft used to hold a detachable spearhead. The mating design and machining is critical; it must stay attached straight and true throughout the spearshaft's flight, but it must also dislodge quickly once forward momentum is gone.

Springbok: The name of a South African national spearfishing team member.

Staggers: A disorder characterized by an unsteady walking gait. Found in South Seas pearl divers, it is believed to be a form of decompression sickness (the **bends**) resulting from freediving in excess of the safe depth and duration diving tables. Also seen in commercial divers who develop vestibular (inner ear) bends often after deep helium-oxygen dives.

Stone shot: A spear shot striking a fish in the brain or spinal cord anywhere in the forward half of the fish; it totally incapacitates the fish, rendering it almost motionless.

Stringer: A device used to hold speared fish. Some are simple metal loops that snap open or closed. Others are shaped metal rods. A common stringer contains a looped line on one end of an 18- to 24-inch cord that is attached to the middle of an 8-inch metal bar. Stringers hold fish between their eyes or through their gills into their mouth.

Sun ball: The image of the sun as seen on print film. Its size varies with the **f-stop** setting.

Swim bladder: A gas-filled organ used by many fish to maintain neutral buoyancy. It's not found in tunas, which need the lift generated by their pectoral fins to support them, nor in sharks, which rely on their high-fat content livers to assist their buoyancy.

Terminal gear: A bluewater diver's rigging, beginning at the spearline and ending with the float. Typically consists of a **trail line, line pack, release mechanism** and a flag-equipped float.

Thermocline: A subsurface strata of water that abruptly drops to a temperature several degrees cooler than the water above. **Bluewater gamefish** species sometimes cruise thermocline edges or can be found in the water just below or above the temperature change.

Thermal debt: The deficit in bodily core temperature seen in progressive hypothermia.

Tide reversal: A small tide change occurring within a large **tide trend**.

Tide trend: The net change from the day's most extreme tidal heights. Generally two trends occur each day, each encompassing a **tide reversal**.

Tourniquet: A lifesaving first-aid device used to control bleeding in the limbs. It's made with a rope loop and a dowel for twisting. Placed over a pressure point, it is twisted tightly to slow hemorrhaging.

Trail line: The line or line-filled tube connected behind the **spear line** or cable. Usually connected to a float, it may simply follow or trail free behind the gun. Used to manage a speared fish or recover a dropped gun.

Tuck dive: The freediver's entry under the water from the surface. His body breaks 90 degrees at the waist and he raises one leg to start the descent.

Tunnel vision: The loss of side vision, narrowing the visual fields to the front. In freediving, this frequently indicates a near-blackout because of low oxygen levels.

U.S. National Spearfishing Championships: A freediving spearfishing competition that rotates venue around the United States and is sponsored yearly by the Underwater Society of America. Regional champion three-man teams compete for the title of national champion and earn the right to represent the U.S. in the **World Spearfishing Championships**.

Vacuum effect: The exit of oxygen from the blood into the lungs of the surfacing freediver, who has consumed most of his oxygen during his dive; ascending, his expanding lungs draw oxygen from his blood. A simplification of the changes in the dynamics of the partial pressures of oxygen, resulting in diffusion from a relatively higher pressure in the blood to a lower pressure in the lungs.

Vertigo: A condition characterized by dizziness, loss of balance and the inability to "tell which way is up." Divers can experience this problem because of shock or injuries to their inner ears; for example, a rupture of the eardrum might allow cold water to enter and cause this condition. It also occurs when one ear equalizes and the other does not.

Video grab: A computer-generated scan converting a video image, stored in analog format, into digital format. The digital image is used to make a still photo from a single frame of video footage. A video recorder makes 30 frames per second.

Welded tabs: See **pinned shaft**.

White balance: A video-recording term referring to the electronic circuitry that assigns colors to the image under various light conditions. White balance must be selected for the appropriate light source—sunlight, tungsten or phosphorescent light—so that colors are accurately represented and as true as possible to color as seen by the human eye.

White pointer: A Southern hemisphere name for the great white shark.

Wings: See **floppers**.

World Spearfishing Championships: The international freediving spearfishing championships sponsored by the world organization CMAS. One three-man team per country competes in this biennial event, held in various ocean-bordered countries.

Index

(Numbers in italic designate illustrations. Numbers in bold designate a major reference.)